High-Impact Learning

High-Impact Learning

Strategies for Leveraging
Business Results from Training

New Perspectives in Organizational Learning,
Performance, and Change

Robert O. Brinkerhoff
and
Anne M. Apking

BASIC
BOOKS

A Member of the Perseus Books Group
New York

Library of Congress Catalogue Card information is available.

ISBN 0-7382-0538-9
Copyright © 2001 by Robert O. Brinkerhoff and Anne M. Apking
Previously published by Perseus Publishing
Published by Basic Books, A Member of the Perseus Books Group

Find us on the World Wide Web at http://www.basicbooks.com

Books published by Basic Books are available at special discounts for bulk purchases in the United States by corporations, institutions, and other organizations. For more information, please contact the Special Markets Department at the Perseus Books Group, 11 Cambridge Center, Cambridge, MA 02142, or call (617) 252–5298 or (800) 255-1514 or e-mail special.markets@perseusbooks.com.

Text design by Tonya Hahn
Set in 10.5-point Minion
First printing, December 2001

Publisher's Note

Organizations are living systems, in a constant state of dynamic evolution. *New Perspectives in Organizational Learning, Performance, and Change* is designed to showcase the most current theory and practice in human resource and organizational development, exploring all aspects of the field—from performance management to adult learning to corporate culture. Integrating cutting-edge research and innovative management practice, this library of titles will serve as an essential resource for human resource professionals, educators, students, and managers in all types of organizations.

The series editorial board includes leading academics and practitioners whose insights are shaping the theory and application of human resource development and organizational design.

Series Editor
Jerry W. Gilley, Colorado State University

Editorial Board

Reid Bates, Louisiana State University

Laura Bierema, University of Georgia

Nathaniel Boughton,
Sonic Software, Inc.

Ann K. Brooks, University of Texas

Jamie Callahan,
Texas A&M University

Neal Chalofsky,
George Washington University

Patrick Combs,
WAITT Radio

Sharon Confessore, Kaiser Permanente

Joseph Davidson, Deloitte & Touche

Peter J. Dean,
University of Pennsylvania

Robert Dean,
Henry Ford Medical Group

Jo Gallagher,
Florida International University

Tim Hatcher, University of Louisville

Pat McLagan, theRitestuff, Inc.

Donna McNamara, Colgate-Palmolive

Ann Maycunich,
Colorado State University

Hallie Preskill,
University of New Mexico

Scott A. Quatro, Dordt College

Gloria Regalbuto,
Ohio Principal Leadership Academy

Nora Ruder, Foremost Insurance

Darlene Russ-Eft, AchieveGlobal

Douglas Smith,
Florida International University

L. Michael Wykes, Steelcase

Robert O. Brinkerhoff dedicates this book to his children:
Robert Joris (Jory), Darcy, Susanna, and Allison.

Anne M. Apking dedicates this book
to her husband, Ted, and to the two most insightful and
inspiring teachers she could have, her children, Leah and Cole.

Contents

Figures and Tables

Tables

Foreword

What problems will this book help readers solve?

Human resource development problems.

U.S. citizens pay enormous sums for human resource development. Approximately $230 billion is spent each year on education, from kindergarten through graduate school. Employers pass on to consumers at least an additional $300 billion per year that is spent to train and develop people to perform competently and prepare for the future.

I mention these numbers to set a context to pose two questions:

1. Are the citizens of the United States getting value for their human resource development money?
2. Would it be possible to get significantly greater value?

My answer to both questions is a resounding "Yes!"

Based on the ability of the U.S. workforce to support a level of productivity and standard of living that is unparalleled in history, I believe the kindergarten through graduate school education is worth every penny, not only to the graduates but also to taxpayers. But as an educator with practical experience in both training and education, I believe that the educational system could and should do a better job with the $230 billion or so spent each year. Elementary schools could and should enable more children to learn to read effectively; the current success rate, nationally, of only 50 to 60 percent of children acquiring reading proficiency is far too low. Secondary schools and colleges could and should enable more students to graduate; the current success rate, nationally, of roughly 50 percent graduating is far too low.

Similarly, I believe that the $300 billion spent in workforce training is worth every penny. Human resources professionals have been able to make effective use of the abundant natural resources in the United States to provide unparalleled opportunities for employment and an enviable standard of living. On the other hand, we have good evidence that it is possible to get better results. I believe better results could be attained without expenditure of "new" money. Let me explain why.

This book describes an approach that can help enormously. I believe, like the authors, that much of the money spent for workplace training and development buys nothing of real value. Even so, I believe that the total result is well worth the cost despite the fact that we waste much of the money! However, as taxpayer and consumer, I would like to see more:

- Training and development professionals working with executives to achieve better results with the same or fewer dollars,
- Cost savings shared with consumers, and
- Cost-saving technologies shared with educators.

I'm an optimist. I believe that it is possible to at least double the productivity of training and development and public education where productivity is measured in results achieved per dollar spent. But please notice that I am saying it is possible, not that it is likely to happen in the lifetime of anyone reading these words. Some educators and training and development professionals already know how it could be done. But there is a long way to go to demonstrate that it can be done reliably and on a large scale and to gather the financial, political, and technological resources to do the job. I am thankful that Brinkerhoff and Apking have written a book that points us all in the right direction. The book describes simply and in detail what can be done to improve the impact of training and development.

The authors advocate a shift in our thinking about training, a shift away from an event-based approach to a performance-based approach. The event-based approach is organized around training events such as courses, workshops, or seminars: Training events are scheduled at convenient times, people sign up for a place, attend, get materials, do activities intended to support learning, and then go on about their work and lives. Both authors are masters of the event-based approach and have enviable reputations for designing and delivering successful training events. Participants leave their events with new knowledge and skill and good feelings about the relevance, applicability, and importance of what they have learned. Participant ratings of the events and the instructors tend to be high. In sum, the authors write about shortcomings of event-based instruction with the authority of masters of the art.

Both authors have asked tough questions over the years: How many partic-ipants use how much of what they have learned in order to perform better, that is, in ways that add value to their organizations? Evaluation results con-sistently show that a few (but not nearly enough) participants use what they learn and perform better in the workplace. Further evaluation has enabled the authors to find out why the training works for some participants and not for others. The logic of training that works is described in Chapter 1.

The logic the authors describe is simple and credible but it requires one to abandon event-based thinking and to adopt performance-based thinking. The goal is not to have successful training events but to enable people to learn to do their work better. Success occurs, not in training but on the job. That simple observation is powerful! Training is a means, not an end in itself. As a trainer and an educator, I want to have successful courses but, according to the compelling logic put forth by Brinkerhoff and Apking, I can no longer measure success by student happiness ratings and test scores. Instead, I must look beyond such measures to see whether students make use of what they have learned to add value in their workplaces. I cannot in good conscience claim success unless the students remember, use, and add value by using what they learn.

I hope that there will be many people who read this book and accept the challenge: Get better results by applying the logic described in Chapter 1. Chapter 1 provides the theme. The remaining chapters provide guidance and examples of how variations on the theme plays out in practice. Chapter 2, for example, shows how to avoid getting lost in the dazzle and excitement of e-learning and stay true to the logic of performance improvement by tailoring e-learning to specific situations. Chapter 2 alone is worth the price of the book—or could be if managers and training professionals were to take it to heart and use the lessons learned there. Chapter 3 provides an example of a common and apparently quite sensible approach to workplace training, then contrasts it with an example of the authors' high-impact approach. The con-trast illustrates five principles of high-impact training. From this point, the principles guide the material presented in the remaining chapters with vivid illustrations and clear direction. Put to use, this book can help readers achieve equally impressive results.

Brinkerhoff and Apking show how we could make the transition from event-based to performance-based training to get the results we all hope for. The authors provide the logic and many examples of situation-based varia-tions. Their concepts and methods apply well to all types of training, includ-ing training we do not think of as being directed at improving workplace performance. The authors provide a lucid discussion of training goals such as fulfilling government mandates and preparing people to deal with emergencies that we hope they will never encounter. Readers can get the results they want by creating additional situation-based variations. It would be gratifying to look back on 2002 as a watershed year. The year 2002 could be the year training professionals see that the glass of value we add is half full, yet we have the capability to fill it to the brim!

—*Dale M. Brethower, Ph.D.*
Emeritus Professor of Psychology,
Western Michigan University

Preface

This book is written for training managers, chief learning officers, educational leaders, performance consultants, and anyone else whose job it is to make learning and training work—to improve individual and organizational business performance.

A wise man is purported to have said that the more things change, the more they stay the same. What has changed a lot in the past few years is the explosion of technology in training and learning, from web-based training to interactive television to palm pilot–accessed CD-ROM disks. What has not changed is the incontrovertible argument that training should produce worthwhile business results. Getting consistent and compelling business results from training—e-learning or traditional—is the single focus of this book.

The challenges that training leaders face today are both the same and changing. As noted, what remains the same is that training leaders must produce worthwhile business results. The change is that they must produce them faster than ever, achieving greater impact from decreasing resources.

But yet another fact has not changed. Training as an organizational function remains stuck with the fundamental weaknesses it has had for decades. Almost all organizational training is a marginal intervention and has only slight effects on performance improvement. The trend to e-learning and other technologies holds promise but offers no guarantee that high-tech training is likely to have more impact than any other sort of training.

The authors of this book have been struggling with the realities of corporate training and development for a combined total of nearly sixty years. Based on their extensive work in evaluating hundreds of training programs and initiatives worldwide, they have discovered a promising set of principles, guidelines, and tools that training practitioners can use to achieve dramatically greater levels of impact from learning interventions. Many client organizations, including the World Bank, Canadian Tire, Anheuser Busch, Qualcomm, Whirlpool, and Compaq, to name a few, have worked with and helped develop the ideas and methods the authors have created. Although such methods and tools have been provided through training and consulting to these and other companies, the authors have not previously had the opportunity to codify and capture these breakthrough techniques in a publicly available book. Until now.

In this book, Brinkerhoff and Apking have taken their innovative work on impactful training and created the high-impact learning (HIL) approach, a comprehensive conceptual framework and integrated methods and tools that training practitioners in any setting can use to help their organizations achieve dramatically increased business results from learning investments. The conceptual framework is based on solid theory and research on organizational learning, as well as the authors' extensive experience. The methods and tools have been developed and refined over several years of intense and varied client work in real organizations. They are proven, practical, and powerful, and have helped many training leaders achieve the status of "local hero" in their organizations.

The book is organized into three sections. In the first section, comprised of three chapters, the authors lay out the conceptual framework and core methods of the HIL approach. In Chapter 1, readers will find the fundamental conceptual argument for and basis of the HIL model. Chapter 2 explains how HIL methods apply to the emerging world of e-learning and electronic technologies. In Chapter 3, the authors present and explain the HIL model, highlighting especially its three major elements.

The second section is devoted to a deeper investigation of each major component of the HIL model. Here, readers will find the practical and proven methods that the authors and others have used to put HIL into practice. Chapter 4 is devoted to the impact map method and tools, a powerful and elegant technology that lies at the core of the HIL approach. Chapter 5 presents and explains the methods and tools for building a clear and highly intentional focus on and linkage to business goals and objectives. Chapter 6 is devoted to principles, methods, and tools for highly effective learning interventions and activities. Chapter 7 presents practical methods and tools for the third component of the HIL process, supporting performance improvement.

The third section of the book concerns putting the overall HIL approach into practice in organizations. Chapter 8 presents a process for creating comprehensive HIL initiatives. Chapter 9 explains and illustrates the HIL approach to impact evaluation, an innovative and practical method for credibly assessing the business impact and return on investment (ROI) of learning initiatives. Chapter 10 shows in detail how the HIL approach can be embedded into an organization-wide system for individual development planning, so that HIL concepts and methods can pervade this essential human resources planning function. In the final chapter, Chapter 11, the authors step back from the HIL methods and tools and provide practical and concrete guidelines for helping an organization make the transition to the HIL approach.

Throughout, readers will find useful and down-to-earth explanation and guidance. The many workshops and presentations that the authors have provided have always earned rave reviews and have been especially noted for their clarity and simplicity. Participants in these sessions often comment on the rare ability of the authors to make powerful and profound ideas elegant and infinitely understandable. This book is no exception to that rule. The authors have worked hard to boil down their thinking into simple words and to illustrate their suggestions and guidelines with real-world examples.

High-Impact Learning

The Challenge
of Training Impact

Chapter Overview

It is a brutal fact that in many organizations, significant financial investments in training lead to very little impact. Consider the fact that during 2000, organizations budgeted a total of $54 billion on formal training, with an estimated $19.3 billion going to outside providers of training products and services (*Training Magazine,* October 2000).

If we define "training impact" as simply the transfer of knowledge and skills to on-the-job performance, research indicates that impact of training is realized only for about 15 percent of all training participants (Tannenbaum and Yukl, 1992). When we define the impact of training more rigorously, such as the application of new knowledge and skills to enhance performance in a way that makes a worthwhile difference to the business, then our evaluation studies typically show even more dismal results.

We believe that this unfortunate outcome of training is due to one compelling truth: Training is defined, in many organizations, as simply the "delivery of events," where the primary role of the training function is to design, develop, and deliver learning programs and services. Performance improvement, on the other hand, is left to the province of line management or becomes the specialty of an elite few "performance consultants."

The key to achieving consistently high impact from training, however, is to integrate performance improvement strategies and tactics into the training process. This is the fundamental premise of high-impact learning, or "HIL," as we refer to it in shorthand in this book.

We start with a basic understanding of the goals of training. From here, we then build to the concept of "high leverage transfer," the application of critical learning in key job applications that is most likely to lead to the achievement of business goals. Finally, this chapter lays the conceptual foundation for the HIL framework, methods, and tools that are explored in the remaining chapters.

The Myth of Training as "Delivery of Events"

Like it or not, and nearly all learning leaders do *not* like it, most organizational training departments and functions are in the "delivery" business. All too often, the learning function has been structured and conceived to "process" employees through learning interventions. Training customers want their employees to have the maximum exposure to learning interventions at the fastest rates and lowest costs possible.

As a result, training is often viewed as a singular, packaged intervention, such as an electronically accessed module, a workshop, a printed workbook, or a college course. The training department's job is to design and "package" these learning interventions (or buy them), then deliver them to their intended recipients. The implicit assumption is that participation in the event—defined as completing the instructional module, sitting through the class, and so forth—is sufficient to achieve learning objectives, and therefore to improve performance. The only role for managers and supervisors within the organization is to grant "permission" for the scheme to operate, granting employees the time to participate. Once participation is complete, there are virtually no other responsibilities on the part of trainees. Nor, and especially significantly, is there any further responsibility on the part of the supervisors and managers of these trainees.

Even though it doesn't work well, or sometimes at all, there are clearly strong forces that keep the "delivery-of-events" model alive today. Suspend belief momentarily and imagine that the event-delivery model really *did* work; then consider the powerful appeal of the following characteristics:

- Learning to perform new skills would be quite painless: All employees have to do is "show up" and participate; all their managers have to do is approve their attendance.
- Training departments could demonstrate dramatic gains in apparent productivity and save huge amounts on training-related travel and housing expenses by converting popular classroom programs to digital materials delivered via the intranet.
- Training departments could significantly streamline the delivery of learning interventions by simply creating a "one-size-fits-all" learning approach to virtually blanket the needs of all employees. To justify expenditures on expensive technology, services, programs, and speakers,

training departments could force-feed training to large numbers of employees, thereby reducing the per-employee costs of the training.

- Busy managers could delegate the responsibility of helping employees learn to the training department (a.k.a. the "fix-it" shop) where the capability to provide appealing learning interventions and programs resides.
- Training managers and others could easily identify which training initiatives and programs are the best based on the numbers of people who participated.
- Training department staff could spend all of their time doing what they do best: designing and delivering training events.
- Training program vendors could spend huge amounts of money developing lavish materials and modules that training departments could never afford to develop themselves, then leverage their investment into large earnings by selling these programs to thousands of companies worldwide who would then need only to "deliver" them.
- Training departments could determine whether all of this was working by asking people to respond to surveys about their reactions to the delivered events, then compare and contrast results to make decisions about intervention and trainer effectiveness.

As the list shows, there is strong appeal for sustaining the myth that organizational training consists primarily of designing and delivering events. Further, the actual training systems that have evolved within organizations and among commercial training vendors and product companies that serve them have sustained and deepened the entrenchment of the "event-delivery" myth.

Despite the attractiveness of the myth and its entrenchment, real learning and performance improvement do not operate this way. If we are to have valuable business results from training, then we need learning that produces lasting effects and leads to behavioral change in critically important job tasks that are linked to important business needs and goals. Getting these sorts of results requires working on and within the performance system of the organization—a far more difficult job than just delivering snazzy learning modules and events.

The Logic of Training Impact

The most common understanding of training "impact" is that training should bring direct benefit to the organization that sponsors that training. Although training may hold some intrinsic value to employees as a benefit, such as a career planning or retirement planning service, training will not be supported by an organization simply as a philanthropic gesture, the "right" thing to do. Nonetheless, part of the total value of training derives from the reality that training is, in fact, a function perceived by many employees as a benefit. This value of training should not be ignored.

Many organizations, for example, promote continuing education of employees by offering to reimburse all or a portion of their tuition in higher education courses. Further, organizations that provide ample opportunity for training and development are perceived as "employee preferred," whereas those that are very stingy with training opportunities are less competitive in attracting and retaining high-quality employees. But this "benefit" function of training is not the major reason that companies support training, nor is it the central concern for high-impact learning (HIL).

The Performance Route to Impact

The fundamental construct of training impact holds that training is, above all, an instrument for improving employee and organizational performance and effectiveness. This rationale for training is based on the easily understood assumption that competent (that is, well-trained) employees should perform more effectively than less competent employees. Note, however, that the emphasis is on *performance,* not simply gains in competence. The impact of training is normally construed as the organizational benefits (such as increased production, greater quality, and reduced costs) that ensue when improvements in competence are manifested in improvements in job performance. This is what has been called the fundamental logic of training (Brinkerhoff, 1987). The logic of training in its generic form is illustrated in Figure 1.1.

As depicted in Figure 1.1, the long-range goal of training is to contribute to organizational goals, such as improving customer satisfaction, increasing market share, reducing costs, and so forth. These organizational goals are achieved through improved performance of employees. The improved performance is enabled when employees use their new learning. New learning is the immediate outcome of a learning intervention. Thus, impact is achieved when this sequence of events is successfully completed:

A. Trainees who lack skills, knowledge, or both participate in a learning intervention, such as an on-line training module or a workshop;
B. trainees complete the learning intervention by having mastered some new skills and knowledge, and then
C. trainees refocus their attention on their primary work and soon try out their new skills and knowledge, then
D. their applications of new learning are supported and reinforced until their performance of one or more important tasks improves, so that

FIGURE 1.1   The Logic of Training

E. one or more key job results (such as a completed order, a produced part, a resolved concern, a work rate, and so forth) is improved, which in turn

F. contributes to the achievement of some business goal, such as improved customer satisfaction.

As Figure 1.1 shows, the impact that results from training is realized only after training-acquired skills are used by trainees in on-the-job behaviors. The immediate outcomes of the learning intervention, if the learning intervention is successful, are new skills and knowledge. In most types of training applications, however, the new skills and knowledge alone do not add value; they must be applied, then nurtured until improved performance can be counted on to consistently produce an important job result.

The route to impact is through performance, in this case. If the new learning does not lead to improved performance, then the training does not achieve impact and the training investment is at risk. For most sorts of training investments this learning-to-performance transition is the principal way in which impact is achieved.

Variations on the Performance Logic

There are, however, exceptions to and variations of this direct learning-to-performance route, and thus a variable range of understandings exists of what constitutes training impact. It is important to discuss these, as the HIL framework and methods presented in this book do not apply equally to all of the variations. Indeed, a major part of the success we have helped our clients realize stems from using the clear thinking about training impact that the HIL framework enables.

Sometimes the purpose of new learning is to build the capability to perform, even though the skills may never be used. Consider the example of a commercial airline providing training to its pilots on how to safely land the aircraft after an engine fails. Passengers who fly with these pilots, and even others on the ground, are safer when the pilots are kept fully competent in this "flameout" emergency procedure. This margin of safety adds value to the service the airline provides, enabling the airline to attract passengers and earn revenues, which help pay for the costs of the training. At the same time, of course, the airline is meeting its regulatory requirements, which in turn are driven by a similar logic. Note that the pilots never have to actually use the emergency skills for worthwhile impact to be achieved. In fact, it is far better if they never do!

To determine the "impact" of this training, we would need to explore first the likelihood of an event occurring that would require the trained behavior, in this case, the aircraft's failed engine. Then we would need to project the magnitude of the negative consequences if the event were to occur and the pilots could not safely resolve it. If, for instance, aircraft engines were 100 percent reliable, then this training could not be impactful. On the other hand, if there is a small possibility that the emergency behavior may be required, and the pilots have been trained and are certified as fully competent, then the competence has greater value. The airline has met its regulatory requirements, and in addition, potential customers of the airline perceive it as safer, or in an actual emergency, the competent pilots may save the lives of the passengers. Therefore, the value added to the core service of the airline as a result of this safety training does in fact justify the cost of the training.

There are other examples that illustrate the logic of training impact that do not rely on the application of new learning into directly related performance. Consider the fundamental logic of training that is intended to indoctrinate employees in an organization's culture and context. In this sort of acculturation "training," there is no expectation of an immediate or even specific application of the learning on the job.

Another key way that training produces impact, but not through direct performance improvement, is in the case of using training to build "bench strength." The logic for this sort of training is that the organization must have a pool of qualified talent ready to move into key positions if they are vacated by attrition. The impact of this training is not realized until a vacancy occurs. If there are qualified internal candidates whose training has provided them with the requisite capabilities to fill the position, then positive impact is possible.

There are further variations of impact logic as well. Some training is provided primarily as a benefit, with no demand for application of the learned skills. For example, a company might provide training in retirement planning or personal financial management. The principal rationale for these offerings is that they are a benefit, with the same sort of appeal to prospective or current employees as any other benefit, such as health insurance. People who avail themselves of this type of training may indeed use it, but there is no requirement for use for the company to realize "impact" from the training. The impact is achieved simply through the perceived popular value of the training. If it is viewed as providing a valuable service, its benefit impact is realized. However, if employees show little interest in it, then this training has little if any benefit value.

But overall, the principal rationale for the value of training is based on the learning-to-performance logic. Organizations require increasingly effective performance from their employees to achieve business goals, to create and maintain a competitive advantage, and to build public support or shareholder value. The realities of the competitive workplace and continued acceleration of change and technology simply leave no alternative: Organizations must train their employees and train them well, so that the greatest possible portion of training leads to improved performance and positive business results.

One of the primary applications of the HIL conceptual framework is to identify the logic of training. The logic of training clarifies the purpose and intent of training, and helps to direct the application of further HIL methods and tools for enhancing the impact of the training investment. Confusion about the logic of particular training initiatives creates murky expectations from the start and increases the likelihood that critical performance factors will be overlooked or mismanaged, undermining impact and wasting valuable time and resources of all stakeholders.

Beyond the Transfer of Training

In the classic lexicon of learning psychology, "transfer" relates to the degree of similarity between skill and knowledge taught during training and their associated tasks on the job. For example, if a North American resident wanted to learn to drive an automobile in the United Kingdom (where they drive on the "wrong" side of the road, steering from the "wrong" side of the car!), training should be conducted in an automobile with right-hand drive. Practicing driving on the left-hand side of the road in a left-hand drive (American) car would not result in high transfer, since there is a mismatch between the training conditions and the performance conditions.

But training transfer as it is construed in human resource development (HRD) has a different meaning, and is well known to every learning leader. In this professional arena, transfer refers to the extent to which training-acquired capabilities are applied to job performance. Transfer, of course, poses a huge challenge, because it is often difficult to achieve. The challenge of transfer—assuring that skills acquired during training are in fact applied in the workplace—rightfully consumes the attention of committed training professionals and has been written about extensively in the HRD literature (see, for example, Broad and Newstrom, 1992).

Of course, transfer is vitally important. We could invest significant resources to help employees learn and to achieve the highest levels of learning possible. But if these same employees did not, for one reason or another, actually apply their skills and improve performance, this investment would lead to no positive impact. In fact, it would have resulted in negative business impact given the wasted resources. We argue in this chapter that transfer, as we typically understand it, is not enough. The HIL approach incorporates the concept of *leveraged transfer,* a significant variation on the traditional transfer theme. To explain the leveraged transfer concept and show how it applies in the HIL framework, we will illustrate with a relevant example.

The "Three Trainees"

This example dramatizes the vital focus of the HIL approach on leveraged transfer. Imagine that you are in a corporate work setting and that you encountered an employee who was engaging in a training intervention, an online learning module, for instance. You initiate a brief discussion with that employee, probing into the following questions:

- What are you doing?
- Why?
- How might you use it?
- What good will it do?

Imagine further that you have this discussion with each of three different employees. You discover that each of the three is involved in completing some training in basic communications skills. Here is what you learn:

Trainee #1. I'm taking some training. Why? Because I was told to do it by my supervisor. See? Here is my name on the memo telling me to sign up. Beyond that, I don't really have a reason why. Will I use it? I don't know. How could I know? I haven't finished it yet. What good will it do? I don't know. I haven't finished it yet. I was told to take it, so I am.

Trainee #2. I'm taking some really good training! I could use it, you could use it, anyone could use it any time, anywhere, for any number of reasons. Will I use it? Oh, yes. In everything I do. It looks *so* useful. After all, communications is really at the core of everything we do, so when wouldn't I use it? Could I name a specific time when I would use it? Let me think . . . pretty much all the time, at work, at home, in my volunteer work. After all, communications is a part of everything all of us do, so I think I'll use it all the time. Do you hear what I'm saying? (There? See? I just used it!). What good will it do? It will make me more effective in everything I do.

Trainee #3. I'm taking training. Why? Well, here in this pharmaceutical company, everything any of us do has to be focused on our overall company goal of getting new drugs to market on time. For me, where I work in the analysis laboratories, our contribution to that goal is cycle time: getting accurate reports to research scientists on time, in the shortest amount of time. Right now, since we are opening a new R&D center next month, our labs will be getting a lot of new orders and assay requests, some of them pretty complicated with different specificity requirements and criteria. I know from my past work with these R&D Ph.D.'s that they're not always real clear about stating precisely the requirements they need, and I'm usually a little intimidated by dealing with them. I would rather guess at what they need than try to talk to them. But when I guess wrong, or don't get the specs clear, then the whole lab analysis is done wrong and has to be redone. That can add many days of rework, which not only increases our cycle time but also doesn't help our customer satisfaction. So . . . I understand that this training can help me learn how to ask questions to get more clarity, confirm understanding, and even be more assertive. I will use it to get orders right the first time.

Clearly, each of the three trainees poses a different transfer scenario and probability. Each of them also represents a sort of archetypal trainee, and further, a sort of archetypal organizational culture. Both the type of trainee and the type of culture in which they work will become the focus of our HIL approach. But before we turn to a discussion of the organizational culture, let's look more closely at the three trainees themselves.

In the case of the first trainee, the transfer likelihood is very low. Apparently there is no understanding of the relationship between the training and the job. Further, there is an implicit understanding that participation in training is only something that meets predominant codes for acceptable behavior, much the same as codes prescribing correct office dress or codes that prohibit stealing office supplies. Training to the first trainee is a code for conduct, not a tool for improving performance.

In the case of the second trainee, the probability for transfer is very high, as there is such enthusiastic acceptance of the role of learning in self-improvement. But again, there is no apparent critical understanding of the job or concomitantly of how communications could be used on the job to achieve important results. So, although it is likely that this trainee will use the training in something, there is no assurance that it will be used with discernment to resolve key business or performance issues. In other words, there is a high probability of traditional transfer. But impactful transfer hinges on whether this second trainee can figure out the most strategic opportunities for application of the learning.

One might argue that if the second trainee really did use better communications all of the time in everything, that this would then also automatically include the most strategic applications as well. From a purely logical perspective, this is true. In reality, however, use of learned skills cannot move immediately to an "all of the time" level, but would follow a learning curve. The risk is great that the skills would be used in nonstrategic applications, leading to little if any positive consequence, and thereby not being reinforced by the workplace performance system.

The third trainee reflects a very different circumstance. This trainee first demonstrates a clear and strategic understanding of the job and can identify how the job is linked to and drives workplace goals. Further, this trainee has identified a particular portion of the job (the order-taking process) that is most important to addressing a particularly important job result: getting orders right the first time. It is also clear how this job result is linked to and helps accomplish a particular work unit objective (cycle time), and therefore how this objective is linked to the important overall organizational goal of getting new drugs to market quickly. Finally, the trainee has identified specific, leveragable skills (clarifying, confirming understanding) that can be learned in training that support job results and work unit objectives. To a large extent, the transfer riddle has been solved before this trainee even begins the skill-acquisition portion of the learning process. As we will explore further, this sort of "intentionality"—a clear focus on and commitment to a strategic subset of learning and performance objectives—lies at the heart of the HIL approach.

Leveraged Transfer

The concept of leveraged transfer is, we believe, a profoundly unique and vitally important principle of the HIL approach. Digging deeper into the example of the "three trainees" will make this clear. Table 1.1 depicts the different levels of understanding of transfer represented by each of the three trainees.

Notice the structure of Table 1.1. There are three major columns: the first, on the left, represents "capability." This reinforces the fact that learning solutions, on their own, can only increase the ability to perform. The next column is titled "performance," and considers the particular job applications in which the new capability can be deployed to help achieve specific objectives. The right-hand column represents "results," in this case, results achieved at both the work unit level and for the entire organization. The structure of the table revisits the concept of transfer and reminds us that training impact (value) is accomplished through a serial process in which learning produces capability, which then must be applied in performance, and that performance is the phenomenon that leads to desired results, which in turn determine the value of the training.

According to the entries in Table 1.1, it is readily seen that Trainee #1 had no understanding of even the immediate learning outcomes offered by the training intervention. There was thus no focus on particular learning objectives, and thereby no focus beyond that on any performance or organizational results. In the many evaluation studies we have conducted over the years, we have to conclude sadly that this type of trainee is in the majority among the organizations with whom we have worked. This simple graphic alone explains the notoriously low rates of impact we have found.

The picture improves somewhat with the second trainee; there is at least some assurance that learning and skill application will take place. Increasingly, and especially in organizations that have placed a high value on learning and develop-

TABLE 1.1   Impact Analysis for the Three Trainees

	Capability		Performance		Results	
Trainee	Key skills and knowledge to be gained from training	How training will be applied on the job	Trainee job results to be improved	Business process objectives contributed to	Business goals contributed to
One					
Two	• Communication skills	• Communicate with others effectively			
Three	• How to seek understanding • How to listen effectively • How to reach agreement	• Probe to get right information quickly • Understand what information scientists need	• Establish accurate order specifications • Set realistic analysis completion expectations	• Reduce rework • Increase accuracy • Reduce cycle time	• Reduce drug development time

ment, we find greater numbers of this sort of trainee. But often, as the "interview" with this sort of trainee shows, there is high enthusiasm but low focus. The culture in which this trainee resides seems to be more focused on learning for learning's sake than it does on learning as a strategic and business-linked tool. Evaluation of training initiatives in organizations with high numbers of this type of trainee typically show strong participation in learning opportunities, enthusiastic commitment to learning itself, but relatively low impact.

The third trainee archetype is not, in our experience, very common (except in organizations that have adopted truly high-impact approaches). There is a clear "line of sight" beyond the learning itself to specific performance applications and important goals. This line of sight is highly intentional and strategic. Looking at it from left to right across the graphic in Table 1.1, there is obvious linkage: connection among the learning, performance, and results elements.

Equally important, there is a right-to-left integrity as well, although this is not immediately obvious in the graphic. That is, the results listed in the right-hand portion of the graphic are not exhaustive, but are delimited to currently important goals that explicitly and strategically link the work unit to the organization. The analysis that lies behind the graphic has determined a single organizational goal to which this work unit makes an especially important and most direct contribution. Moving from the right to the center column, the analysis has identified and focused on the relatively small set of job objectives and tasks that, for this particular individual (Trainee #3), are the most important contributors to the unit's goal of cycle time. In other words, the analysis represented in Table 1.1 has isolated the job tasks and results, for this person's job, that afford the greatest leverage for improving cycle time in the unit.

Notice also that the information in Table 1.1 is not only specific to the job (lab analyst) but is also specific to this particular individual. If the particular behaviors specified in the middle column are improved, then we have the greatest opportunity to improve cycle time that *this particular* person can make. As you will remember from the "interview," Trainee #3 had an especially hard time coping with Ph.D. scientists when taking orders, preferring to guess at specifications rather than risking any sort of confrontational interaction. Thus, the best use that Trainee #3 can make of the training, given that cycle time is the overall goal, is to improve the order-taking portion of the role, aiming at getting more orders right at the beginning. This is the transfer—the specific and high-leverage application of learning with the greatest probability of contributing to business goals—that we aim for and that we use HIL methods and tools to achieve.

In later chapters, we will provide more detail and guidance as to how readers can use the HIL framework, methods, and tools for identifying and actualizing leveraged transfer from training systems and initiatives. There is a twofold purpose for the HIL approach: one primarily tactical, and the other more strategic. Referring again to the "three trainees" concept, HIL is used tactically within particular initiatives to increase the number of Trainee #3–type learners we have, and to assure that the high-leverage learning applications are in fact nurtured and supported in actual job performance. Strategically, the HIL approach is aimed at building the capability of the organization to gain more business value from learning investments. The HIL strategy seeks to build an organizational culture in which Trainee #3 is the rule, not the exception.

Understanding Training Impact

Before beginning a detailed exposition of the HIL model, it will be helpful to extend our discussion of leveraged transfer and look at the concept of high-impact learning from one additional perspective.

We referred earlier to the "line of sight" apparent in the example of the third trainee. Figure 1.2 begins to re-create this notion in more detail.

Here, we see one long horizontal arrow that represents a particular job position or a team role. As you can see, the organization expects specific performance results from this job position or team. Further, the individual performance results achieved by employees and teams leads to the achievement of a business goal, such as increasing customer satisfaction, decreasing costs, or improving market share.

FIGURE 1.2   Anatomy of High-Impact Learning

In Figure 1.3, we have now isolated a smaller "chunk" of this job position or team role. The smaller shaded components each represent a job task for the job or team role that is critical to achieve the desired performance results; we have called these "high leverage" tasks because they leverage performance results. In other words, if the employee or team could improve performance on these critical job tasks, there would be a direct impact on the performance results and thereby a direct, positive impact on the business measures of the organization.

FIGURE 1.3   Anatomy of High-Impact Learning

Learning-Performance Intersections

Figure 1.4 now adds "Learning Opportunities, Resources, and Tools" to the graphic. This illustrates the array of learning resources, such as e-learning modules, performance support tools, workshops, and so forth that are available in the organization. The bars that connect upward from the learning resources and intersect with the high-leverage, critical job tasks form "critical learning-performance intersections."

Here is the key point of the graphic: Impact from training occurs when . . .

- people as individuals or as a team learn . . .
- how to perform some part of their job more effectively, and . . .
- that improved performance drives achievement of an important business goal.

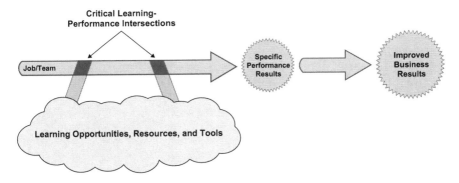

FIGURE 1.4   Anatomy of High-Impact Learning

Notice that this explanation of impact does not depend on the sheer *quantity* of learning. In a traditional approach to training, trainees are supposed to learn *all* of the objectives contained in a learning intervention. But according to our definition, there will be impact only if something that they learn is especially needed to improve performance on a key, high-leverage job task. One trainee could learn a lot from a learning intervention, but if that learning does not support a high-leverage task—or if that trainee could not sift out the high-leverage learning from all the rest of the learned stuff— there would be no chance for impact. Conversely, another trainee may only acquire a fraction of what was taught, but if that bit were exactly what was needed to perform a high-leverage job task more effectively, then we would be on the road to impact.

This was the case with Trainees #2 and #3. The second trainee was likely to learn a great deal about communications but was far less likely to have identified critical learnings that could be used in a targeted way to improve performance related to a key business goal. On the other hand, Trainee #3 had focused exactly on the learning needed to drive an improvement in order-taking accuracy, which was already known to be the task most likely to result in an improvement in cycle time. Overall, Trainee #2 might learn and use the content more extensively, but only Trainee #3 will achieve valuable impact.

Producing High-Impact Learning

The final version of this graphic analysis of training impact adds additional job and team roles.

In Figure 1.5, there are now multiple job and team roles, representing the many people who may participate in learning interventions. Notice also that

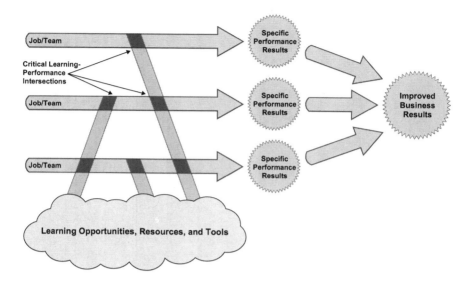

FIGURE 1.5   Anatomy of High-Impact Learning

any job or team role may have more than one critical intersection, meaning that there may be more than one particular task that is identified as a high-leverage transfer opportunity. But notice also that no job or team has more than two or three such targeted intersections. It is a corollary principle that impact is most likely to result when the focus is specific and is linked to a manageable performance improvement opportunity.

The graphic in Figure 1.5 implies as well that all impact is individual. Training works only when individual people learn something, then use it in a highly leveraged application. High-leverage applications are typically not generalizable or common among many job roles. Job and team roles may be similar (sales representatives, for example, are all doing the same sort of job). But the individuals in these roles will have unique personal strengths and weaknesses (recall that Trainee #3 was not very good at coping with research scientists) and specific performance improvement needs related to their particular job circumstances. Because this is the case, the HIL approach includes methods and tools to identify the unique high-leverage performance learning needs for all individuals.

It is useful to view the HIL methods and tools from the perspective of the notion of intersections. The challenge is to create learning systems that focus on both the horizontal and vertical dimensions shown in Figure 1.5. On the horizontal dimension, we look to HIL to help identify, clarify, and focus on particular high-leverage applications that exist at any given point in the dynamic context of the organization and its competitive environment. As goals, processes, and the people in roles change, learning needs and opportunities change. The HIL approach contains methods and tools to enable learning leaders to continuously analyze and clarify these horizontal connections among job roles, tasks, results, and important organizational goals.

On the vertical dimension, the HIL approach seeks to enable intersections of high-leverage tasks with effective learning resources. Thus, there are HIL methods and tools for helping to identify and define the key high-leverage learning needs for each individual in the organization, then systematically enable individuals to access the learning resources they need to improve performance, in just the right amounts and at just the right time. Finally, the HIL approach includes evaluation to assess how well the system is working, what business impact it is helping to achieve, and what needs to be done to build the organization's capability to get increasingly greater impact at better efficiencies.

Chapter Summary

Making training work is all about being sure that learning drives performance, since it is performance, not just capability, that contributes the most to impact from training. But performance is a complex and elusive phenomenon and is driven by more factors than sheer capability. The HIL approach is based on the concept of leveraged transfer, wherein learners focus on the strategic few performance improvements that are most likely to lead to achievement of key business goals.

HIL methods and tools are aimed at helping to determine and clarify these high-leverage opportunities, then create the learning and performance support methods that will best ensure impact. Finally, there are tactical and strategic aims to using the HIL approach. Tactically, we want to accomplish learning that drives improvement on key performance that in turn drives demonstrable business impact. In the longer run, we aim to build our organization's capability to gain increasingly greater impact returns on training investments. As the organization becomes more capable of achieving learning to performance, costs of tactical learning initiatives go down (since "intersections" are more tightly focused), learning-to-performance cycle time decreases, and more learning and performance management resources are free for the development of breakthrough innovations and virtuosity.

Does the E-World Change Everything?

Chapter Overview

E-learning is a powerful concept that is sweeping through, around, and over the training world. It is a technology with huge potential and can be used to significantly improve the impact of training, at the same time dramatically reducing costs. E-learning is also just a tool, and like any tool, it can be misused and wastefully applied. In fact, used incorrectly, it can subvert and undermine the impact of training. In this chapter, we begin by defining and explaining the concept and methods of e-learning as it can be used to enhance learning and performance. In the second section, we outline a number of ways in which e-learning can be used effectively in HIL solutions. We then turn to a brief look at the pitfalls and drawbacks of the e-learning revolution. Finally, we close the chapter by summarizing the ways in which e-learning can be used to leverage the HIL process, improving the performance and business impact return on training investments.

What Is "E-Learning"?

Casually defined, "e-learning" refers to training that is offered on and accessed electronically through the Internet or an organization's intranet, which is often otherwise referred to as "on-line learning" (Hambrecht Report, March 2000). However, defined more specifically, and as we will refer to it in this book, e-learning refers to a larger set of electronically formatted learning resources and activities. This more broad definition is sometimes referred to with the acronym TEL, or "technology-enabled learning." In our book, however, we will use the term "e-learning" to refer to the broad spectrum of TEL methods and tools.

From a purist perspective, technology is not at all limited to electronic formats. According to Webster's dictionary (1999), technology refers to any systematically applied science, tools, or both. By this more traditional definition, technology could refer to the use of an overhead projector, film strips, or a set of procedures, such as using behavioral objectives or an ISD (instructional systems design) process. But in keeping with more current usage, e-learning includes all the TEL media that are based on digital (that is, electronic and computer) technology. Therefore, when we refer to e-learning, we look beyond instructional media deployed through the Internet and intranets to CD-ROM and other transportable media for use at a workstation or from a laptop computer. We also consider distance learning tools such as one-way and interactive television, computer-based instruction, electronic performance support systems (EPSS), and all other digitally reproduced learning tools, procedures, and objects to belong to the family of e-learning opportunities.

On the other hand, "classroom" learning refers to the traditional instructor-led training that takes place in a contained physical space. It is not useful to think of this traditional mode as "instructor-led," since there are some e-learning delivery methods that employ instructors (CD-ROM modules or television courses, for example). Henceforth in the book, we will define classroom learning as learning activities that are conducted in a single physical space at a defined time, and typically that involve groups of participants.

This brings us to the single, most differentiating dimension between e-learning and classroom learning. Although classroom learning is inherently conducted synchronously, in other words, learners access the instruction at the same moment in time, e-learning is not limited to one particular time or physical space. Many forms of e-learning can be flexibly accessed at any time or from any disparate location, asynchronously.

Figure 2.1 further illustrates this concept. Asynchronous versus synchronous learning on the vertical axis. The horizontal axis depicts a range of low tech to high tech as it relates to learning media. Within the four quadrants of the matrix, we have placed a variety of learning media that includes both traditional classroom instruction as well as different types of e-learning. As you can see from the illustration, traditional and e-learning forms of instruction can be delivered both synchronously and asynchronously. What we will address next in this chapter, as well as throughout this book, is the art of crafting a "blended solution" that leverages the media, be it e-learning or otherwise, taking advantage of its best applications. Specifically, in Chapter 6, "Effective

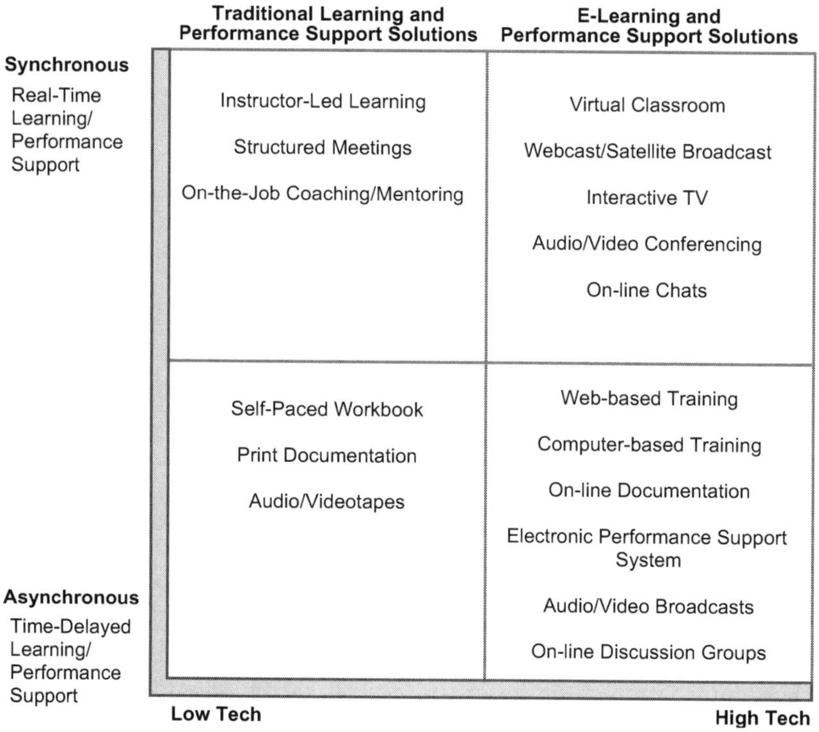

	Traditional Learning and Performance Support Solutions	E-Learning and Performance Support Solutions
Synchronous Real-Time Learning/ Performance Support	Instructor-Led Learning Structured Meetings On-the-Job Coaching/Mentoring	Virtual Classroom Webcast/Satellite Broadcast Interactive TV Audio/Video Conferencing On-line Chats
Asynchronous Time-Delayed Learning/ Performance Support	Self-Paced Workbook Print Documentation Audio/Videotapes	Web-based Training Computer-based Training On-line Documentation Electronic Performance Support System Audio/Video Broadcasts On-line Discussion Groups
	Low Tech	**High Tech**

FIGURE 2.1   High-Impact Learning Solutions

Learning Interactions," we explore the range of learning media in detail. Let's now take a closer look at the concept we refer to as blended solutions.

Blended Solutions

Just as variety is the spice of life, a mixture of learning solutions nearly always is more powerful than a single approach that attempts to do it all. Within the HIL approach, we refer to this mixture of learning media as a "blended solution." A blended solution is simply a set of instructional components that combines e-learning with classroom learning, communication, and performance support tools. A blended solution affords the benefit of using the most appropriate mix or blend of instruction, performance aids, and communication to create the optimum learning and performance improvement experience. A management training initiative we recently designed for a large multinational telecommunications corporation provides an excellent illustration.

Managers needing this training were globally dispersed, and the traditional method of bringing them into a single, multiday course was far too expensive, too slow (not responsive to being available exactly when it was needed), and virtually impossible to schedule owing to managers' stressed calendars. Further, the skills addressed (how to distance-manage globally dispersed virtual teams) were badly needed, and there was little time for a lengthy development process. The blended solution had these components:

- An on-line "chat" between managers and their managing directors to clarify the critical business objectives in the manager's unit, and the most important tasks to be accomplished to achieve those objectives.
- An on-line assessment of skill levels completed by the managers, their directors, and one or more direct reports.
- One or more basic knowledge and skill modules keyed to and driven by the assessment, to be completed on-line, that would build a fundamental skill and knowledge base in distance management techniques, issues, principles, and so forth.
- Participation in a facilitated problem-solving (classroom style) workshop with a small group of managers facing similar business challenges, which closed with the completion of an action plan and a continued learning plan to strengthen skills needed to initiate the problem solutions arrived at in the workshop.
- Action plan sharing among both directors of the managers and other managers addressing similar issues.
- The creation of a learning "community" among the managers facing similar issues, who could provide support, interaction, feedback, and so forth. An electronic bulletin board and e-mail supported these learning community contacts.
- Additional learning modules, performance aids such as coaching checklists, and knowledge coaches were provided, as aligned with the action plans.
- Additional skill-building workshops or courses were available in the managers' home locales.

As you can see, the total solution was much more than a single classroom workshop, as before. The new process was more thorough, far more individualized, and contained a blend of electronic and classroom learning methods and tools, as well as tools to facilitate communication and networking. This sort of process exemplifies the best of e-learning melded into a "blended solution," a solution that provides more impact and greater access than its classroom-only predecessor.

It may seem at first blush that because these blended solutions are more complex and lengthy, they are more expensive than traditional training. But this is usually not the case, since classroom training time is almost always reduced, which dramatically lowers costs. At QUALCOMM, for instance, classroom training is dedicated only to interactive skill building; all "information" training elements are provided electronically. In this manner, participants spend less of their valuable time in the classroom, and learning impact—as well as ease of access—is enhanced. It is true, however, that blended solutions span longer periods of time, since they intersperse practice, on-the-job application, networking, and so forth, among the structured periods of more typical training. This is more aligned with how learning and performance improve, however, and clearly adds power and impact to the experience. It also adds advantages in convenience to learners, since they are in more control of when and how they learn.

A Three-Part Structure

It is also worthwhile to note that the overall structure of the blended initiative can be viewed in three major phases.

The first component in our example leveraged e-learning to establish the conditions for more in-depth skill building, providing participants with a business focus for their learning, and establishing a fundamental capability in the management competency. In the second component, participants were involved in classroom activities intended to develop more complex skills. The development of skills such as these almost always requires the sort of hands-on practice, responsive feedback, and group interaction that only a classroom experience can provide. The classroom experience provided the social interaction, networking, and community building that deepens learning, and also assured the continued interaction among participants that helped to support their ongoing learning as they struggled with discovering and mastering new managerial capabilities. The third component of the initiative again relied

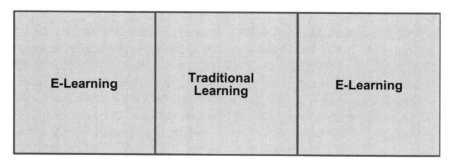

FIGURE 2.2   Blended Solutions

primarily on e-learning technologies; they gave participants maximum flexibility in driving their own further learning and allowed them instant access to resources and performance support as they were needed.

This three-part structure is quite common in blended solutions. The e-learning technology lets learners build individual focus and readiness and enables them to assess their own circumstances and tailor their initial learning. As learners discover more in-depth skill needs, they can use additional e-learning resources to plan further learning strategies. Typically, however, for many learning needs, there is a point in the learning journey where a classroom experience is needed to practice skills in a safe environment and leverage the social interaction and sense of community that group learning experiences provide. After engaging in this sort of intense group learning, participants enter a phase where they need to try out skills in their own work settings and begin to experiment with application, trial, and error. During this stage, new learning, regardless of how capable people felt when they completed their classroom experience, is very fragile; it is not uncommon for learners to retreat to old behaviors after a first few discouraging attempts at something new. During this phase, e-learning technologies are especially useful and efficient, as they put control of learning back into the hands of the learners and let them access the sort of help they need when the need arises. Typically, too, interventions during this phase need not be lengthy, so e-learning technology is especially helpful, as it enables rapid access to "bite-size" bits of instruction, helpful tools (such as checklists and process guides), and sympathetic advice and support from fellow learners or identified experts and coaches.

Readers will also notice that this three-part structure is very similar to the structure of the HIL process, which we review in detail in Chapter 3, "The High-Impact Learning Model." You will see that e-learning and HIL are highly compatible frameworks and together provide a powerful technology for achieving business results from learning investments.

Applications and Advantages

E-learning methods, especially when combined with the massive and worldwide Internet, offer sweeping huge advantages to organizational learning and performance. Some of these advantages are relatively immediate and obvious, such as reducing costs of travel to central classroom training, electronic file generation to enrich and ease administration of training, and providing individualized and rapid access to learning resources. Other benefits are more profound and will take more time to emerge.

- Freeing training personnel from mundane and poorly leveraged training tasks to enable them to invest in activities with greater value

- Democratizing training by putting more power in the hands of learners
- Providing more powerful performance support tools and methods that can decrease cycle time in learning, so employees become more competent more quickly
- Improving operational efficiencies by applying emerging industry standards to create "best practices" in the design, development, and implementation of learning

It is important for learning leaders to understand these advantages, so that they can leverage them with the HIL approach for even greater impact. Further, it is a fact of life that most strengths are also, at the same time, potential weaknesses; understanding these vulnerabilities (which we discuss in the next section) further enhances our capabilities to leverage the power of e-learning. But first, we review advantages of e-learning.

Unlimited and Individualized Access

We have already noted one of these: the "just what's needed, just in time" access to learning and performance support tools. This advantage is so great that it is probably not possible to overestimate it. Sales representatives, for example, can access immediately updated information about their own products, competitor activities, and customer profiles from laptop computers mere minutes before making a sales call. Computer technicians troubleshooting a customer's server can refresh their understanding of diagnostic procedures, greatly increasing their accuracy of performance and sharply decreasing the time they would have to spend accessing complex written manuals. Medical personnel in remote locations can access real-time expertise from specialist doctors, immediately applying their just-in-time learning in lifesaving procedures. The list could go on forever, and new applications are emerging daily.

For decades, educators and trainers have searched for methods and tools to individualize learning, and have often been frustrated by the classroom model, in that the classroom economy requires large group sizes to defray per-trainee costs of instruction. The classroom model virtually requires that all trainees move through the training process at roughly the same pace, all working on the same topics and materials at the same time. The e-learning model eliminates this requirement and affords a truly individualized approach. With e-learning methods and tools, individual employees in an organization can not only access learning when they need or want it but can also tailor that learning to their own particular learning needs and styles.

This should not be construed to mean that e-learning is always a superior alternative to classroom learning. Good classroom learning, of course, can offer a dynamic, fluid, changeable environment to match the needs of the learners, given an attentive, qualified instructor and a flexible instructional design. On the other hand, static e-learning modules aren't "intelligent" and are less pliable to flex to the needs of the individual learner. For these reasons, we almost always promote the use of blended solutions in our work and likewise almost always build choices of learning methods into learning systems.

In our earlier example of a blended solution, for instance, a manager could choose from a number of learning modules and experience those particular elements that he or she felt best addressed the development capabilities identified from the assessment. The learning department in this organization had "exploded" already existing training programs and workshops into the smallest elements (knowledge objects) and then arrayed these elements into menus that were keyed to capability development needs and objectives. Imagine, for example, a manager who wanted to learn about distance management techniques such as how to conduct a meeting using two-way television. This manager could search the learning systems bank and find the following resources:

- A video clip of a manager conducting such a meeting
- An annotated version of this video highlighting the key skills and techniques the manager employed
- A self-instructional module on the principles and methods of successful distance meetings
- Several reading articles on the topic
- An on-line "coach" who would discuss and provide feedback on a manager's plan for conducting a key meeting
- An on-line expert who would agree to observe a manager's attempt at conducting a meeting, then provide critical feedback and suggestions for improvement

Not only can learners pick and choose the learning modules they want, they also can build them into unique combinations. For the first time, learners can create their own learning solutions, blending the available resources into the solution that works best for them.

Large-Scale Distribution

E-learning methods and tools enable an organization to rapidly disseminate key learning opportunities to broadly dispersed global audiences. The distributed computer network, either within an organization or over the Internet, allows any learning program or activity to be scaled to any size of audience, from a small local group to the entire worldwide organization. Further, the cost of scaling it to a large audience is negligible, once the learning module is developed, since it is just a matter of making it accessible through already existing data systems (assuming, of course, that the hardware and software infrastructure is already in place). In addition, this electronic infrastructure allows immediate dissemination of revised and updated information almost effortlessly.

The United States Navy was an early adopter of e-learning, and provides a dramatic example of the scalability of e-learning methods and tools. Imagine the navy's business scenario: employees scattered liberally all over the globe, and many on ships at sea, hugely separated from central classroom learning spaces. Add to this the tremendous training and learning burden of the navy; in times of peace, military service is virtually constant training. Finally, add in the fact that the navy requires intense learning, as the personnel demands are such that young neophytes with no navy operations skills must be quickly trained, then must be involved in ongoing advanced training to fill the many layers of upper ranks of the organization. E-learning to the rescue. Using wireless transmission of e-mail and Internet access, as well as television and distributed CD-ROM disks, the navy is able to operate a widely dispersed and highly accessible "learn at sea" program that enables personnel to engage in highly effective learning from a seemingly limitless number of remote sites. Prior to electronic means, of course, the navy had operated a distance education program, but this was all paper-based learning by mail. (Just imagine the logistical nightmare of managing the production and distribution of information and learning in this low-tech environment!) The new technologies enable a far more rich training environment, with a more attractive and effective array of teaching and learning modalities.

Cost Savings

A very prominent feature of e-learning that is much loved by chief financial officers is the dramatically reduced cost of providing training to large, dispersed audiences. Consider, for example, the case of a computer services company that offers a two-week workshop provided at its corporate headquarters for technicians in troubleshooting one of the company's key products. Using this delivery strategy, the company must pay for travel and per diem expenses for all attendees, a cost of about $6,000 per participant; with 400 participants per year, the company spends $2.4 million just moving participants to and from the training session. Now imagine that this entire workshop can be offered via the Internet, wherein technicians complete self-instructional modules covering all of the knowledge components of the learning, observe videotaped versions of repair and troubleshooting cases, and actually practice troubleshooting via computerized simulation from their laptops. They then receive CD-ROM versions of technical support manuals to guide and support their application on the job. In one year, this direct training cost can be reduced by $2.4 million. Once the cost of developing the e-learning solution is covered, this training cost saving is available year after year—and this is only from one of the many courses offered by the company.

Clearly, e-learning affords potentially huge cost savings for providing necessary training to broadly dispersed audiences. This potential for cost saving has provided tremendous impetus for the development of e-learning and has made it easy for vendor companies who create e-learning content to prepare impressive return-on-investment (ROI) arguments for their services. As many readers will recognize, quality and effectiveness risks are encountered in conversion to e-learning, as we will discuss in the next section. But it is likewise clear that the cost-saving benefits of e-learning have been a formidable force in driving rapid conversion, and edicts from chief financial officers to force training departments to initiate conversion of classroom training to e-learning are commonplace.

Competency Tracking

Many companies are adopting electronic tools and methods for administering training and integrating these with e-learning systems. These have a number of advantages and applications. Because e-learning is accessed electronically, it is a simple matter for e-learning activities to be tracked and logged, allowing administrators to quickly summarize how often, how long, when, where, and by whom training is participated in and completed. Records are automatically generated and, likewise, automatic summary reports and analyses can be quickly produced.

Having analyses of learning participation and completion is extremely helpful not only in administering training operations but also in determining what pockets of the organization might need more or less training attention. It is also an advantage to be able to compare learning rates and acquisition to emerging business issues and opportunities. A company could, for example, determine quickly which field division had the greatest number of employees with a certain capability, thus directing business operations to the field division with the greatest capability for handling that business.

This business-competency linkage capability extends to the individual employee, as competency acquisition can be monitored and summarized at any time. Using electronic competency tracking tools, a company can determine almost instantaneously which employees have completed which competency acquisition activities. This enables, for example, the IBM company to assemble a sales team of individuals with a unique blend of competencies to address an emerging business opportunity with a potential client. In another example, a call center that coordinates automobile towing services for all of Canada can monitor weather conditions (an emerging blizzard, for example), predicting call center loads, then bringing in the staff with the competencies needed to handle the expected rush of calls. This same call center company also has coordinated its call distribution software with its competency profile database, so that calls are automatically routed to a person with the right capabilities to handle the unique circumstances of each inbound service request. A customer calling with a question about insurance coverage for a Ford minivan with an overheated radiator is routed to speak to a person who is qualified (because that person successfully completed a particular learning program) to handle Ford product service requests in Montreal.

This linkage of competency to performance needs and therefore to business objectives is, of course, an attractive feature for the HIL approach. High-impact learning is predicated on accurate business linkage, and e-learning tools provide the potential for accomplishing this linkage rapidly at the individual performer level.

Workplace Locus of Control

E-learning has the potential of putting much of the learning access system into the hands of employees, reducing or even removing any bureaucratic steps and barriers. This is a powerful force indeed and has potentially far-reaching benefits. In the most immediate sense, administrative demands on training professionals are reduced as electronic systems do more mundane record generation automatically and as learners take on more independent learning responsibility. This gives training professionals more available time, which (following an HIL model) can then be invested in the higher leverage effort of strengthening relationships with business customers and deepening their analysis and understanding of the relationship among business issues, performance improvement opportunities, and learning needs.

E-learning provides line managers and their employees with the tools needed to better manage performance and continuously identify emerging learning needs that can drive performance improvement. This direct access to the methods and tools that drive learning and performance has the potential for more rapid and accurate identification of important needs and can therefore presumably increase the effectiveness of learning and performance improvement initiatives. Again, this application and outcome of e-learning is not only highly compatible with an HIL approach but furthers it, as it moves training and learning into a tighter linkage to the business issues of the organization.

Flexible Performance Support

E-learning systems make an array of on-the-job learning and performance support aids available to managers and employees. Consider, for example, an engineering and architecture firm with whom we worked that is a national builder of municipal parking structures.

This company, in its unusual niche in the market, has a large amount of proprietary knowledge that forms a valuable base of intellectual capital for the organization. It is also faced with the issue of a growing market and needs to quickly bring newly hired engineers (all with no experience in parking structure design) up to speed on company expertise. At the same time, business demands are such that virtually all learning must happen on the job, as there is no time for a lengthy preservice training program, nor would the profit structure of the business allow large amounts of time spent in a non-revenue-generating activity such as training.

The solution is an electronic "knowledge bank" that provides working engineers access to "bite-size" bits of learning and performance support, such as a project checklist, engineering criteria, and so forth. This system is supplemented with e-mail and teleconference access to veteran specialist engineers and architects within the company who can provide brief consultation and advice from remote and to remote locations, on an as-needed basis. Using these e-learning tools, the company is able to maintain its project schedules, yet at the same time embed brief learning and performance consultation support almost seamlessly into the work process. At the same time, they protect and enlarge their intellectual capital, an important source of competitive advantage in this specialized business.

Another client company, one of the largest providers of office furniture and work environments in the world, uses an on-line support tool for globally dispersed salespeople. In this business, there are literally over a billion possible combinations of product models, styles, layouts, and features that can be configured for any customer, far more than any single person or team could possibly learn in several lifetimes. On the other hand, price limits imposed by a customer may limit the combinations, and complex production and engineering constraints must be added into the mix to come up with a workable bid for a customer.

The solution we helped this company implement is an on-line simulator that can be accessed by any salesperson anywhere in the world. The salesperson, using a laptop computer and an easy-to-learn program, can create a number of possible virtual combinations for a customer, all of which can be vividly and attractively portrayed on the screen. The program then is linked to the company's manufacturing and production database, which will modify the virtual combination to accommodate installation schedule and cost constraints. This system has greatly reduced initial product training demands, yet lets sales activities continue (which drive revenues) in the field to quickly and accurately meet customer needs. At the same time, salespeople are learning as they work out combinations, and with each successive sale they become more proficient and expert. This sort of performance support system provides a "safety net" that maintains a minimum level of adequate performance while it successively builds competence. Again, we see clear and direct linkage to business needs, and learning is rapidly transformed into effective performance.

As all of the applications and advantages summarized in this section show, e-learning can be a powerful enabler of HIL approaches. In many cases, it allows faster learning times, which immediately improves business performance, since it reduces time and money spent in a non–revenue-producing activity such as training. In other cases, e-learning supports more effective translation of learning into performance. In other instances, e-learning methods put access to and engagement in learning in the hands of line employees, which in turn provide tighter linkage to business needs and issues. In sum, e-learning is a tremendously valuable tool with almost unlimited potential. But like any tool, it can be misapplied. Given its seductive advantages, the likelihood of misuse is very great, and growing every day.

In the next section we look closely at the potential weaknesses and faults of e-learning. They are numerous and significant. If we do not pay heed to overcoming and avoiding them, e-learning can actually reduce the effectiveness of training and run totally counter to the goals of high-impact learning.

Issues and Obstacles

The training profession has always been vulnerable to the criticism that it is aimed more at delivering training than it has been at achieving results. In their book *Training for Impact* (1989), James and Dana Robinson labeled this phenomenon the "training for activity" trap. They noted that many training departments seemed more concerned with the number of training hours they provided and the number of trainees they processed during those hours than they were with the results that the training led to. Later publications (for example, see Brinkerhoff, 1987; Brinkerhoff and Gill, 1994; Swanson and Holton, 1999; Robinson and Robinson, 1996) further developed the training-as-activity notion into a prescription for training departments to focus their efforts on performance rather than just learning. Indeed, the premise of this book is an extension of the same issues, since the HIL approach is likewise a methodology for assuring that learning investments pay off in performance improvement that impacts business results.

The forces that have driven the cautions given in these earlier works have not gone away. Much of training still suffers from a lack of focus on performance. Many training departments are still burdened by budgeting, measurement, and accounting structures that force a focus on production of training hours and programs rather than accomplishment of business results. Much training is still as disconnected from business needs and objectives as it ever was. In short, the weaknesses inherent in training operations remain in some cases as strong as ever.

Unfortunately, there is nothing inherent in e-learning technology that assures greater performance results from training than any other training technology. The reality is that e-learning is only a tool, and as such it can be misapplied as readily as it can be used effectively. Even more dangerous, the huge potential of e-learning makes it so attractive that it is probably more likely to be misused than not. Our purpose in this section is to highlight some key cautions about e-learning, as they must be especially recognized and addressed by practitioners wanting to adopt the HIL framework, methods, and tools.

Cost Savings Versus Performance Results

Perhaps one of the greatest problems with the migration to e-learning is that it has become a *rush* to e-learning. We have encountered a large number of companies that are jumping on the e-learning bandwagon as if it were the only way to go. This rush has been driven by many factors, but primary among them is money (which comes as no surprise). On the company users' side, the cost savings available by reducing travel to training sessions has been strongly attractive; it is difficult for a chief financial officer or a training director to turn down an immediate opportunity to demonstrate dramatic savings to a cost-conscious leadership.

On the other side of the equation is a large and growing band of fiercely competitive vendors, ready to convert any and all training content to digital format. Alongside these conversion vendors are an equally powerful assortment of technology companies that build the hardware and software platforms from which e-learning initiatives are mounted. As we noted earlier, it is not unusual for companies to issue edicts to their training departments prescribing a conversion rate demanding, for example, that within a year, no less than 50 percent of all training must be done via e-learning. Harried training directors can find any number of vendors willing and ready to accomplish these mandated goals, and the rush is on.

Without careful attention to design and an unrelenting concern for performance improvement, it is just as likely as not that an e-learning initiative will be ineffective in achieving business-important performance improvement.

True, it may cost less to deliver this weak training (though after infrastructure and conversion costs are added in, this may not be true). We see no strategic advantage, however, in doing poor training for less money. Cost savings are worthwhile, of course, but are not and should not be the goal of training. The goal of training, e-learning or otherwise, is performance results that make a difference.

Choices, Choices, Choices

One of the strengths of e-learning is that it makes available a broad array of learning topics, media, and schedules to employees. This is also a key weakness. As we noted, training has always been subject to the risk of being disconnected from business goals and objectives. To some extent, linkage between business goals and learning activities is more controlled in the classroom paradigm, since there is more control over participation. As the choices of learning options grow exponentially and the access system becomes far more available, the risk of unlinked learning increases. What is to assure, for example, that the e-learning activity in which an employee engages is important, linked to a key performance need, will be supported by that employee's supervisor, and will be likely to lead to business impact?

We would not argue with the philosophical notion that any learning is probably worthwhile. Learning is always "good," and to be learning is probably healthier than to not be learning. But at the same time, from an organization's need to grow competitive advantage, some learning is clearly better than other learning. The key, then (and this is fundamental to the premise of HIL), is to build systematic methods and tools into learning operations that consistently and accurately steer learning to achieve the greatest possible strategic value, for the learner as well as the organization. As the choices and options increase, then so must our attention to steering mechanisms, to counter the risks of investing learning time—an always limited resource—in low-leverage activities.

Cultural Clash

E-learning is part of a larger transition to an electronic workplace and business environment. Organizations vary as to how far along they are toward making a transition to paperless tools, instantaneous communication, and the broad access of the e-business world. But chances are most organizations are not as far along as they could be, and it is also virtually a guarantee that some parts of the organization are further along than others. Thus, to some extent computer applications and electronic tools are still an emerging capability, and some employees will not be as comfortable or as fluent as one might wish.

On the other side of this is the pervasive culture of the older, classroom-based training approach. This is a deeply rooted culture, as virtually everyone in an organization was raised from earliest childhood in a classroom approach to education. So, it is a knee-jerk response for most people to equate learning with classrooms. This culture has also insidiously invaded the workplace, and most training in most organizations, although it may be transitioning, is still largely classroom based. If it not classroom based today, chances are it was not too long ago. When these two cultures—the new electronic workplace and the classroom-based training approach—are added together, they create a formidable barrier to effective learning and performance support.

For example, consider a company with whom we recently worked that had invested large sums in building and disseminating electronic learning modules to be completed by individual employees at their workstation in their "spare" time. Despite the investment and impressive technological array of learning tools and options, the single greatest barrier to effectiveness was simple use of the system. Time and again, employees were interrupted from learning or discouraged from beginning modules in the first place by managers who felt they should be engaged in more "productive" endeavors. From the managers' perspective, when they saw people engaging in learning modules, they saw them essentially with time on their hands and directed them to other activities. "Since you're not too busy, why don't you . . ." was a commonplace directive heard time and again.

From an HIL perspective, here was a system that paid a lot of attention to the design and deployment of learning opportunities but spent far too little time working to create an environment that could leverage those opportunities into practice and results. Importantly, the managers were not professedly antilearning. In fact, many had been strong supporters of learning programs in the past; they were just used to having employees who were engaged in learning being somewhere else—not visible to them, and certainly not readily available to be redeployed into mainstream work activities.

From the employees' perspective, we have also heard the lament that when you really need to learn something, the classroom is the best way. This tells us that there is not as much learning potency as is ascribed to the e-learning approach. People like it for its flexibility and convenience but may not think that it really works to produce lasting results. Leveraging the many potential advantages of e-learning will require an adoption of a different mind-set about training, one that does not equate learning with a classroom. Further, our studies on the completion rates for e-learning modules show distressingly low percentages. These low results may be attributed to the latitude that e-learning affords the learner, who, lacking the controls of the classroom, will not work as hard.

Passive Methods

The predominant mental model that drives the design of many e-learning modules is the old classroom model. That is, when it comes time to create e-learning methods, practitioners have viewed the task as principally one of *conversion;* taking the classroom training program that has been in place for many years and converting it to electronic modules. Thus, for example, if our communication skills program had three objectives and six modules, then the e-learning version of that program will have the same structure, and the content, exercises, and examples will remain essentially the same. The result of most conversion approaches to e-learning design is very weak, uninteresting, passive, and ineffective learning. Too many e-learning programs become a dump for content, and consist of page after page of reading matter, livened up with clever graphics, sounds, and illustrations. Not only will these approaches not work, they will build resistance and frustration among users, which will spill over and create a low-expectation, negative attitude toward all e-learning methods.

The proper paradigm for creating e-learning is not classroom instruction but performance support and improvement. According to this mental model, we should ask the question, "How do we help people learn from their performance?" rather than "How do we teach them this content?" This model will lead us to look at the performance environment of employees, understand their opportunities and obstacles, then design a system that fits into their primary tasks, responsibilities, and workplace system. This will also ensure that the e-learning activities require performance from the participant, such as solving problems, analyzing information, collecting data about themselves or others, responding to questions, and so forth. One of the advantages of e-learning is that it is both individually accessed and it is designed to be accessed from the workplace. The method should take advantage of this setting, working with it and within it, rather than trying to somehow digitally transport a classroom into the workplace. So, for example, a customer service module might ask a participant to try out one or more of several options for responding to customer queries, then to take a minute and ask the customer for reaction and feedback. The employee might then be directed to reflect on the feedback and choose to develop (in another module) more skill on the technique that seemed to work best. A classroom setting would never allow this sort of instant experimentation, but it is natural and obvious within the e-learning capability.

Lack of Social Interaction

Classroom training and other synchronous approaches that engage groups of people in a common experience have a powerful side effect of creating opportunities for socialization, providing networking contacts, and creating a sense of community. These social interactions, and the opportunity to have them, are probably a fundamental human need and value. They are also valuable in learning, as people who are having difficulties can share their feelings of inadequacy and come to the comforting knowledge that they are not alone nor unusual. Further, people learn well from one another and, being simultaneously engaged in a difficult learning task, can turn to one another for advice and encouragement. Groups of learners can also see how others approach a problem and perhaps discover a way that they might want to try, or that they might want to avoid. Finally, classroom learning also affords a dynamic and flexible learning environment that allows subtle connections to be made, hard-to-anticipate questions to be answered, and extra examples to be presented. In other words, classroom learning can be customized to the needs of the audience attending at the moment, based on their specific needs and performance requirements. Even the most exquisitely designed e-learning module cannot simulate this type of rich learning environment.

The power of groups for social learning and support is well known and highly valued. E-learning approaches that attempt to make all learning individual and that deny opportunities for the social "retreat" that classroom learning provides are probably doomed to fail in the long run. On the other hand, there is probably no learning initiative that could not be strengthened by the inclusion of some e-learning methods, particularly in the building of basic understanding and in the provision of real-time performance support and feedback. The trick is to leverage the e-technology for what it is good for and to avoid overusing it is as a blanket solution. The old adage of the "law of the hammer" is worth our heeding: When you teach someone to use a hammer, every problem starts to look like a nail.

It's All About Design

In sum, our position in this book is that e-learning is a tool for learning and instruction, perhaps the most profoundly powerful tool that has come along since the invention of the printing press. But it is still a tool and must be used correctly. Effective learning will always contain inherent challenges, such as:

- What learning is most needed to drive desired performance and results?
- What specific competencies do people need to master to achieve these results?
- What learning approach, with whom, will work best?
- When and how should we provide learning activities?
- How can we help motivate and inspire learners?

- What obstacles and opportunities will learners confront in their work lives?
- How can we best support performance improvement?
- How will learners, and those who help them, measure their success?
- How can we assure that learners tap into and leverage their current experience and expertise?

Again, we should note that there is nothing in particular about e-learning methods and tools that addresses any of these critical design questions, nor does e-learning pose any prima facie solutions. The challenge is to design solutions that work and that make a difference. The correct approach for the training leader who wants to make a difference to the business must begin with understanding the business case and performance requirements of the training challenge. This creates the vision of the end solution: What will we have when we have something that works? Then, one proceeds through the more traditional design process to identify learning needs, performer characteristics, performance requirements, and so forth, putting together the right combination of tools and methods that will get the quickest and best learning opportunities in place, in a way that is most likely to drive performance improvement.

Avoiding Either-Or Choices

We rarely encounter learning and performance scenarios where we must make an either-or choice between e-learning or classroom instruction. Almost always, as we've noted, we create solutions that include a blend of classroom components, along with technology-enabled learning and performance support, as well as essential communication tools. We would almost never, for example, rely solely on a classroom-only approach. At a minimum, the classroom approach will be blended with some medium for interaction between trainees and their supervisors, to revisit and clarify business objectives, to focus performance improvement targets, and to assure a clear "line of sight" between learning outcomes and performance and business goals.

Where there is a need for people to develop complex skills that involve a high degree of interpersonal interaction, we defer to classroom methods for some if not all of the skill development process. Consider, for example, the skill of conducting an effective coaching session. This is the sort of skill application that requires "steering" information based on the verbal and nonverbal reactions of the fellow participant, a sophisticated skill that entails keen observation, empathetic listening, and so forth. Although it may be possible to develop an electronic simulation with the range and power of branches and feedback options, we would find a simple, old-fashioned group session to be the best choice.

Clearly, before attending this group session, it may be good for participants to read a bit about the issues and challenges of coaching, to learn some fundamental skills about coaching techniques (for example, asking open-ended versus closed-ended questions). It will also be good for participants to identify their particular business goals and analyze how performance of key roles in their chain of direct reports addresses those business needs. After in-depth skill development in group settings, it may also be useful to have participants use the Internet and e-mail to share successes, ask questions of experts, and so forth, to support continued refinement and extension of their skill. These e-learning options would be built around and within a larger design that incorporated the live group training session.

One of the real benefits of the e-learning capability is that it lessens the demand on the group session, as so much else can be accomplished through the technology-enabled distance learning methods. In a classroom-only approach, the classroom activity has to include all of the learning elements: establishing objectives, clarifying needs, focusing business goals, soliciting supervisory involvement, forecasting application needs and performance obstacles, and action planning, for examples. Given this burden, the classroom vehicle bends and nearly breaks, leaving nowhere near enough time and mental attention for the crucial classroom-only task of practicing skills, forming relationships, and receiving feedback. When the classroom vehicle is relieved of these burdens through parsimonious application of e-learning methods, huge gains in productivity and efficiency are made, and a truly powerful learning-to-performance process emerges.

Determining how much of what types of e-learning support to provide, how, and when, as well as to design a powerful classroom-based experience, are, of course, the design challenge. But HIL thinking and design principles will help address this challenge. The result is powerful learning that works, and works quickly and efficiently, to impact performance and business results.

A Process Approach for E-Learning

It is easy to fall into a framework where e-learning is conceived as electronic bits of instructional content, or "knowledge objects." Indeed, to fully leverage broad accessibility and to enable optimum individualization, it is right to explode learning content and modules into the smallest logical components. This lets users access only those elements that are most useful to them, and also to get in and out quickly, which reduces cycle time in learning-to-performance. On the other hand, e-learning will not be fully effective unless it is embedded into a learning and performance improvement process.

The earlier example of a blended solution provides an excellent illustration of a process approach to deploying e-learning. This example can also be easily interpreted in the three-part structure described in the first section of the chapter. According to this structure, the first portion of the process was dedicated to establishing a clear focus for the performance improvement and business impact that was the target for the learning initiative. This first part of the process also included basic instruction, to build the knowledge foundation and prerequisite skills necessary to fully exploit the in-practice, feedback, and reflection that constituted the middle portion of the process. In the final portion of the process, e-learning tools were used to refine skills, guide application, support performance improvement, and provide access to the performance support job aids, expert resources, and other tools that constituted a knowledge base that could be readily accessed by the continuing learner.

Good design that leverages e-learning technology will conceive of performance improvement as a cyclical process, wherein challenges and obstacles to performance are identified and clarified, competency levels are assessed, learning is strategically focused on high-value objectives, skill practice and reflection are facilitated, and ongoing performance support is provided. This larger process requires careful design in itself, and the system that surrounds it must likewise be tapped for support and resources. In the management training process, for example, the design also included means to solicit the involvement of senior managers who were to review and affirm business goals. Likewise, the process was designed to be compatible and integrated with performance review tools and procedures.

In sum, good and thorough design is the task that we as training leaders face, just as we did before the advent of e-learning. The challenge has always been how to best structure and deploy the myriad tools and methods that the current technology provides, so that learning provides the maximum return for the resources invested. It is no different with e-learning. Whether the e-world works for us or against us will be determined by the quality of our design efforts.

E-Learning and HIL

E-learning technology can greatly enhance the HIL approach and fits it exceedingly well. With e-learning, we can increase the speed and ease of instruction and provide far more flexible and powerful performance support than ever before. We can develop and deploy instructional tools and methods faster than ever and provide a much greater degree of individualization than has been previously possible. The transfer of learning to the workplace, previously a burden borne by learners, can now be eased, since e-learning enables employees to address transfer issues before they engage in learning, by selecting only those instructional modules and activities needed to address performance improvement goals.

Perhaps the greatest contribution of the e-learning capability to the refinement of the HIL approach is the extent to which e-tools and methods can be used to integrate the learning-to-performance process. In earlier versions of HIL that we developed for the classroom learning paradigm (see Brinkerhoff, 1989; Gill and Brinkerhoff, 1994), we partitioned the training process into "before" training, "during" training, and "after" training segments. This segmentation was very helpful at that time, as it helped training leaders recognize that by the time trainees arrived at a training session, the business impact they might achieve from that training was already largely fixed. That is, if they didn't know exactly why they were there, what they were learning for, how they would use what they learned, and if their supervisors were not prepared to support their postlearning application of new skills, then the training could be pretty well discounted as having little impact potential. Likewise, if after the training there was no system in place to nurture trial application of the new learning and provide the supervisory feedback and support for performance improvement, then the impact of the training would be further diminished.

This partitioning of the training process into temporal "zones" was helpful, in that it spurred learning leaders to pay attention to more than just the classroom phase of the training process. As we pointed out, the classroom phase was probably the part that already worked quite well, and there was little leverage to be gained from improving it. If, however, learning leaders could improve the focus and readiness of learners to use new skills in intentional performance improvement efforts, then the overall process would be far more likely to produce impact.

In the old classroom paradigm, what was done before arriving at training was "prework," a label that immediately relegated it to something that was of low importance, a mere bureaucratic inconvenience that could be readily ignored. In the e-learning paradigm, learning starts when the learner engages the learning resources. Work done first is not done "before" learning, it is just the early part of the overall process. Likewise, performance support is not some afterthought that is tacked on, such as a rushed action planning activity crammed into the last ten minutes of a workshop. In the e-learning paradigm, the learning process simply continues, transforming itself into changing methods and tools at the learners' commands. This blurring of the temporal distinction is powerful and greatly aids us in our quest to plan, design, and implement learning as an integrated and seamless performance improvement process: the heart of the HIL concept.

Chapter Summary

Over the years, technology has truly expanded our toolbox for delivering learning more efficiently, and at a lower cost. More important, technology-enabled learning delivery methods have allowed us to improve our strategies around how learners learn. Now, instead of having to force-fit all learning experiences such as content and opportunities to practice and receive feedback into a single learning event, we find that we have a multitude of learning delivery mechanisms at our disposal and can instead create a blended solution that leverages the media to its best application.

But, as with any new set of tools, we are wise to recognize technology-enabled learning methods for what they are and to understand both the advantages they offer and the potential obstacles and issues they can raise. Although e-learning can reduce overall training costs in comparison to classroom instruction, we cannot underestimate the instructional value that can be achieved in the classroom in terms of the richness of practice and feedback opportunities, networking among participants, and so forth. Simply converting all instruction from one medium to the other will only result in doing poor training cheaper.

Therefore, using a variety of media in a structured, performance-oriented manner will achieve the best learning, resulting in improved employee performance that will lead to positive business impact. This notion of a blended solution is one we will investigate in more depth throughout the upcoming chapters.

The High-Impact Learning Model

Chapter Overview

What makes learning "high impact"? What enables learning to be converted into enhanced capabilities that in turn translate into improved job performance and the achievement of organizational goals? What are the elements and ingredients that set the high-impact learning approach apart from our traditional efforts to train and educate employees? It is the aim of this chapter to answer these fundamental questions.

As you will see in this chapter and in the chapters to come, the HIL approach leverages some powerful principles and tools to achieve this conversion of learning-to-capability-to-performance-to-results.

We begin this chapter with the stories of two learners, each in a similar job role. One follows a comprehensive but typical learning process, and the other engages in a high-impact learning approach. As we analyze and reflect on the learning experiences of these two employees, we are able to derive five key principles that define learning as high impact.

Following the discussion of these principles, we illustrate and describe the HIL model and its component parts, including assumptions regarding how the several components of HIL can and must work in unison, seamlessly, to achieve true business impact.

Two Learning Stories

Before we begin our stories, let's establish a bit of background about the two learners. Each of them is a new financial advisor with a major company that offers financial services and products to individuals and families nationwide.

Their major role is to contact potential new customers and sell them their financial planning service, and to provide ongoing financial planning assistance to current customers. In a response to market trends, the company has begun to refocus its energies toward increasing the level of customer service and satisfaction, as the competitive environment increasingly demands that financial planning companies retain their customers as "customers for life." Whereas the old market environment focused on selling as many initial financial plans as possible, the new thrust is to build long-lasting, trust-based relationships with customers. New advisors still have to sell, however, since acquisition of new customers remains a critical part of their job.

In response to the new strategic direction, the company has modified its employment policies, replacing commission-based compensation with more stable salaries to discourage turnover, and has instituted new measurement systems to assess customer satisfaction and quality of service. It has also offered new training opportunities, one of which—"Emotional Management Skills"—is intended to help advisors work more effectively with their current and potential customers. This course helps advisors to be more confident in acquiring new customers, to build greater trust and to better understand customer issues and needs, and so forth.

Imagine that we have two different advisors, Pat and Lynn. Each is relatively new. Although each works in a different regional market, their performance goals and the business needs of their regional market group are virtually identical. Here are their training stories.

Pat's Training

Pat's manager announced some particular training opportunities at a staff meeting and described how this training was a part of the company's new focus on customer satisfaction and retention. Pat's manager also noted that it would be a good idea for everyone to try to take advantage of and complete the training when they had a chance. The manager handed out a brochure from the training department that outlined instructions for getting on-line, both to learn more about the training services and also to actually participate in some of the on-line modules. Ending with final words of encouragement about the relevance of the training to the new business strategies, the manager moved on to other topics.

Not long after the meeting, Pat went on-line and visited the training web site. There were a lot of options for on-line modules as well as some group training sessions that were offered regionally. Also on the web site was a recommended training sequence for new advisors. Pat noted that some modules looked especially relevant, particularly modules about using emotional skills to help book more appointments with potential customers (something that all new advisors had trouble with, as almost everyone hated "cold calling"). There was also a group session on applying communication skills with current customers to build more trust. Pat signed up for a couple of the electronic modules. Pat also sent her manager an e-mail requesting permission to go to the regional session next month, as building trust with customers was key to increasing revenues in accounts. Pat decided to start the on-line modules that evening after work. Meanwhile, there was a reply to her e-mail from her manager, saying that it was okay to attend the group session but noting that it would be better to wait three months until the office vacation schedule slowed down.

Pat liked the on-line modules. They were interactive, and the tests showed that Pat had indeed mastered all of the principles of emotional skill management and had also identified the "emotional triggers" that most interfered with her own concentration abilities and kept her from listening closely to others.

There was an assessment that Pat could complete herself and could also send to her manager and another advisor who knew her well for their input. Pat sent these out and, in fact, got a quick response back from her friend. However, because of schedule conflicts, Pat's manager was unable to complete the assessment. He did take the time, though, to assure Pat that she was doing well in her appointment rate and that she should keep working on trust building.

Three months later, Pat went to the workshop and thought it was excellent. Her understanding of the principles from the on-line modules, just as promised, made her feel immediately comfortable in the discussions. There were opportunities to participate in role-play exercises on a variety of business process applications, and Pat took the time to try each one of these, wanting to get as broad an experience with the methods as possible. She thought they all looked useful, but because she participated in a lot of different exercises, she never really felt competent in any one in particular. She was surprised, though, that her final test score in the workshop was in the top third. Despite not feeling totally competent, she had mastered the workshop objectives. The feedback from other participants was helpful, and she was sure she could keep trying some of the techniques on her own back at work. At the close of the workshop, the session leaders reminded participants of the on-line modules that could be accessed to develop deeper knowledge in each of the applications. Pat made a note of all of these and promised herself she would try them out soon.

Things were quite busy when Pat got back, and her commitment to try out additional modules kept getting sidetracked. She did try out a couple of the techniques she had practiced in the workshop with several customers but couldn't really tell what impact they were having. At the workshop, they recommended that Pat ask her manager to sit in on an advising session and use a checklist that she could download from the training site. But Pat felt uncomfortable asking for extra help. Besides, her manager had not mentioned anything substantive about the "action plan" she had completed at the workshop. He did acknowledge having received it, however, and offered some encouraging words about hoping that Pat followed through with her plans.

Lynn's Training

After a staff meeting to discuss the new customer-focused strategy, Lynn's manager asked each new advisor to use the "assessment" option on the training web site to talk over implications of the strategy for advisor performance. Lynn reviewed an "impact map" on the site that showed the five most critical portions of a new advisor's role. The web site them prompted her to complete a personal assessment of the components she had the most trouble performing. Lynn immediately zeroed in on the "making new appointments" task, as this was especially hard for her. She hated cold calling, and was increasingly upset when people she called were irate over being disturbed. She forwarded the assessment to her manager, as the site directed her to do.

Two days later, she received an e-mail from her manager suggesting they have a telephone conference to talk over the assessment. In this call, her manager agreed with Lynn that scheduling appointments was an issue. As the impact map showed, the task of "making appointments" was directly linked to acquiring new customers and in fact accounted for 32 percent of the success of new advisors. Her manager noted that Lynn's close rate once a meeting was held was excellent—one of the highest in the office. In other words, once she had a meeting with a customer, Lynn was very good at making a sale. Further, her trust and satisfaction ratings from current customers were high. But on the issue of making appointments, her rate was quite low, and so they agreed that this would be the improvement focus for Lynn: to increase her weekly appointment rate with potential new clients from her current average of three or so to more than six.

Visiting the training web site, as her manager suggested she do right away, Lynn quickly found a series of three modules that focused on using emotional intelligence skills to overcome feelings of personal rejection and to persevere in making calls. The modules were good. They engaged her in listening to recordings of sales calls and analyzing her own reactions had she been the advisor on the call. Further modules prompted Lynn to complete exercises to identify her own "trigger" scenarios that raised her emotional reactions, then suggested techniques she could practice in real calls.

When she finished the three introductory modules, she sent her completion message to her manager. Her manager replied and suggested that she enroll in the regional skills practice workshop next month. When she logged on to the workshop enrollment site, she was given a template to write scripts for different calls that she felt were especially hard to handle and to bring these scripts with her to the workshop.

The workshop was not easy, but Lynn found it very useful. She practiced her call role-plays over and over and began to feel comfortable with the techniques for managing her own reactions. By the end of the sessions, she was able to score acceptably on the skills application tryout test, using the self-management skills to empathize with customers, and bolster her own commitment to keep trying despite rejection. She learned not to take a rejection personally and to understand that many people are busy and stressed.

At the close of the workshop, she prepared a customized assessment checklist from the master version they used in the session. This checklist was keyed to the particular techniques she felt were most useful to her. As suggested, she e-mailed a copy to her manager and requested that her manager sit in on some calls as soon as she got back.

The feedback sessions with her manager were very helpful. She found it was much harder to actually use the skills in a real call, but observations from her manager helped her maintain her focus. By the fifth call, she felt much more effective. Her manager suggested they track her meeting schedule rate for the next three weeks, using a format he downloaded from the training web site. He also requested Lynn to e-mail him a list each day of every call she made, whether it was successful or not, and to aim for not giving up on calls until she had booked at least one appointment. He also asked Lynn to post her call records using an anonymous code on the electronic "bulletin board" that the office maintained for all their advisors, so she could compare her rates with everyone else's. Even after a week, it felt good for her to see her rates of calls at least keeping pace with the others. Though her success rate was still not where it should be, at least she knew she was trying! Thanks to not giving up, she always got one appointment per day.

After three weeks, her manager surprised her with a dinner certificate for two to one of her town's best restaurants. This bonus was given to acknowledge her perseverance and the fact that by the third week she was scheduling more than one appointment a day. Her manager asked another advisor to sit in on Lynn's calls the next week and to use the checklist to give her feedback. This helped even more.

Today, it is gratifying to Lynn to know she has finally solved her cold-calling issues. She still thinks it is the least likable part of the job and would rather not do it. But she can manage it now and has learned to manage her reactions and persevere despite the inevitable rejections. Also, she volunteered to be part of an evaluation study of "success stories" that the corporate training department conducted and has been invited to participate in the regional workshops as a "visiting expert" who can tell her story to others who struggle with the same issue.

Comparing the Experiences

Clearly, Pat and Lynn had substantially different experiences. Pat's experience is similar to what we might have predicted for Trainee #2 from Chapter 1. There was some learning over a broad range of possible applications, though we did not see any tightly targeted and successful applications in Pat's job performance. Lynn, on the other hand, had focused her learning on a particular high-leverage application (increasing appointment rates). As we saw, her learning continued on the job and she began to see some significant success. Analyzing the two stories and comparing them provide an excellent vehicle for identifying and understanding the key elements of the HIL approach.

Table 3.1 affords a side-by-side comparison of these two experiences and includes a list of the key and defining elements of Lynn's high-impact learning story. Following this comparison, we will "roll up" the features defined in Lynn's high-impact story into the five key principles of HIL.

By reviewing the analysis of the two stories shown in Table 3.1, (page 47) it is easy to see the major ways in which HIL plays out in the design and implementation of training. It is also easy to see why the likelihood of impact increases dramatically in the HIL approach. We will turn now to an explanation of the five key principles of high-impact learning, which are listed in Table 3.1 under the heading "key elements." Then we close the chapter by presenting and discussing the process model for HIL, highlighting the fundamental methods that practitioners can use in implementing their own HIL initiatives.

The Key HIL Principles

These five key principles guide all of our HIL practice. Because the principles are applied somewhat differently in any particular application, depending on circumstances, we will point out the particular ways in which the principles were applied in the story of Lynn's experience. Finally, although each principle is defined and explained separately, in practice, they overlap, interact, and blend together.

Principle One: Strategic Leverage

The HIL approach is guided by the notion that it is almost always more effective to focus our efforts on a few strategic actions rather than seek to be comprehensive. So, for example, if we work with a company to develop a training plan, we would first work to understand the organization's strategic direction. Based on this understanding, we would determine where we could score the biggest win through high-impact learning by identifying the most critical

TABLE 3.1   Comparison of Two Training Experiences

Key Element	Lynn's High-Impact Experience	Pat's Traditional Experience
Strategically Leveraged Learning Objectives	A single objective defined as improving performance in a high-leverage portion of her job: making calls for appointments. This objective required the development of a new capability: more resilience in emotionally coping with rejection. Learning objective was individualized to her particular circumstance.	Not focused on any specific element of job performance; more generally to "master" all of the objectives addressed in the learning activities in which she participated.
Business Linkage	Clear line of sight and specific connection between learning objectives, performance objectives, and organizational goals.	No clear line of sight or focus on any particular business objectives; only very general connection between organizational strategy and learning content.
Focus on a Learning-to-Performance Process	The entire experience was a coordinated performance improvement process with seamless connections between goal-setting, learning, and performance support activities.	Conceived and managed mostly as "events" with separate, disparate elements.
Learning Intervention Design	Included procedures for • Targeting performance improvement • Individualizing learning objectives • Coordinating self-instructional elements with group learning facilitator-led activities • Interactive learning activities • Opportunities for practice with feedback • Action planning with measurable objectives • Access to further learning as needed	• Included some interactive learning • Learning objectives and practice were not individualized • Learning objectives were "owned" by the program, not by the individual learners • Action planning was not prominent • Little measurement and feedback

- business goals, that are driven by
- processes, which are linked to
- job/team results, in order to develop a
- plan to support learning of the most critical (but not all) competencies that will drive
- performance improvement and goal achievement.

Or, for example, if we work with a single employee, we would identify the most important performance results to be obtained, then link a few key competencies to the desired outcomes. In Lynn's case, you will note that her learning was focused on a single, high-leverage performance improvement objective. There were surely other ways in which she might have improved her performance, but we know that improvement is most likely to actually be accomplished where there is a tight focus. So this is where Lynn and her manager started.

Our learning and performance support resources are limited and must be leveraged against the most influential drivers of business goals. If we strive for eliminating all performance gaps and fulfilling all learning needs, we will seriously dilute the impact our resources can have and lose focus on the most important intent of learning.

We are guided in HIL to identify strategic leverage in terms of what will be the most valuable to the business. This is not because individual interests and goals are not important. On the contrary, readers will see how these play into HIL in Chapter 10, "High-Impact Employee Development Planning." But business linkage is always of paramount importance, for it determines the amount of organizational attention that can be invested at any given moment. This takes us to the next key principle.

Principle Two: Deep Business Linkage

Much is said in the training literature and among training vendors about achieving "business results." But in reality, this notion typically infers a logical but superficial connection between training content and business goals. For example, if a company has launched a strong strategic thrust to improve customer service, then we can be sure there will be lots of energy invested to get employees engaged in customer service training topics. In the HIL approach, business linkage pervades all aspects of the training design, development, implementation, and evaluation process and is directly linked to individual performance.

As mentioned and illustrated in the first principle, business goals determine the primacy and priority of training initiatives. Then linkage between overall organization goals and organization elements (functions, business units, and work units, for example) is determined to identify strategic leverage opportunities. Next, the critical linkage among job role and team processes and job and team results is defined. Finally, linkage is determined and defined at the individual performer level, so that each specific learner (Lynn, for instance) has a specific performance improvement target.

This performance improvement target is linked both "outward" through work unit objectives to an important business goal, then "inward" to one or more personal capability development needs. This creates an individual learner objective linked to performance and business goals.

Notice how business linkage is paramount in the definition of learning objectives. In Pat's training experience, which was essentially nonbusiness linked, her objective was to "learn as much as she could." Then she was on her own to attempt to figure out linkage. In Lynn's case, however, her learning objective was explicitly linked to a focused performance improvement objective, which was in turn driven by a business goal.

Business linkage continues through training implementation as learners revisit and reclarify what they are learning and reconfirm how these learning objectives connect to the business. Linkage is also reinforced in performance support and managerial involvement, in the form of action plans and follow-up activities that reinforce the connection to business goals. In Lynn's case, her involvement in the learning process began with a focus on improving her frequency of scheduling meetings, which was connected to customer acquisition and retention (key parts of the overall business strategy). She practiced these skills and traced her success by monitoring a critical work unit performance measure, "meetings scheduled and held." Finally, her success in contributing to business objectives was recognized and rewarded.

Principle Three: Systematic Learning-to-Performance Process

The HIL methods are based on the notion that learning and performance improvement are integrally related. Learning provides the capability to perform more effectively; performance provides the opportunity to deepen and extend learning. Performance improvement is the goal of learning and cannot happen consistently and efficiently without careful preparation and focus, practice and feedback, and support and encouragement.

Figure 3.1 illustrates a very simple but compelling premise of high-impact learning: True learning must be applied in the real world (performance). Further, attempts to try out and perform new skills and knowledge on the job typically lead to a deeper understanding and comprehension of those skills and knowledge. This "learning-to-performance" cycle provides a powerful mechanism that builds increasing capability that leads to continuously improved competence.

Lynn's experience showed several cycles of this learning and performance integration. First, her learning objectives were based on an analysis of her performance, seeking especially an intersection between a performance objective that was linked to a business goal and a capability improvement need that could be addressed through targeted learning activities. This part of the learning-to-performance process culminated in a learning plan and related performance improvement objective. Then Lynn began to build her awareness and knowledge of emotional intelligence in targeted learning modules based on real-world job experience. She then formally analyzed her performance with an assessment that helped her identify more specific strengths and weaknesses and focus her learning on some specific performance objec-

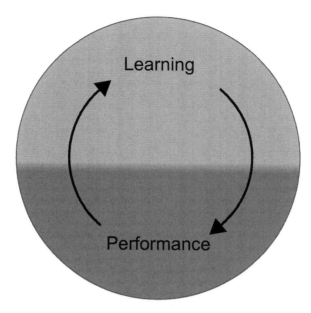

FIGURE 3.1   The Learning-to-Performance Process

tives (key aspects of the call process and related emotional reactions). Her process continued with guided practice on real job scenarios and performance feedback, then moved more formally into the performance environment as she set improvement objectives for her actual work with clients. Feedback and coaching extended her learning and strengthened her capabilities, until her performance reached the targeted levels (at which point she became reinvolved in additional formal learning processes).

Although the learning management that guided and supported Lynn's experience was invisible in the story, it is important to note that it was based on careful learning design and development. The planners and designers that created the instructional system that enabled her successful experience were guided by a holistic perspective; they focused not on creating separate "events" but on providing integrated performance improvement and learning processes with seamless connections among goal setting, formal learning, practice, and application.

Principle Four: Integration
with Performance Support Systems and Factors

As we noted, performance improvement is the target of the HIL approach. We recognize, though, the complexity of performance; it is driven not only by capability but by other intrapersonal factors such as attitude, expectation, motivation, and values. It is also driven by a host of external factors, such as workplace culture, management, information, feedback, measures, support tools and devices, rewards, incentives, and so forth. In fact, the sum of these other factors, and sometimes only one of them alone, can completely derail performance, in spite of the most targeted and business-related learning systems.

Given this complexity, the HIL approach includes a determined effort to first identify the key performance factors that will either enhance or impede applications of learning, then design methods and tools that will help assure the successful achievement of performance improvement objectives. Many of the key factors are embedded in and operated by what we call the "performance system" of the organization. We enclose this phrase in quotation marks, because we know that much of this system is often undefined and, therefore, many parts of it are not overtly managed. Official job objectives and incentives, such as sales commissions and performance bonuses, are part of the intentionally structured system. But other key elements are part of the informal and unarticulated (but very recognizable and powerful!) system, such as attitudes and pressures demonstrated by coworkers, habits and behaviors of managers, workplace cultural values, and so forth.

The HIL approach always includes an analysis of these factors and efforts to manage or cope with them. Sometimes tools are created to support positive factors or to counter negative factors. In Lynn's example, for instance, the learning system provided her a checklist for assessing call behavior, because there was no such feedback system in the workplace. Yet the negative reactions that built up call after call were a powerful disincentive to making yet more calls. Sometimes we only make learners aware of factors that we cannot do anything about, on the assumption that arming them with this knowledge may help them strengthen their resolve or discover ways around obstacles. Sometimes we make specific recommendations to alter formal system factors, such as initiating an incentive or reward program.

Sometimes in extreme cases we decide not to move ahead with learning processes, because we know that the workplace environment is so toxic that it will squelch performance improvement despite the best-learned capabilities. We should add that this is very rare. To avoid this kind of failure, we suggest pilot tryouts of new learning in specific parts of the organization where we know conditions are more favorable, or we can work constructively to make performance system changes. This way, we avoid the overly toxic environments, hoping that success in one area will provide us with the credibility and evidence on which to base recommendations to make changes in these more negative settings.

Principle Five: Exquisite Learning Solutions

We choose the word "exquisite" in describing the HIL approach to the design of learning solutions for its particular meaning in reference to ". . . the finest quality . . . keenly sensitive and responsive" (Webster, 1999). Learning solutions comprise the multitude of learning interventions and tools that are made available to employees in the organization, for example, on-line modules, workshops, games, simulations, and print materials. This principle of exquisitiveness subsumes a considerable amount of expertise, since the creation and implementation of effective learning solutions is a complex combination of art and science (as we will see later, in Chapters 6 and 8).

Exquisite learning solutions are based on and reflect the following characteristics:

- All learning solutions are iterative and evolving; none is final, and improvements are continuously sought.
- Employees can learn just what they need, when they need it.
- Access to learning is as easy and nondisruptive as possible.
- Learners are treated with integrity as respected adult individuals.
- The most effective methods and techniques with multiple learning modalities and technologies are employed.
- Learners are actively engaged in the most effective blend of content, practice, feedback, and reflective activities.
- Learner interaction and involvement are promoted.
- Opportunities exist for participants and other stakeholders to provide feedback and critical reactions to learning leaders.

Note again the definition of the adjective "exquisite." A key meaning of this term as we use it is the notion of *responsiveness.* Exquisite solutions are not necessarily expensive, fancy, flashy, or intricate. On the contrary, they may be simple and unpolished in appearance, especially in early iterations. They are always the best solution for the needs and circumstances that drive them and in all other respects responsive to the environment of the performer. "Less than perfect" learning solutions that are available when needed are always better than fancier versions that arrive too late. The most simple solution is almost always the best choice.

As we conclude our review and discussion of the five principles of HIL, readers should recognize that the principles are not independent. They interact and overlap in any given application. The principle relating to the quality of learning solutions (Principle Five), for example, subsumes all of the other principles, since business linkage, strategic focus, adherence to a learning-to-performance process, and so forth, must be provided for in each learning intervention. Nor are the principles equally emphasized in any particular application. Principle Four (Integration with Performance Support Systems and Factors) might demand, for example, an especially speedy solution because of an acute organizational crisis. Imagine a company that has suffered a damaging fire in one of its factories and must quickly relocate production to a different facility where the workers are not familiar with the production procedures and tools. This performance context will require trade-offs with the principle requiring exquisite designs, since the business and performance scenario require such a rapid solution. But in any context and any situation, all of the principles must be considered and addressed, or impact will be threatened.

The HIL Process

In Chapter 1 we presented the conceptual framework underlying the HIL approach, wherein impactful training is characterized as an "intersection" of high-leverage job and team tasks and results in learning that enables performance in those tasks. In Chapter 2 we explored the promise of e-learning technologies and also reminded readers that although these technologies offer great opportunities, they cannot inherently assure high impact. We have also, to this point in the book, looked at the key characteristics of HIL and the principles that those characteristics embody. In this closing section of this chapter, we present and explain a process structure for the overall HIL approach. As you will notice from the table of contents, the next section of this book is organized according to these components to fully explore the defining elements of the HIL process.

Figure 3.2 portrays high-impact learning as three major elements: creating focus and intentionality, providing learning activities to enhance capabilities, and supporting performance improvement. These three process elements characterize the core of the HIL approach and are always a part of HIL strategies and interventions. You will also notice that these components encircle a fourth element at the center of the graphic, which is labeled "Business Impact." It is the effective application of the three elements that results in our overall aim: achieving significant positive business impact.

Notice that the elements that lead to business results are contained in a larger shaded circular shape in the figure. Successful achievement of business impact requires that all three elements be structured and managed as a coherent process. It is useful to think about the three elements as critical portions of the process, but none is truly separate; none is more important than another, none can be done without reference to the others, and the separation between them is for purposes of illustration only. In practice, as was evident in the story of Lynn discussed earlier, distinctions among the process elements become blurred, as the overall process is managed as a seamless whole.

Typically, in most current and traditional approaches to training, the only portion of this process that is explicitly defined and managed is the provision of learning events and activities. In other words, the training department's re-

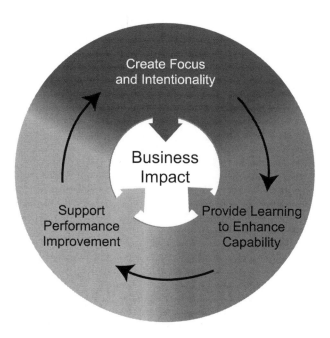

FIGURE 3.2   High-Impact Learning

sponsibility is to provide employees with learning opportunities, such as workshops, electronic modules, and so forth. After they participate in these activities, they are "on their own" to apply the newly learned skills on the job, and any support they might receive would be the responsibility of their supervising manager in particular or of the entire performance management system in general. In addition, there would typically be no explicit intervention with these employees that would help them articulate the linkage between the learning to be provided and any specific individual performance and business improvement objectives.

In this traditional approach, it is highly likely that many learners who participate in learning interventions will not really know exactly why they are engaged in training, and they will have no clear and compelling focus that drives their learning. It is further likely that after participation in training, another large proportion of trainees will not use their learning in any sustained and focused applications that lead to business impact.

Both of these realities, lack of explicitly linked learning purposes and a performance context that is not explicitly managed to engender application of new learning in job performance, drastically impair the impact of training. The HIL approach is specifically conceived to counter these obstructive forces. More specifically, the HIL process is based on several assumptions about training and training impact, which are described next.

Assumptions of the HIL Process

1. Improvements to the "learning activities" portion of the HIL process are the *least* likely to yield increases in business impact. In traditional approaches, learning activities are the most thoroughly developed and managed portion of the overall process, and chances are this portion of the process may be about as effective as it needs to be.
2. No matter how strong the learning activities portion of the process is, if learners do not have a clear focus on exactly what they need to learn and how it will improve important performance, are not supported when applying their learning in improved job performance, or both, then the overall process will yield little if any positive business impact.
3. When learners fully understand what they need to achieve from learning and pinpoint how they will use their learning to improve performance, they are more likely to actually apply learning in ways that will help the business. Thus, strengthening the "focusing and intentionality" portion of the process can yield dramatic gains in performance improvement and business impact.
4. Strengthening the "supporting performance improvement" portion of the process likewise affords great leverage. New learning is fragile and is easily abandoned in the face of workplace pressures and demands. For example, consider us, the authors, both of whom are enthusiastic if not expert tennis players. We may learn a new stroke or hitting style in a tennis lesson and feel comfortable on the lesson court using that new stroke. But in the pressure of an actual match, if we try the new stroke and lose point after point, we will quickly revert to our old style, simply because it is safe and comfortable. Employees need early and frequent opportunities to try out new learning, and they need responsive feedback to motivate them to keep trying when success is not immediate.
5. Management of all of the three key portions of the high-impact learning process cannot be ignored or left to chance. Consistent performance and business results can be assured only when all three portions of the process are linked and integrated and the entire process is managed as a seamless whole.

Integrating High-Impact Learning Process Elements

Given these assumptions, we can see how any HIL initiative must be constructed to encompass all three key process elements. We will clearly need to provide robust and constructive learning interventions, so that employees can expand their knowledge and acquire new skills. This is a very familiar part of the training challenge. We will also need effective methods and tools that enable learners and their managers to engage in dialogue to identify performance improvement objectives and clarify the linkage between these objectives and important business goals. Then the learning objectives that will drive key performance and business improvement can be established and linked to one or more learning opportunities. Finally, the performance context must be considered to identify factors that might inhibit or enhance performance. The performance support needs for each performer must be addressed with the correct supervisory guidance, measures, performance aids, and so forth.

In earlier evolutions of our high-impact approach, we also worked hard to build in "before" training activities, such as discussions with managers and the creation of impact maps to clarify performance objectives before people "entered" a training intervention. We still use these tools and methods, though they have been refined considerably.

However, as we discussed at the close of Chapter 2, the e-learning trend has helped us see that chronological separation of the process elements is not helpful and is based on the old paradigm of training as "events." We have thus tried to purge from our vocabularies such terms as "before" training, and even the notion of "prework," because terms like these are rooted in dysfunctional concepts. ("Prework" is typically defined as tasks trainees are assigned to complete prior to a formal training session, such as completion of readings, an assessment instrument, and so forth.) We also know, of course, that learning does not wait to begin until after prework is done; good "pre-work" is, after all, vital learning. Performance support does not start "after" training, nor does thinking about goals and expected performance results happen only "before" learning. Clearly, the conditions for successful performance improvement are created throughout the learning process. Managerial support, for example, begins to be built when learning needs and expected results are clarified and continues through interactions between learners and managers as training activities unfold.

Revisiting the story of Lynn, the financial advisor portrayed earlier in the chapter, we can see more clearly how the process elements are melded and managed seamlessly.

Creating Focus and Intentionality

This portion of the HIL process began as Lynn learned more about the company's strategic goals, then continued when her manager met with her to discuss how advisors needed to contribute to strategy. The assessment Lynn completed on-line and the impact map she reviewed prior to the assessment further focused her learning objectives. Later, when Lynn met with her manager to discuss her assessment results, her focus sharpened further, as together they formulated specific and measurable performance improvement objectives. Lynn then began completing some individual web-based learning modules. From these, she determined that she needed to master particular skills, such as identifying and working with her personal emotional "triggers." This was, again, a further sharpening of the focus of her learning and gave her specific ways that she could apply learning in her job to improve her results in booking meetings with clients.

Her learning continued to evolve a new focus when she registered for the "live" workshop and was directed to a web site to develop role-play scenarios and scripts that were tailored to her particular circumstances. More focus yet was created when Lynn customized her own performance assessment scale for use on the job, and this focus was further tightened when she and her manager agreed on some new performance objectives derived from her assessment dimensions. At this point we left the story, though it was clear that Lynn's learning to improve her performance in scheduling meetings and understanding client needs would continue to evolve through successive iterations of learning and on-the-job trials, in turn shifting her performance goals as her capability grew.

Providing Learning to Enhance Capability

Learning activities were woven throughout the chronology of Lynn's experience. She began her journey with instruction from her manager to develop her understanding of the company's shifting strategic direction. This instruction, although brief, was not unstructured, as it was supported by a sound presentation plan and integrated collateral materials. Several learning options were available, including an array of self-instructional modules accessible from the intranet, as well as optional "live" workshops. Some learning solutions were very simple, such as a self-instructional checklist, an annotated worksheet, and a guided self-assessment. Others were more complex, involving simulations, exercises, one-on-one interactive discussions and feedback, and group interactions.

Regardless of their complexity or simplicity, all learning solutions were integrated within an overarching structure driven by Lynn's particular learning needs and performance improvement objectives. As Lynn's focus and goals shifted and sharpened, the learning solution system likewise responded with alternative choices, paths, and activities. Each separate learning intervention was a part of a larger systemic architecture, and each also shared a common basis in foundational principles of learning and instructional design. Finally, learning interventions were interspersed with opportunities for self-reflection, tryout, feedback, and coaching.

Supporting Performance

From the very start of Lynn's story, it was evident that her learning was driven by and focused on performance improvement, not just acquisition of skills and knowledge. Each iterative step in the process laid the groundwork for supporting performance. In many instances, there was a role played by her manager, which not only helped focus her learning but also created commitment to and a common interest in Lynn's success. Some instructional activities included performance support tools, such as checklists, worksheets, and feedback guides. Some activities, such as the application plan Lynn completed in the skill workshop, included specific components that required action on the part of others, such as a peer or Lynn's manager. Together, all of these methods and tools helped assure that Lynn would receive the maximum amount of encouragement, guidance, feedback, and recognition for her attempts to actually use her learning in ways that would drive business impact.

Chapter Summary

This concludes our "high level" look at the HIL framework and methods. In the next section of the book, we will review one HIL process element at a time, providing in-depth guidelines, examples, and tools. Specifically, we will begin the next section by examining a critical HIL metatool that allows us to clearly illustrate the direct "line-of-sight" that must exist between employees' performance and key business indicators. Chapter 4, "Mapping Linkage to Business Goals," will describe this metatool, the impact map, and will provide numerous examples of the variations this important tool can take.

Then in Chapters 5, 6, and 7, we will in turn take a close look at each of the HIL process elements that help us to achieve business impact: Learner Intentionality and Focus, Effective Learning Interactions, and Performance Support. Again, you will see how these components work together seamlessly to improve performance that leads to positive business impact.

The final section of the book will provide guidelines and practical approaches for putting the HIL approach to work in your organization, giving specific attention to the design of HIL initiatives, impact evaluation, individual development planning, and how to manage the transition to an HIL approach.

Mapping Linkage
to Business Goals

Chapter Overview

Business impact is both the intended result of HIL and lies at the heart of the HIL approach. Over our many years of trying to get more business impact from learning and training, we have created the concept and tool of "impact maps," first published in *The Learning Alliance* (Brinkerhoff and Gill, 1994). These maps have come to shape the way in which we think about and document business impact, whether it is at the very beginning of an HIL initiative or at the very end when we are assessing our results. Impact maps are not just an invaluable tool but are inseparable from the HIL process. We use impact maps to analyze the business impact that is needed from learning, to identify learning and performance requirements, to clarify expectations for learning results, to communicate learning plans and goals, and to guide measurement and evaluation. Further uses for impact maps have evolved among the many companies and organizations that have adopted an HIL approach, and new applications are evolving yet (some of these additional uses are addressed in Chapters 9 and 10).

In this chapter, we explain and illustrate the impact map process and the variations of impact maps that we use in HIL. We define the concept and tool of impact mapping by presenting and dissecting an example of a basic impact map. Following this basic example, we explain and discuss the generic, conceptual structure of all impact map variants. We then proceed to illustrate the several core impact map variations, explaining how each is used for different HIL purposes. Finally, we close the chapter with a brief list and some of the primary ways in which we use impact maps to help achieve an HIL approach to training.

What Is an "Impact Map"?

Simply put, an impact map is a visual representation of the linkage, or the "line of sight," between a job position or a functional role and how the capabilities (skills and knowledge) for that role influence key business results of the organization. In other words, the impact map shows how learning is linked to "impact." We've selected the word "map" to describe the tool because it is very analogous to a road map, in that it shows the direction in which performance must be driven to achieve the results and business objectives necessary to accomplish worthwhile organizational goals. The impact map shows the route that learning takes, through performance, to business impact.

We'll look first at an example of an impact map, as this is the best and most simple way to understand the concept. Following the example, we explore the basic structure that underlies all impact maps, regardless of their particular application.

Impact Map—An Example

Table 4.1 provides an example of a typical impact map. Readers will find the example somewhat familiar, as the impact map in Table 4.1 is based on the financial advisor job exemplified by Lynn in Chapter 3. Remember that Lynn works for a major company that offers financial planning services and products to individuals and families nationwide, helping them invest their money in ways that will meet their financial planning goals. Recall further that Lynn's company has refocused its strategic direction with the goal of improving customer service and satisfaction to retain their customers for life. In response to the new strategic direction, the company has taken numerous actions, including offering new training opportunities, such as "Emotional Intelligence Skills," intended to help advisors work more effectively with their current and potential customers. This training is meant to help advisors to be more confident in acquiring new customers, to build greater trust, to better understand customer issues and needs, and so forth.

The first column, "Job Role," simply lists the job position or role that we are mapping, in this case, financial advisors. The next column, "Competencies/Skills," lists specific skills, knowledge, competencies, and capabilities that are provided in the training initiative; in this case, these are the trust-building communications skills (how to listen with empathy, reframe reactions, manage emotions, and so forth). The next column lists "Critical Actions." These are the job behaviors in which a financial advisor could apply the skills built by the training initiative. The next column lists the "Key Results" that would be improved or achieved if the skills were used in the ways shown in the previous column. In this case, we can see that advisors

TABLE 4.1   Impact Map for Financial Advisors

Job Role	Competencies/Skills	Critical Actions	Key Results	Unit Business Goals	Company Goals
Financial Advisors	How to listen with empathy How to positively reframe emotional reactions How to manage emotions during stressful interactions	Booking new appointments	Increase in appointments booked from three per week to six or more per week Increase trust of customers	Increase acquisition of new customers	Increase in sales Increase in revenues Increase in customer satisfaction and trust

could book more appointments and could increase the trust of customers with whom they meet. The final two columns list the business results to which the advisors' improved performance would contribute. The next-to-last column (Unit Business Goals) shows that an advisor's improved performance would lead to an increase in the number of new customers acquired, a key business goal for the regional sales office in which advisors work. Looking further to the last column, we see that this unit business goal contributes to the overall company goals of increased sales, increased revenues, and increased customer satisfaction.

The impact map illustrated in Table 4.1 shows, in a simple and direct way, what a financial advisor can learn from the training provided, how that learning would be used in performance improvement, and how improved job results could contribute to improved business performance. There are some other key features of this simple impact map that we should point out.

- The map is strategic, not comprehensive. It does not show all of the learning objectives from the training program, nor does it show all of the advisor's job responsibilities, nor even all of the job behaviors in which the training could possibly be used, nor all of the office's and company's business goals. It points out only the most important and critical among these.
- This particular map shows only one job role (a financial advisor) and one particular training initiative (trust-building communications). Other map variations, as we'll soon see, can show different sorts of information.
- Entries documented in the Key Results column are typically personal performance indicators that employees can monitor and use to adjust their own performance; they are the results that employees directly control and produce.

- The impact map provides clear and simple answers to several "why" questions. What about this learning is important? How can it be used? If it were used in this way, what good would it do? How would it help the business? (Notice that these are important questions, often asked by customers of training.)
- For each column, the entry in the column to the left of that column is always, and must be, a *necessary* contributor to achieve the entry in the column to the right. But it will almost never be a *sufficient* cause for the entry to the right. That is, for example, the skill is necessary for the performance improvement, but may not alone be sufficient to enable it. Likewise, the performance behavior must be needed to bring about the result, but again may not be sufficient. Impact map information must always meet the "necessary" criterion, but because impact maps are not comprehensive (they are strategic), impact map information will almost never meet the "sufficiency" criterion.
- The final column, "Company Goals," should answer the final question of, "So what? Or "Who cares?" because it lists the high-level, strategic goals for the organization. Entries in this column should satisfy the final question of the value of this training. If someone were to read the entries in the final column and still wonder, "Well, so what? Who cares?" then the impact map analyst has not pushed the analysis far enough. Typically, the goals listed in this column are much like what you might find on an organization's balanced scorecard, relating to

- Sales and revenue
- Profitability
- Cost containment
- Customer or shareholder satisfaction
- Employee satisfaction or morale

Fundamental Impact Map Structure

All impact maps share a common, core structure, as graphically portrayed in Figure 4.1.

FIGURE 4.1   Fundamental Impact Map Structure

The basic structure of an impact map has only three core elements: capability, performance (or behavior), and results. This core structure is inherent to the nature of training and training impact. The immediate result of a training intervention (when it works) is learning, or the acquisition of new skills and knowledge. But acquisition of new skills and knowledge represent only capability. That is, if we learn how to do something, we have the capability to perform in a new way. For value to occur, we have to change our behavior and use the new capability in performance. Further, our performance must be aimed at worthwhile results. Results, finally, are the arbiter of the value of training impact. If results are sufficiently important, then training has had worthwhile value.

Results are often defined at different levels, depending on the complexity of the organization in which learning initiatives are being implemented. In the simplest of organizations, immediate job results might be valuable of and by themselves. Imagine, for example, a dentist in a one-doctor dental office. Further imagine that our dentist might participate in training to learn a new method for acquiring dental patients. Table 4.2 shows an impact map for the dentist's training.

TABLE 4.2   Impact Map for a Dentist

Capability	Performance	Results
How to use marketing tools to recruit new patients	Use tools in marketing efforts	New patients

Assume the dentist goes through the training and learns the new method. In other words, the dentist has acquired a new capacity. Now, the dentist uses the new methods (performance), and the result is that the dentist acquires new patients (the result). In this case, the result of the new performance is, directly and immediately, a worthwhile organizational result, and the training would be deemed to have had valuable impact.

But consider a larger, more complex organization. Oftentimes in a more complex organizational setting, one person's performance results will then contribute to another result, which must in turn contribute to another result before impact would be deemed valuable. This more complex organizational scenario is depicted in the impact map in Table 4.3.

The financial advisor, for example, who books more appointments has achieved a significant result, but this result has no immediate business value. Organizational impact is achieved only after the appointment leads to an acquired customer (a next result), and that customer is retained long enough to generate revenues (yet another result). It is often the case that immediate results must lead to subsequent results before worthwhile organizational im-

TABLE 4.3   Complex Results Impact Map

Job Role	Capability	Performance	Job Result	Work Unit Result	Sales Result	Organizational Result
Financial Advisor	How to communicate to build understanding and trust	Use trust-building skills in initial calls to prospects	More appointments booked	More customers acquired	More financial plans sold	Increase in revenues

pact is achieved. That is, results lead to results, which then may lead to even more results. Again, readers should note that the results that lead to results must be necessary for the subsequent result but may not be sufficient.

In our impact map core structure, results are results, regardless of their level. In practice, however, we will often differentiate the level of the result, using the particular language of the client's context and organization. Thus, for example, readers will find examples of impact maps that refer to job level results, work unit results, process objectives, division results, and so forth. In any impact map, the entry the farthest to the right on the map must represent a result that has prima facie value to the most senior leaders in the organization; it must justify the training investment. Thus, in practice, we may encounter impact maps with several levels of results depicted, simply because it requires this many levels of analysis to explain impact on a final result that will be recognized by the leaders of the organization as "worth it."

This chain of learning producing capability—capability applied in improved performance and performance-enabling valuable results—is the fundamental value premise of training. This value chain shows clearly, simply, and directly how the training is linked to impact. Any disconnect in the chain would impede value. That is, if learning did not occur, then the desired performance improvement would not happen. Likewise, if the desired performance improvement did not occur, then the desired results would not be produced. Further, the value of training is dependent upon the logical validity of the links in the chain. If, for example, the learning that might occur from training is not sufficient for new performance, then value will be frustrated. Or if the performance that learning might drive would not lead to the right sort of results, then value is again frustrated. And finally, if the results that improved performance produced were not worthwhile results, then value is again frustrated.

Because the impact map uncovers and explicates the essential logic of training value, it is a valuable tool for many purposes. Here are some of the uses for which we have applied impact maps or the impact map structure.

- Evaluating the logic of a planned training initiative, to see whether it makes sense, or is likely to be worthwhile.

- Explaining the intent of training to an interested party, such as trainees' managers or senior managers.
- Figuring out what about a training initiative to measure to assess whether it is working as planned.
- Explaining learning objectives to trainees in a training program.
- Having trainees think through how they might best use some new learning.
- Designing (or analyzing) an overall curriculum to see how it aligns with business needs and goals.
- Analyzing the job roles in a work unit to determine training needs.

Impact Map Variations

Every impact map is different, since each map always reflects the particular learning circumstance in which it is applied, and each likewise employs the language and terminology of the client's organization. Thus, for example, what one map labels as a "Key Result" might be called a "Job Output" on another map. In this respect, there as many impact map variations as there are clients with whom we work. But it is also true that there are several typical impact map variants, each with its own particular structure (but all based on the common core structure discussed in the preceding section) and each depicting a different sort of analysis. In this section, we present and explain the several fundamental variations on impact maps as we typically apply them in HIL.

We have already presented the single role/single learning intervention impact map, as this was our example in the previous section (Table 4.1). As you will recall, this impact map depicted a single job role, that of a financial advisor. It showed how that particular job role might leverage a single particular learning intervention, training in trust-building communications techniques. The single-role-single intervention impact map is probably the most simple of all maps.

Multiple Job Role/Single Learning Intervention Impact Map

In this map variation, there is still only one single learning intervention analyzed. This map shows, however, how people in several different job roles might adapt, adopt, and apply this learning.

It will be helpful, before we present the map itself, to provide a few words about the business setting, a pharmaceutical company. The business function in the example is the Quality Control Laboratories, a division of the company that provides analysis services to both research and development (R&D) scientists and to managers in the manufacturing area. Each of these two customer groups needs periodic and regular purity and compound assay analysis services, to check the quality of pharmaceutical compounds and to determine chemical changes that might occur over time. The laboratories division is a 24/7 operation that receives orders, then conducts assays and other technical analyses, providing detailed technical reports back to customers. Because of regulatory laws, peer reviews are required for all analysis operations and reports, to double-check all work. Finally, the laboratory section of the quality control division is organized into "areas" by the type of pharmaceutical to which it is dedicated (such as infectious diseases, central nervous system drugs, and so forth). Each area is then divided into several laboratories, which are the actual work units in which employees reside.

This company was providing communications training (a popular vendor-supplied program) to all lab employees. Senior managers were particularly concerned because recent staff reductions had decreased overall lab staffing and increased the amount of work that was being done across shifts by ad hoc teams that were continuously formed and reformed as workloads demanded. Effective communications, it was hoped, would reduce problems and improve general work morale as well as productivity.

Table 4.4 presents the impact map created for this training. In this map, you will notice that there are three job roles depicted: laboratory operators, peer reviewers, and shift supervisors.

Review the map in Table 4.4 and take special note of the following observations:

- Arrows on the map show the connections among map elements. Only the most significant, high-leverage connections are shown.
- This map shows two levels of organizational outcomes: laboratory unit objectives and quality division goals.
- The initial learning outcomes for the three roles are all the same, since all job roles will be attending the same training, a "canned" program.
- The map shows only a few, high-leverage applications of the training for each role. These are the ways that we, the analysts guiding the implementation of the program, determined that the company could get the greatest impact from the training.
- Even though this intervention was initially conceived of as a "one-size-fits-all" training and all of the learning objectives in the program were the same, each job role will apply them differently. For example, laboratory operators will listen closely and ask questions to confirm understanding during peer review sessions. Peer reviewers will mostly use the skills of providing nonjudgmental and balanced feedback and asking questions to confirm understanding while giving peer reviews. These two applications of training "combine" to facilitate the key

TABLE 4.4   Multiple Job Roles Impact Map

Job Roles	Learning Objectives	Critical Job Tasks	Key Results	Lab Unit Objectives	Quality Division Goals
Laboratory Operators		Ask questions to confirm order specifications	Accurate order specifications		
Peer Reviewers	How to listen effectively	Listen closely and ask questions during peer reviews			Provide accurate analyses that meet customer needs
	How to use questions in interpersonal interactions	Seek to understand, not explain and defend during peer reviews	Constructive, accurate, and efficient peer reviews that do not waste time in defensiveness	Provide timely and accurate reports to customers	
	How to provide non-judgmental feedback	Provide non-judgmental feedback during peer reviews		Reduce rework	Satisfy customers
Shift Supervisors	How to confirm understanding	Ask questions to confirm accuracy and completeness of work-in-progress	Complete and accurate shift transitions	Reduce cycle time	Reduce operating costs
	How to present clearly and effectively	Provide complete and accurate shift-end reviews			
		Ask questions during shift-change to assure understanding of all shift-end issues			

result of achieving accurate and constructive peer reviews that will not engender defensiveness, thus negatively affecting cycle time.

- Laboratory operators will also use the skill of asking questions to confirm understanding when taking orders from R&D scientists, so that rework due to inaccurate order specifications will be reduced.
- Shift supervisors, however, are building different capabilities for providing accurate and complete end-of-shift briefing to the incoming supervisor, and clearly communicating and understanding shift work-in-progress and objectives. Our analysis with this client showed that shift transition issues were the single greatest cause of errors and rework. Further, as an incoming shift supervisor, they also need to ask questions to clarify and confirm understanding of work-in-progress.
- All applications of training eventually converge to enhance only a few critical business results.

Single-Role/Multiple-Learning Intervention Impact Map

Sometimes a particular business issue dictates performance improvement needs for a single role in the organization. However, there is no single learning intervention that is sufficient to drive the needed performance improvement. For purposes of illustration, we will refer again to the pharmaceutical laboratory operation referred to in the preceding section. Imagine that the laboratories division has undergone some major change, wherein new drug products have been introduced, and these new products require new analytic processes, using new equipment. These changes will require considerable training for laboratory analysis operators, involving learning several new capabilities that will be applied in several job behaviors. The map in Table 4.5 portrays this scenario.

Impact Map for a Laboratory Analyst Operator

The impact map in Table 4.5 introduces several changes and variations. First, notice that the map is for a single role, and that the name of this role (laboratory analyst operator) is provided at the top of the map, instead of in a column on the map. Notice also that the first column is labeled "training," since this map depicts three separate learning interventions, all provided for laboratory analysts. In this particular client circumstance, there was a critical need to have laboratory analyst operators be quickly prepared to work with a new product that had been acquired and was being rushed to market to meet an especially urgent market demand (an emerging epidemic). The company had "patched together" some existing training opportunities, using product orientation materials provided by the acquired company, and equipment and analysis procedures training provided by a vendor from whom new equipment was purchased. The map in Table 4.5 shows how this training would be combined to drive the performance needed to meet the business goals created by the market demands.

Notice that there is not a "one-to-one" linkage between the key skills learned in the training and the job application behaviors. Again, arrows are used to show the linkage among map elements. Analyst operators, for example, will combine their knowledge of product and formulation requirements with their equipment training to properly set up the new equipment to conduct the analyses required by customers. This map, like others, shows only the most strategic elements, to simply communicate the essence of how training opportunities will be deployed to meet pressing business needs.

Single-Role/Multiple-Competency Impact Map

This next variation is similar to the preceding map in that it focuses only on a single role. In this map, however, there is no particular training intervention portrayed. Instead, this map variant (shown in Table 4.6) shows the overall

TABLE 4.5   Laboratory Analyst Operator Impact Map

Training	Key Skills	Critcal Job Tasks	Key Results	Lab Objectives	Quality Division Goals	Company Goals
Product Orientation	Understand treatment protocols	Set up equipment to match needed analysis protocols		Accurate reports	Satisfied customers	
	Knowledge of formulation variations		Timely and accurate reports that meet customer requirements	Improved customer satisfaction		Launch a new and urgently needed product
Equipment Training	Setup and calibration	Adhere to all safety regulations and requirements		Reduced cycle time	Analyses and reports that assure quality	
	Routine maintenance					
	Safety procedures	Conduct accurate analyses				
Analysis Techniques	Analysis processes	Prepare complete and accurate reports				
	Report formats					

set of capabilities needed for effective performance in this job role. We use this sort of map when we want to show the overall capabilities needed for performance but have not yet begun to align the capabilities with any particular learning interventions and opportunities.

The job role shown in Table 4.6 is for a project manager in a financial services company (called anonymously here the ABC Company). Notice that this project manager works in a central project office that is responsible not only for managing projects but also for developing project management services and tools throughout the organization.

Notice also that the map has defined five critical actions for project managers. These are not a comprehensive list of all job responsibilities but are a summary-level analysis of the most critical job accountabilities. There is a set of key skills (capabilities) for each of these critical actions. The key skills are also not comprehensive, but only the few most important skills were identified for each critical action. Again, we note that impact maps are strategic, and not comprehensive. In this organization, it was important to identify and clarify a smaller set of highly important skills, as these maps were eventually used to drive a curriculum plan for the entire organization. In fact, similar single-role, multiple-capability maps were produced for each of thirty-three manager roles in the organization. On any of these maps, the "company goals" column was, of course, the same. The maps had to show, however, exactly how, through what key results and work unit goals, each role was important and contributed to the overall company goals.

TABLE 4.6 Project Manager Impact Map

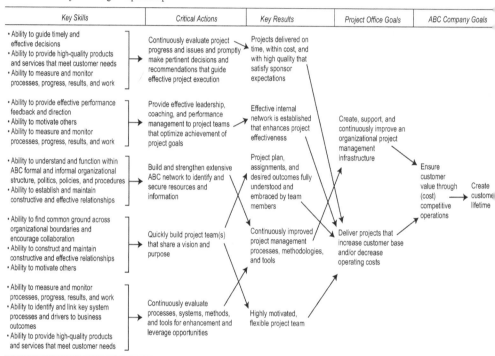

Key Skills	Critical Actions	Key Results	Project Office Goals	ABC Company Goals
• Ability to guide timely and effective decisions • Ability to provide high-quality products and services that meet customer needs • Ability to measure and monitor processes, progress, results, and work	Continuously evaluate project progress and issues and promptly make pertinent decisions and recommendations that guide effective project execution	Projects delivered on time, within cost, and with high quality that satisfy sponsor expectations		
• Ability to provide effective performance feedback and direction • Ability to motivate others • Ability to measure and monitor processes, progress, results, and work	Provide effective leadership, coaching, and performance management to project teams that optimize achievement of project goals	Effective internal network is established that enhances project effectiveness	Create, support, and continuously improve an organizational project management infrastructure	
• Ability to understand and function within ABC formal and informal organizational structure, politics, policies, and procedures • Ability to establish and maintain constructive and effective relationships	Build and strengthen extensive ABC network to identify and secure resources and information	Project plan, assignments, and desired outcomes fully understood and embraced by team members		Ensure customer value through (cost) competitive operations
• Ability to find common ground across organizational boundaries and encourage collaboration • Ability to construct and maintain constructive and effective relationships • Ability to motivate others	Quickly build project team(s) that share a vision and purpose	Continuously improved project management processes, methodologies, and tools	Deliver projects that increase customer base and/or decrease operating costs	Create custome lifetime
• Ability to measure and monitor processes, progress, results, and work • Ability to identify and link key system processes and drivers to business outcomes • Ability to provide high-quality products and services that meet customer needs	Continuously evaluate processes, systems, methods, and tools for enhancement and leverage opportunities	Highly motivated, flexible project team		

Multiple-Role/Multiple-Capability Impact Maps

We have also used impact maps to analyze and summarize the way in which several job roles in a work unit interact to accomplish the goals of that work unit. For example, we examined the several job roles in a national beverage company that operated through several hundred distributorships dispersed across the United States. The company (which we call, for purposes of this example, Barking Frog Beer) was going through some significant organizational change to increase sales and capture more market share. Further, the company was considering the adoption of a broad leadership development initiative, since senior management believed that the aggressive new growth and change strategy would overly stress the current capabilities of leaders at all levels in local area distributorships.

Our analysis quickly revealed that Barking Frog Beer had adopted three fundamentally different change and growth strategies, each of which was applicable to a subset of local area distributors. One strategy for growth was to acquire smaller distributorships, absorbing them into the Barking Frog operation. This strategy was useful in quickly expanding markets, such as rapidly growing suburban areas, where immediate and large growth was needed to serve an exploding population of new grocery and convenience stores. The second strategy was to grow through expansion of the sales force. This strategy was most applicable for distributors serving markets that were expanding at a slower rate, where greater service of accounts was needed. The third growth strategy was the most modest, applicable to markets that were not expanding, but where greater market share could be achieved. In these distributorships, growth was to be accomplished by increasing the effectiveness of the current sales force, providing training in aggressive new sales techniques and introducing new sales incentive programs.

It also soon became clear to us that the leadership challenges for area distributorships would be relatively different, depending on the principal growth strategy being implemented in the distributorship. The impact map presented in Table 4.7 summarizes the results of our analysis. (This impact map was, by the way, included in our proposal to this client and was also referred to extensively throughout the presentation of the proposal to define leadership development needs.)

This impact map is similar to the map presented earlier in Table 4.4, which portrayed a single training intervention for multiple job roles. What is different in the map in Table 4.7, however, is that intermediate business goals differ (according to the growth strategy for the distributorship) and also that there is no single and discrete training intervention represented. In this map, we simply used the Key Skills, Critical Actions, and Key Results columns to show how the different growth strategies necessitated different sorts of leadership capability applications.

TABLE 4.7 Impact Map for Leadership Training at Barking Frog Beer

Participants	Key Skills	High-Leverage Application of Skills	Key Results	Wholesaler Goals	Corporate Goals
Sales Managers **Operations Managers**	How to: · Delegate tasks to competent and committed warehouse staff and sales team leaders · Conduct coaching with corporate standards teams	Empowering teams to achieve corporate process standards	Achieving standardized operation in newly merged distributorship	Operations: · Reduce costs · Reduce shrinkage · Reduce downtime · Achieve corporate compliance targets	
Sales Team Leaders	How to: · Diagnose development levels of new sales reps · Direct and coach early sales efforts · Conduct future coaching	Training, directing, and coaching new sales reps	New hires performing at excellent levels quickly		· Increase sales volume · Increase market share · Reduce costs through streamlined operations
Sales Managers				Sales: · Increase volume · Increase market share · Increase retail shelf space (presence)	
Sales Team Leaders	How to: · Direct shelf space acquisition process · Conduct coaching during "ride alongs" · Secure and implement performance improvement agreements	Coaching and managing performance of current sales teams	Creating sales expertise and excellence in growing markets		

This differentiation was very useful to the client, as it meant that no one single leadership development (read "one-size-fits-all") approach was desirable. Rather, the distributorships should be engaged in different leadership development programs, driven by the fundamental differences in the leadership challenges they would face according to the growth strategy they would pursue. Notice in the map in Table 4.7, for instance, that the principal leadership challenge in a distributorship employing an acquisition strategy is to quickly stabilize operations, helping the newly acquired though deeply experienced staff to understand and follow the Barking Frog Beer procedures and policies, with a minimum of stress and disruption. This meant that operations managers and sales leaders would need to form and provide effective leadership to "integration teams" that would then implement the newly integrated work processes. The leadership challenge in a distributorship using a hiring strategy would face very different challenges, teaching and leading large numbers of staff who are new and inexperienced in the beverage business.

Thus the middle portion of the impact map in Table 4.7 differs according to the three principal growth strategies. Yet the distributorship job roles are the same, since all distributorships are organized in the same way. The far right-hand portion of the map is also the same, since all distributorships, regardless of their principal growth strategy, are pursuing the same corporate goal of increased market share, the "holy grail" of the beverage distribution business. This impact map (Table 4.7) was very useful to senior leaders at Barking Frog, since it clearly showed that their initial plan to purchase and implement a single leadership development program was ill advised and did not address the realities of their business scenario.

Constructing Impact Maps

The impact mapping process is relatively simple and is essentially a data gathering and analysis activity. Like any other data gathering activity, it begins with seeking information, using the common procedures of interviewing, reviewing documents, asking questions, and simply listening. Sometimes, we will already know enough about an organization and its operation to just go ahead and sketch a draft impact map based on what we already know. In other cases, we know next to nothing and have to go to considerable lengths to educate and inform ourselves before we feel anywhere near comfortable in creating an impact map. We use different approaches to gathering data depending on our access to information sources, familiarity with the industry represented, and the amount of trustworthy knowledge our sources and contacts have. Though our methods differ from client to client, it is possible to provide some general guidelines.

Start with What You Know

Take whatever knowledge you have about your client and the business needs and circumstances of the organization, and sketch out an impact map based on what you already know, regardless of how sparse or inaccurate it may be. Use this as a starting point, fill in missing information, and revise inaccurate assumptions as you go. Asking questions of others is always an imposition, and the more you have cataloged and confirmed before you begin, the better. Further, reviewing what you already know and structuring it into the impact map format helps you organize your thinking and efficiently focus your quest.

Keep Refining the "Scope" of the Map

Take some time at the beginning of your mapping quest and identify and confirm the boundaries of the information you need. Then continuously revisit and redefine the scope of the map as you gather information and learn more. Will your map, for instance, need to portray the entire organization or just one business unit? Are you going to need to include all business goals and issues, or should you focus on just one or a few? How many key job roles will it be necessary to include? Should you focus on one learning intervention or open the scope of the key skills to a broader range of capabilities?

Some of these questions will be determined early and will not change. For example, we recently completed an evaluation of a core supervisory learning program for a major company. The scope of this mapping process was always limited to the supervisory role and supervisory capabilities. But several times, as we learned more about the organization and its goals, we changed the business units and divisions that we analyzed. It became clearer as we went ahead that supervisor roles and challenges differed in fundamental ways from work unit to unit, and business goals were likewise quite different across the units.

Tap Different Layers and Sources

Since impact maps represent different levels of the organization, from overall company goals to individual job or team role behaviors and capabilities, it is almost always necessary to tap into information sources at different organizational levels. You can often get high-level goals and overall strategy from a review of an annual report or a visit to a company's web site. From here, you may try to hold brief meetings with senior leaders to confirm and revise your understanding of critical issues. Often mere fifteen-minute meetings over a cup of tea or coffee are all that we can get, and they are likewise almost all that we need.

Information about key job roles and work processes is often available from organization charts and can be confirmed with senior leaders or midlevel managers. Information about critical actions and core capabilities takes longer to gather. We have found that the best sources for collecting this information are employees that actually hold the position being mapped, as well as their direct supervisors, managers, or leaders. This is not unlike the typical type of research interviews an instructional designer would conduct with subject matter experts (SME) or exemplary performers to collect content for the design of learning. When conducting such interviews, it helps to get access to especially knowledgeable and informed sources.

Listed below are some of the key questions we might employ during our initial information gathering efforts to identify business goals and critical business issues.

- What two or three business goals are critical to the company? To our client? Other leaders? To employees?
- How do these goals align with stated strategy?
- How thoroughly communicated are the strategy and goals?
- What time frames and market cycles shape and drive these goals? What deadlines exist?
- What is the current status of achievement against these goals?
- What would improved performance on these goals be worth to the company and others?
- What does this organization do to establish and maintain competitive advantage?
- What issues, obstacles, or barriers stand in the way of achieving these goals?
- What opportunities exist that you may be able to leverage to help achieve these goals?
- How does the culture of this company help achieve goals? How does it hinder performance?
- How effective are managers and other leaders?

The questions listed below will help to gather information regarding critical work processes within the organization.

- Which work processes have the greatest influence on the critical business issues, goals, or both?
- How is the effectiveness of those work processes measured? Are these processes currently meeting expectations? If not, why?
- What factors, internal and external, influence the performance of these work processes?
- What changes, either internally or externally, will have an impact on these processes?

- Which job positions or teams have the most influence on the business issue or goals identified?

The questions outlined below help to identify critical job roles and tasks that have the greatest influence on critical work processes and business issues and goals.

- What makes these job positions or teams critical to the business goals?
- What outcomes must these job positions or teams produce?
- Why are these outcomes important to your business goals?
- How would we measure these job or team outcomes?
- What three to five things must performers in these job positions or on these teams do well?
- How do these actions produce the results?
- What are the essential skills, knowledge, competencies, or capabilities required to perform the critical actions well?
- What are the most common causes of performers not being able to complete a critical action well?
- What aspects of employee performance are complex or not performed frequently?

Keep It Brief

Typically, we have found that meetings to discuss a specific job role with the intent to create an impact map generally take fifteen to thirty minutes. Remember, impact maps will provide us with an understanding of the overall context and set of performance expectations attached to a job position. They are not competency models or exhaustive inventories of required skill and knowledge for the job. Again, they are intended to be strategic, not comprehensive.

Don't Try to Construct the Impact Map
During the Data Collection Interview

It is not recommended that you attempt to create the actual impact map as the interview is in progress. Instead, it is far more efficient to focus attention on the information being offered and to carefully construct probing questions that will yield all of the data you need to build an accurate and complete impact map later. (The exception to this rule is using a group of employees to create an impact map during a facilitated impact map exercise.) This is especially true for novice "mappers" who may struggle with deciding in which column specific pieces of information belong, as opposed to truly listening to the data being discussed.

You will find that simply taking notes or even tape-recording the meeting will result in better, more complete data. You may also wish to conduct the meeting paired with another mapper. While one of you is focused on facilitating the meeting and managing the interview, the other can be documenting the information. Having two present at the data collection meeting is also beneficial later, when constructing the map, so that you have someone with whom to confer when questions arise.

Don't Follow a Lockstep Procedure

Our experience is that the people whom we interview all have different styles and preferences for thinking about and talking about their work. Some are very "results" focused, whereas others may think most about what they do and how they do it. Others yet prefer to concentrate on what they know and how they have been prepared. We have found that the best approach is to start with a few overall probe questions (such as "Tell me about your job," or "In essence, what is this job all about?"). As you proceed, you refer to your mental image of an impact map, and gently steer the conversation to the areas of information you are missing. Forcing the conversation to follow your thinking model may suppress information as well as frustrate your interviewee. Follow their lead, and listen.

It is very easy to steer a conversation to another portion of an impact map. Whenever you wish to move an informant to talk further "to the right" on the map (toward results), ask, "Why is that important?" or "Why do you do that?" When your conversation is too focused on the right-hand portions of the map and you need to go farther "left" toward actions and capabilities or preceding results, just ask, "How do you do that?" or "What does it take to do that?" Remember that "Why" questions steer you to the right, toward results and goals. "How" questions steer you to the left, toward actions and capabilities.

Whenever you do not understand or the information you are getting is too vague or general, ask, "Give me an example."

Listen and Think First, Map Later

This is similar to the caution to not try to construct a map during an interview. But we expand this cautionary note to proceed in an iterative fashion, listening and probing for information, sketching draft maps (either mentally or actually), then going back for more information later. Like many research activities, the people you interview do not necessarily provide you with the information you want, in the sequence that you want it. Instead, information gathering is often a messy business, with golden nuggets of information buried beneath bushels of irrelevant clutter. This is especially true in impact mapping, wherein your output, the impact map, is by definition a tightly focused, spare, and strategic view.

Typical discussions with employees regarding their jobs are likely to lead to detailed and intertwined lists of tasks, activities, skills, accomplishments, and behaviors necessary to do their job. To help you sort the wheat from the chaff, you may find it helpful to review your draft work of a preliminary map before you begin and to keep a mental model of a map in your mind as you proceed. These will help you to focus on the nuggets of information you're looking for.

Another problem comes from the fact that organizations use a variety of terms and definitions as they describe their work processes. In fact, this organizational "language" is likely to have a direct bearing on the titles used for the various columns of the map, which will vary from application to application. The point is that the title does not matter as long as the information recorded reflects the fundamental categories of capabilities, performance behaviors, and results at different levels. Again, as long as the information in the column defines the most impactful capabilities, actions, and results, the specific column heading label is not important.

Strategic Purposes for Impact Mapping

As we noted earlier in this chapter, the overall purpose of the impact map is to clearly and succinctly understand and portray how capabilities link to and drive business results. But the reasons and applications for knowing this linkage differ. In practice, we use impact maps for a variety of purposes. In this closing section of the chapter, we will briefly overview some of these more common and major purposes and applications. In later chapters we expand greatly on some of these purposes.

Shifting Requests for "Training"
to a Performance Improvement Focus

Training leaders often get requests from managers throughout their organizations to deliver specific training to targeted groups of employees who they believe are not meeting performance standards. Frequently, however, managers view the "problem" as lying with the employee and take the narrow perspective that training can "fix" these employees by giving them some new skills and knowledge. Using an impact map in dialogue with these sorts of managers will reinforce that it is your intention to "fix the problem," but that you will focus on employee performance, not just a training solution. Using impact maps in all discussions and communications about training and learning assures that the focus on performance and business results is maintained and reinforced.

Aligning Curricula with Performance and Business Needs

Many companies have crafted elaborate curriculum designs or architectures, or even corporate universities, with recommended learning paths and access systems for employees to provide them learning resources to build the competencies that have been identified for their job roles. Although these systems and resources may have great potential, they are often at risk because of their static nature, appearing to prescribe the same learning opportunities and needs for all employees, regardless of the dynamic nature of business conditions and organizational changes. Impact maps, when created and updated on a regular basis, can help clarify the linkage among the many choices and options in the curriculum architecture, steering employees and their managers to the right choices to meet current performance and business improvement needs. (In Chapter 10, we provide detailed guidance on how the HIL process, and impact map, can be used to guide individual development planning, a common feature in large training systems.)

Linking Core and Soft Skill Training to Specific Performance and Business Goals

Many organizations have invested in and continue to implement large, "one-size-fits-all" programs. The strength of such programs is that these core skills have a broad range of potential applications and can be used almost anywhere, at any time. This diffuse focus is at the same time the inherent weakness of such training, since their business impact depends on whether the skills are used in important, leveraged applications. Defining impact maps for differential organizational units and job or team roles can help tremendously to create a focus on the right content and assure relevant practice and feedback opportunities that relate to the critical job tasks of the performers.

Focusing Evaluation and Measurement

Impact maps clarify outcomes and objectives across the learning and performance spectrum. They identify the expected causal sequence of learning and performance, from initial learning outcomes to performance behaviors to job and thence to business results. These sequential intersections and indicators are very useful in planning measurement and evaluation, to monitor whether a learning initiative is on track, to assess learning, track performance changes, and so forth.

Reframing the Perception of the Training Function

Learning leaders and their training functions have long suffered from the presumed malady of being "out of touch" with business needs and realities. Unfortunately, a review of most communications from a training department, such as catalogs and training usage reports, reinforce the perception that training is an "event delivery" business. The pervasive use of impact maps can begin to change this perception, since they clearly place the focus of training on linkage to performance and business results. Notice that nowhere on an impact map is there any mention of the "how" of training, or training activity. Impact maps are all about performance and business; using them widely and consistently in all training function communications can go a long way toward establishing the perception that, like the maps, training is all about performance and business.

Chapter Summary

Impact maps are a flexible and powerful tool to help us to begin creating learner focus and intentionality. They help to create that line of sight for employees, managers, and the organization at large between capability, performance, and business results. The needs that can be addressed within an organization are numerous. However, in every case, impact maps help to create a shared vision of training and the role it plays.

In Chapter 5, we will continue to investigate this notion of creating focus and intentionality and the degree to which this task actually resides in the hands of the learners themselves.

Creating Learner Intentionality

Chapter Overview

One of the fundamental principles that define high-impact learning is the "line of sight" that must exist and be made explicit between the employee and the goals and business measures of the organization. This linkage and connection is absolutely critical because it identifies and defines the context for all learning within that organization. It is this essential set of connections between the employee and the organization's goals and learning that sparked the invention of a new term we refer to as "intentionality." Learner intentionality represents the understanding that a learner creates and shares with other key stakeholders, particularly the learner's manager, about exactly how any potential learning is linked to both performance objectives and business goals.

Business impact from training hinges eventually on individual adoption of learning into performance improvement efforts. Simply put, if people apply what they have learned in training to important job behaviors, then training can lead to impact. If they do not use their learning to drive performance improvement, then the training investment comes to a screeching halt. Our goal in HIL, then, is to do what we can to assure that each and every individual who participates in training will indeed use that training in one or more valuable performance applications.

In this chapter, we share the methods and tools that we have used to achieve this HIL goal. The chapter begins with an example of intentionality to explain and illustrate the intentionality concept, including its basis in research on learning effectiveness. From there, we move on to highlight the particular advantages of intentionality in creating and managing successful training endeavors. We close the chapter with an explanation and illustration of methods and tools that readers can use in their own applications.

Learner Intentionality: An Example

To illustrate the concept of intentionality, we'll revisit the story of Lynn, the financial advisor who we introduced in Chapter 2. As you remember, Lynn focused her learning in this way: She started with an overall performance improvement objective of increasing the number of appointments she could book with potential financial planning customers. As you may recall, Lynn did an excellent job of closing sales with new customers once she got them into a meeting, and she also was very good at establishing rapport and creating a sense of trust in those with whom she met. But acquiring new customers required making "cold calls," calling people whom she had not met and asking them for an appointment. This was a weakness for Lynn, and her success hinged on whether she could improve this capability.

So Lynn's learning quest started with this performance goal: to get more meetings with potential customers. By using an assessment tool and reflecting on feedback from her manager, Lynn was able to identify some emotional management skills that would help her, if she were to learn them. These skills (identifying her emotional "triggers," controlling fear, and reframing rejection so that she did not take it personally) would help her to persevere and make more calls. As she began to evolve a learning plan for these skills, she targeted a more specific performance objective: to keep making calls each day until she had booked at least one appointment.

Then, as she got into her training, she practiced making simulated calls, using a script she had created and a willing partner to role-play customers. This learning activity entailed more specific performance outcomes, which focused on keeping the call proceeding smoothly, while controlling her feelings of rejection. So, as we can see, there was a cascade of performance improvement objectives and associated learning outcomes, each successively more specific than the next. All of these learning and performance objectives were linked together, however, by an overarching performance improvement objective, which was to schedule more appointments. This objective was, in turn, linked to a business goal: to acquire more customers. This business goal was likewise linked to higher-level business goals related to successfully working with acquired customers to sell more financial plans, increase the total assets she managed, and earn profits for herself and the company.

This successively integrated and linked set of learning and performance improvement objectives formed the focus for Lynn's learning. It also represents what we would call "intentionality." More precisely, the cognitive understanding of this linked set of objectives in Lynn's mind is what we refer to as intentionality. Intentionality is a mental construct in the mind of a learner. As such, it organizes the attention of the learner and keeps the learner focused on goals (goals that, not accidentally, are linked to business goals valued by the organization).

A Basis in Learning Research

Intentionality is simply a new term with a specific application in the HIL framework, though it is not a brand-new construct. Educational psychologists and other learning researchers have identified and studied similar constructs and shown them to be effective in making learning more successful. For a recent summary of this research, see Tracey et al., 2001.

Brinkerhoff and Montesino (1989) conducted a study in a major Fortune 100 company in which they provided a structured intervention for randomly chosen trainees enrolled in company-sponsored training programs targeted on a variety of "soft" skills. Their interventions were aimed at increasing "intentionality" by having trainees and their supervisors engage in a thirty-minute discussion intended to identify a performance-linked learning outcome for each trainee, prior to the training sessions. In this study, they found that training transfer (application of skills after training) was significantly higher for trainees who completed this intentionality-building exercise.

This and previous research indicates that these "advance organizers" and other readiness factors seem to positively mediate learning effectiveness.

Therefore, we cannot claim to have invented the construct of intentionality, only the term. But we think we have perfected the notion and developed it into coherent methods and tools that learning leaders can use and that we have used with considerable success over the years. The HIL approach hinges heavily on the careful and consistent application of these tools, so that each learner has developed a strong sense of and commitment to his or her own intentionality: a crystal-clear focus and reason for engaging in learning.

To further clarify the concept, Table 5.1 provides some examples of intentionality based on some recent work with a range of business clients.

The alert reader will notice that each of the examples in Table 5.1 involves multiple trainees who are participating in the same general learning experience. Yet each trainee has a distinctly different intentionality—that is, each will learn his or her own particular application for the skills taught. This leads us to a key feature of the HIL intentionality concept: It enables truly individualized learning (though the learning delivery method is often classroom instruction!).

TABLE 5.1   Examples of Intentionality

The Setting
Learners are supervisors in a public agency who provide counseling and medical services to war veterans. The agency wanted to increase participatory managerial practices, as these were perceived as enablers to better customer service and satisfaction.

Examples	
Frank, a supervisor of eligibility technicians, will learn how to use "dialogue," a method and tool for increasing verbal participation among members of organizations. Frank will use the dialogue tool for soliciting ideas and opinions from all participants in staff meetings. Better ideas and opinions are needed to broaden the base of common knowledge among these technicians so that they can address veteran questions and eligibility issues more quickly.	Yvette is also a supervisor who is learning how to use the dialogue method. She will use it with a peer group of supervisors from other areas in the agency to raise and discuss issues of redundancy and lack of cooperation, with the goal of creating a "one stop" service concept. More cooperation among the functional areas will increase speed of service and reduce duplication that frustrates veterans and adds time and cost to service.

The Setting
The audience is the administrative support staff in a global development and poverty reduction agency that provides loans and financial consultation to Third World countries. They are participating in a workshop to learn how to use a new software application that combines word processing, graphics, and spreadsheets.

Examples	
George provides support to agricultural experts whose key task is to conduct meetings among ministers of agencies in foreign governments. They need graphic presentations that simply and clearly portray development goals and fiscal resource plans. He needs to e-mail instructions back to the central agency during breaks in meetings, then receive presentation quality graphics within two hours or less. George will learn how to quickly produce and e-mail these complex graphics on a moment's notice.	Francesca provides support to the central training unit. She needs to quickly summarize attendance records from a variety of data sources and merge these into daily reports to managers in many disparate locations. Above all, she must provide timely and accurate reports, as these data drive budget allocations for training missions.

The Setting
Chemical analysts in a pharmaceutical laboratory (part of the quality assurance division of a major pharmaceutical company) are receiving training in basic communications and literacy skills, provided by a local community college.

Examples		
Franz is an analyst who receives orders for assays from research scientists. These scientists often do not complete their orders, and Franz needs to develop skills to ask probing questions to assure clarity and completeness of his understanding. His goal is to get orders right the first time, as errors in initial orders account for a 30 percent increase in cycle time.	Georgette is a "checker" analyst, whose primary role is to provide a peer review of draft reports and provide feedback to the analysts who must finalize the report (this peer review is a regulatory requirement). Georgette needs to learn how to use basic communication skills to provide feedback clearly, without using judgmental language. Defensiveness in her audience often leads to resistance and outright arguments, which add unnecessary cycle time, as well as workplace stress, which introduces more errors.	Hans is an analyst who provides calibration and maintenance to analyst teams to help them keep their equipment operating accurately. Equipment modifications and upgrades are made weekly, sometimes more often. Technical manuals (on CD-ROM disks) are updated, and Hans must read these accurately and quickly, then clearly communicate calibration instructions to the teams with whom he works. If he does this well, errors in analysis and resultant cycle time can be significantly reduced.

Individualized Learning via "Mass Customization"

It is possible to apply the concept of "mass customization," an approach that many retail and service businesses employ using the Internet and other e-resources to achieve individualized learning. "Mass customization" refers to tools or applications that are available to all users that allow them to tailor a system to their personal needs. For example, Lands' End, a mail-order clothing retailer, uses a mass customization approach when it provides software tools to allow an individual shopper to create a virtual electronic replica of him- or herself that is true to body shape and size. Shoppers create this electronic model of themselves by entering data about their height, weight, coloring, and dimensions into a special program. Using this electronic replica, shoppers can then "try on" clothes and see how they, as individuals, look in the clothing. In this way, Lands' End uses mass retailing efficiencies to purchase, stock, and deliver clothing but provides tools to enable individual shoppers to customize their shopping experience to their own objectives.

We can apply the parallel of this mass customization thinking in the HIL approach, using the notion of intentionality. In a traditional instructional design approach to training, the training program "owns" the learning objectives. That is, the program specifies the objectives for the learners, and they are the same for all learners participating in a particular training program or initiative. Imagine, for example, the workshop referred to in Table 5.1, wherein software training is provided for development agency support staff. In the traditional approach, this workshop would have objectives such as "how to open and edit a file," or "how to create and save an e-mail attachment." These objectives are specified at the level of analysis of the program and would be the same for all participating trainees. The scenario is very different within the HIL framework.

In the HIL approach, each individual learner has his or her own individual learning and performance application objective. For example, again referring to Table 5.1 and the software training, one person's objective was to "learn how to use the software to prepare accurate and complete graphic presentation elements." Another trainee had this objective: "How to use the software to create accurate and timely data summaries incorporating data from disparate locations and sources."

HIL learning objectives have a distinct and unique structure. The HIL learning objective structure is always of this form: how to use the learning to do a particular portion of the job more effectively. Notice that the objective is not just to learn something, nor is it to learn all of something. It is clearly and simply how to use some new learning to perform some particular portion of the job more effectively. As we noted in Chapter 3, this manifests the HIL principle of "deep business linkage." Trainees in an HIL experience are there

TABLE 5.2 New System Application

Learner	HIL Objective	Typical Objective
Learner A, an internal sales representative who takes telephone orders	To reduce cycle time in preparing order report summaries so orders are shipped more quickly	How to use new software application TurboMail
Learner B, a support staff member who coordinates the work of external sales representatives	To prepare weekly e-mail sales call schedules so that all accounts are covered to improve customer satisfaction	How to use new software application TurboMail
Learner C, a shift supervisor who coordinates work of internal sales representatives who take telephone orders in a twenty-four-hour call center	To prepare staffing assignments to reduce customer wait time	How to use new software application TurboMail

SOURCE: Adapted with permission from *High-Impact Learning Systems: Fundamentals*, International Learning Works (1998) – Copyright held by TSI Consulting Partners, Kalamazoo, MI 49009

for a particular and unique individual purpose, whether they are participating in the "same" experience or not, and that is to learn something that will enable them to perform some key, highly leverageable job function more effectively. Of course, the part of the job they are going to perform more effectively is that part of the job that is most linked to a particular business goal, such as to reduce cycle time or to increase customer satisfaction.

Table 5.2 provides an example of HIL learning objectives as they are compared to more traditional learning objectives. Notice in Table 5.2 that there are three learners, each participating in a system application skill training activity intended to teach participants how to understand and use the applications in specific job tasks. All of the learners have different jobs in the same customer service function of a large retailing company. Their work unit's overall business goal is to provide more accurate service, to reduce rework and increase productivity, and to improve customer satisfaction.

Again, notice that the typical learning objectives are the same for everyone, since they "belong" to the training program. In the HIL approach, the learner has created and "owns" the learning objective. The HIL learning objective is focused on improving a particular aspect of job performance which is linked to and drives a business goal. The HIL objective creates intentionality, and helps assure that learning will indeed lead to performance improvement that makes a difference to the business.

Individuals Achieve Training Impact

We know that any business impact we achieve through training, regardless of the kind of instruction we deliver, is a function of individual action. If individual employees apply their learning in ways that help the business, we get impact. If they do not, then there is no impact. For every employee that uses training in a way that is linked to a business result, we will see a resulting impact on business measures. Our goal, then, is to get as many employees as possible to apply their learning in the most value-added ways. We accomplish this by creating clear intentionality for each individual learner/performer. These individuals are then empowered to leverage the training resources of the organization in ways that are most likely to lead to desired business impact.

We have found it helpful in understanding and applying the HIL concept to discard the familiar notion that there is such a thing as *a* training program. In the HIL reality, a training program does not exist; there are only individual learners whose needs are to be served. In this respect, there are as many "programs" as there are individuals participating in learning. According to the HIL framework, each learner is participating for a different and unique learning purpose—his or her own individual intentionality—and thus is experiencing a unique learning experience, despite participating in a group session.

Imagine this: You are standing outside a training room in a corporate training building, looking in through a glass window so that you can see the action inside. Imagine further that you are looking in two such windows—one into a traditional classroom training event, and the other into HIL classroom training. Each might look exactly the same. That is, in both learning environments, you might see a group of employees sitting at tables, working with materials, with an instructor standing at the front of the room, gesticulating, pointing out features on a screen, and so forth. Yet in the HIL classroom, if you were looking out through the eyes and mind of any individual trainee, that trainee would tell you that he was there learning one thing, and yet another trainee would tell you something different, and so on for each trainee in the room. Indeed, each would be experiencing a "different" learning program, the difference being created by the intentionality of the individual trainee. Each different participant may be receiving the "same" learning content, but each interprets it through the lens of his or her own intentions; each has a different line of sight through the content to a uniquely owned and individual performance improvement objective.

This construct of intentionality is a key to the power of the HIL approach. By working very hard to create clear, distinct, and sharply focused intentionality in the mind and motivation of each individual learner, we harness the best that the learning experience can offer and leverage the learning for the maximum possible business linkage and impact. Ideally, we would have truly individual learning for each and every employee, with learning experiences tailored uniquely for each one of them. But the reality is that we need, for purposes of efficiency, common learning resources that have been created to serve larger groups of employees. By working with each individual to identify unique performance improvement goals that can be achieved through the common learning, we are able to leverage the learning at the individual level.

Advantages of Intentionality

We believe that our HIL process of creating a high degree of intentionality pays off in several important ways. In general, as we have discussed, it provides a means by which we can individualize learning. But what good does this accomplish? In the following pages, we highlight some of the benefits that we and our clients have experienced.

Creating a Strategic and Empowered Learner

Learners with a high degree of intentionality know where they are headed and why. The ideal training circumstance would be to provide each and every employee with a "personal" trainer, in much the same way that some physical fitness enthusiasts now employ a personal trainer to individually lead and coach them through their fitness sessions. But there is one huge drawback to this notion: cost. Although learning may be important, no company could possibly afford a personal trainer for each employee. The solution to the cost issue has been group training, a far more efficient way of "distributing" learning to large groups of employees. Thus, companies create training programs that are organized by the type of learning and the category of trainee they are intended to serve. And so we have "Supervision 101," a course for new supervisors, or "Finance for Nonfinancial Managers," or "New Sales Representative" training, and so on. The efficiency principle reaches its greatest obvious extension (and some would believe absurdity) with the popularity of the vendor-supplied training program. In the vendor-supplied scenario, we now have a single training program that can presumably be used by any company, from manufacturing to high tech, from sales to production, anywhere in the world. These more efficient approaches to training rest on the assumption that there are common learning needs among similar groups of employees, and thus that a "one-size-fits-all" approach can be effectively employed.

But as all of us know, a one-size-fits-all approach typically never quite fits anyone. Our experience tells us that in any training program in which we have participated, there are always some parts that are more relevant to our particular needs than others. Thus, the "smart" learner will know how to sort wheat from chaff, delve more deeply into what is relevant and worthy, and ignore or reject that which is not. The ability to sort learning wheat from chaff is more important than ever with the advent of e-learning, which dramatically explodes the choices available to learners, making the capability to choose the right learning more vital than ever.

The HIL approach is based on the assumption that there are really no purely one-size-fits-all solutions, that all learners represent individually unique learning and performance improvement needs. To be sure, there may be similarities among needs, and thus grouping for provision of training can allow us to leverage efficiencies. But within the HIL approach we must distinguish between the need for efficiency and the resulting impact on training effectiveness. Therefore, to ensure training effectiveness as measured by the resulting business impact, we incorporate the method of intentionality. The highly intentional learner can be strategic, focusing especially on the parts of learning offerings that are most relevant, paying less or no attention to those things that are not currently needed. The reality is that this is the way things are anyway. In a group training session, no one can pay equally focused attention to all things all of the time. (Research, in fact, has shown that the typical human attention span has a duration of about thirty seconds.) Managing attention, then, becomes a powerful tool for learning. The HIL approach puts the attention management task in the hands of the learners, enabling them to make the individually strategic choices that will best leverage their time.

Managing strategic attention is less obvious and more difficult to achieve in the group classroom training setting. However, in the e-learning scenario, it is very obvious since learners and their supervisors must make correct choices from an ever-increasing array of options, then persevere to complete learning modules. To manage strategic attention in the e-learning setting, we can install methods and tools into the system that will help create the intentionality needed to focus and direct learning. In the classroom setting, the challenge is more problematic, but again we have developed HIL methods and tools for creating the intentionality that is needed. (The next section of the chapter explains and illustrates these methods and tools.)

The highly intentional learner is also a more empowered learner. Learners with a clear focus on exactly what they need and a deep understanding of why they need it are also learners who will not shy away from doing what must be done to get what they need. The highly intentional learner will quickly notice when training is not being helpful and will act decisively to redirect the learning. Highly intentional learners do not sit back and suffer or "tune out"; they take charge of their learning and get what they need.

More Efficient Consumption of Learning Resources

Empowered and strategic learners drive waste out of learning systems. Since these learners and their supervisors are clear about what specific learning is needed, they manage access and consumption in a lean manner, taking only what they need. This point might best be illustrated through a metaphor: Imagine two different customers in a buffet-style restaurant, one being highly conscious of diet and nutrition, the other simply choosing food based on taste and preference, with no understanding of personal nutritional needs. The second customer will fill a plate with anything and everything that looks appetizing, vaguely hopeful that the foods chosen will cover at least some of his or her nutritional needs. The intentional eater with a clear understanding of precise nutritional needs will select low-fat, high-fiber foods and will also consider the carbohydrate and protein makeup of the foods to ensure a healthy balance. This nutrition-conscious customer will leave off the plate foods that are high in calories, fat, and sodium, as these choices derail the eater's quest for a healthy diet.

Let's return now to thinking about how this analogy pertains to learning systems: The traditional training program approach typically loads the "training buffet" with all possible content available, so that there is at least *something* that each learner will find relevant. We have found that as organizations transition to the HIL approach, their consumers of learning become more strategic, and like our nutrition-conscious eater, become more selective and discriminating. In response, training providers become more knowledgeable of these learners and their needs and begin to stock the training buffet more strategically, resulting in reduced content and training contact time.

Increased Commitment

Learner intentionality is identified and documented through a dialogue between learners and their supervising managers. Statements of intentionality are often then shared with senior line managers and also with the leadership of the training function. (The process of creating intentionality statements is explained in more detail in the following section of this chapter.) Because the process of intentionality formulation is interactive and open, with "public" dissemination of results, it tends to build awareness and commitment among the stakeholders who participate in the process. Learners, for example, discuss and explain their ideas about intentionality to their managers, and in this process come to a better understanding of their own expectations for the applicability and importance of learning. Managers provide input about their expectations, which are then reacted to and accommodated by the learner. As in any instance of dialogue, this communication helps to articulate unclear or additional expectations, which leads to higher levels of mutual understanding and commitment.

The statements of intentionality created by learners and their bosses clarify and specify expectations for performance that follow new learning. In this respect, they extend the "line of sight" from simple participation in training or acquisition of new skills to behavioral definition of planned performance objectives. They serve as a form of contract or agreement about how training will be used in job performance that serves both to define the expected performance and to provide a basis by which the performance can be tracked and assessed. Learners and their managers are thus more accountable for fulfilling these implicit contracts, which also serves to increase commitment. In a more traditional, non–HIL training setting, the implicit contract between learner and manager typically only extends to the learner's agreement to attend the training and to the manager's agreement to permit the learner to attend. In the HIL intentionality process, however, the implicit contract extends well beyond attendance to concrete specification for learning outcomes, applications of learning outcomes, and expected impact on performance and business results.

"Hardening" Soft Skills

In the training world, interpersonal capabilities such as listening, managing conflict, clarifying expectations, and so forth, are often referred to as "soft" skills. "Hard" skills, on the other hand, are those more concrete technical capabilities, such as using spreadsheet software, performing preventive maintenance, calculating average daily balances, or performing troubleshooting operations, to name just a few. Though one could be hard-pressed to find a literal definition of these popularly employed terms, the key distinction seems to be that it is easier to observe, measure, and assess "hard" skills than "soft" skills.

Another distinction is that hard skills typically have a clearly delimited range of applicability. That is, one's spreadsheet skills are useful only when one is creating or using spreadsheets. Soft skills, on the other hand, have a broad range of applicability. One can use listening skills, for example, in an almost endless range of applications; listening skills can be used in almost all phases of endeavors at work, at home, in leisure activities, in volunteer work, in church work, and so on. This tremendous range of applicability is at once both the strength and weakness of soft skill training.

On the strength side, we can argue the great value of the skill by reciting the long list of opportunities to apply the skill. At the same time, because the range of opportunities to use the skill is so broad, it may be quite difficult to tell someone else specifically when and how their application of the skill would be the most useful. But clearly, it is the case that some uses of the skill are more productive than others. Consider listening skills, for example. Exactly to what and to whom, when and where should someone listen more? Should we listen more to conversations in the hallways on our way to and from meetings? To the radio in our office? To a stranger complaining about service in the company cafeteria?

In this respect, intentionality is probably most important and most beneficial in the instance of the "soft" skills, such as communications, listening, leadership, and so forth. Creating a dialogue to focus intentionality will help learners determine the strategic value of the soft skill, being more wise about when and where it is most useful in achieving work, personal, and business goals. In this sense, a dialogue about intentionality "hardens" the soft skill, giving learners explicit behavioral expectations for their performance and focusing the range of possible applications to those that are most strategic. In classroom training, clarification of intentionality helps facilitators formulate examples and provide more explicit and actionable advice and guidance to learners.

Creating Intentionality: Methods and Tools

As we have noted, the primary method for creating intentionality among learners is dialogue. That is, in the HIL approach, we aim to promote and facilitate interaction and discussion between employees and their managers as to why some learning is important and how it can be helpful in achieving performance improvement objectives. We use particular tools and methods to accomplish this, which we will explain and discuss following an overview of the basic approach.

Intentionality Discussions

The basic approach for creating intentionality is a structured dialogue between a learner and his or her manager. There are variations on this approach, but it is useful first to explain the steps and elements of the basic intentionality dialogue. In essence, the intentionality dialogue is intended to raise and clarify answers to the following questions regarding a potential learning initiative:

1. To what business goal(s) does the learner's role most need to contribute?
2. Why is/are the business goal(s) important?
3. What results of the learner's job should be added, deleted, maintained, or improved in order to best contribute to the business goal(s)?
4. What critical performance tasks should be added, deleted, maintained, or improved to best produce or improve this result or results?
5. How would this learning contribute to improving performance?

The dialogue should seek not just to answer each question, but especially to establish the key linkage among the several elements raised by the questions. Recall Lynn, for example, the financial advisor we exemplified in Chapter 2. We saw that Lynn and her manager agreed that Lynn should participate in some emotional skills training to

5. learn how to better manage her emotions and reactions
4. during telephone calls to solicit financial planning appointments, so that
3. she could book more appointments, in order to
2. sell more financial plans, thus contributing to
1. office revenues.

At the end of the intentionality dialogue, the learner and manager should have a clear and shared understanding of what is going to be learned, how it will be applied, and what good it will do.

Notice that the five elements of our example from Lynn's learning experiences directly connect to the five questions that make up our intentionality dialogue. Further, you can see that these questions can be ordered and integrated from the "bottom up," as in the example of Lynn's experience, or from "top down." That is, we could start with a scenario where the learning intervention and outcomes are not previously decided but will be determined by starting with an analysis of business goals and the results and behavior that drive them. Or we can start with a known learning intervention, such as a workshop on communications skills, then work from the last question upward to try to pin down a worthwhile performance result and business goal to which that learning could contribute. In this "learning is a given" approach, however, we assume that the particular learning initiative we started with would be abandoned if indeed there was no worthwhile goal to which it could contribute.

But again, returning to the argument about the broad applicability of "soft" skills, it is most likely that any job incumbent could find a worthwhile way in which a basic and core skill such as listening or interpersonal trust building might be deployed. The HIL approach accommodates and promotes either of the top-down or bottom-up scenarios, as we realize that in many instances, certain training programs and initiatives are mandatory or otherwise broadly disseminated. The challenge in these bottom-up instances is to find the application for the learning that yields the greatest leverage against the most important business need.

Ideally, these intentionality dialogues should take place as early in the learning process as possible, since they create a strategic focus and steer the remainder of the learning initiative.

Facilitating Intentionality Discussions

We employ several methods to facilitate the intentionality discussions described in the previous paragraphs. The method to be used depends entirely on what the learning leader perceives will work best to achieve the most complete discussion. At the same time, the choice should be based on what will be practical and elicit the greatest cooperation.

The first choice to be made is whether to facilitate the discussion or to simply provide tools so that the discussion can be self-guided. When a small number of intentionality discussions are to be conducted or when the participants are relatively senior managers, we tend to use a process whereby the learning leader (or some other qualified person) facilitates the discussion. This is done most typically by telephone, in a joint conference call that might last for twenty to thirty minutes.

For example, when a large telecommunications company was providing leadership training to senior operations managers, we scheduled and facilitated a call between each manager to be trained, and his or her manager, typically a vice president. The scheduling was coordinated by an e-mail message to both of the parties, in which we explained that the purpose of the call was to discuss the upcoming leadership training and to identify the goals that the training should address. We also asked each of the participants to think through, before the call, their responses to several questions.

- What were the most important business issues or challenges that the senior leader was hoping to address or accomplish in the near future?
- What contributions to this goal or issue were needed from the manager who was to attend training?
- What particular leadership challenges did this entail? (For example, managing a new department, downsizing staff, introducing a new technology, providing guidance to virtual teams at a distance, and so on.)

During the call, we solicited their responses to these questions and facilitated a discussion based on their responses. Our aim was to get them to agree on one or two key challenges and business objectives that were most important, then to close the discussion with a promise to provide them a summary impact map that would capture their conclusions and would also help focus the upcoming training experience. (Impact maps, as you remember, were discussed in depth in Chapter 4, "Mapping Linkage to Business Goals.")

When a senior manager directs more than one person who will be participating in training, the intentionality discussion may then be conducted in a group conference call. In working with a pharmaceutical sales organization, for instance, all sales representatives in each district (on average, about five to seven sales reps per district) were to participate in leadership training. In this instance, we scheduled a group telephone conference among the sales representatives with their respective district manager. This was especially helpful, since the sales representatives each worked in different locations and thus were able to participate in this call from their home offices. As usual, we preceded the call with an e-mail message to prepare the group. In this case, we asked the district manager to begin the call with a brief five-minute summary of the business goals and challenges facing the district. We then asked the sales representatives, as a group, to describe ways in which they saw themselves making contributions to those goals. Again, as faciltiators of the call, our role was to keep the discussion moving, to try to reach agreement and closure, and to provide a summary. As before, we promised to follow up the call with an impact map for each participant and reminded them to bring the impact map to the training session.

Intentionality discussions can also be facilitated in face-to-face meetings, though we rarely use this approach, because it is time-consuming and difficult to schedule. Also, it is rarely the case that all of the participants in training are in the same local area, making face-to-face meetings unfeasible.

Another method to manage the intentionality discussion is to provide tools and a forum for the discussion, without facilitating it directly. The discussion between trainees and their managers can be scheduled to occur face-to-face, by telephone, or even electronically, using e-mail or some other medium. In one company, for example, intentionality discussions are conducted electronically using "chat room" technology. In this case, participants use instant response messages to discuss the upcoming training. Following this discussion, each participant drafts an impact map, which is then reviewed by the manager. In support of this approach, we typically supply a list of discussion questions, as well as an impact map template for participants to follow. The rule again is: whatever will work. The advantage of the nonfacilitated approach is, of course, that it is more efficient, since it does not require the time and energy of a third party to facilitate. The disadvantage is that there is less control over the quality of the discussion, or even whether it happens at all.

Intentionality Impact Maps

We have often used a tool, a personal impact map, as a way to document the intentionality discussion. Figure 5.1 portrays a personal impact map, again using the earlier example of Lynn, the financial advisor.

Notice that the personal impact map retains the general categories of the impact map we described in Chapter 4. That is, the map defines and describes how capability (learning outcomes) will be used in performance to

Key Skill and Knowledge Capabilities	High-Leverage Tasks/Actions	Performance Improvement Targets	Business Outcomes
1. How to identify my emotions 2. How to positively reframe my emotional reactions 3. How to manage my emotions during stressful interactions	Booking new appointments	Increased booking of new appointments from three per week to six or more per week	Increased sales

Training: Emotional Management Skills   Trainee: Lynn, Financial Advisor

FIGURE 5.1   Personal Impact Map

create worthwhile results. In the case of the personal impact map shown in Figure 5.1, we see that Lynn has identified three learning outcomes to be mastered during her emotional skills training.

1. How to identify her own emotions.
2. How to positively reframe her emotional reactions.
3. How to manage her own emotions during stressful interactions.

She then plans to apply these newly learned skills during phone calls with potential customers. The result she expects to achieve from this application is that she will book more appointments.

We caution readers to not be misled by the simplicity of the personal impact map shown in Figure 5.1. As a tool, we want it to be simple, clear, and, especially, to be easy to complete. What is most valuable, however, is not the tool but the dialogue and understanding that it represents between a learner and a manager, since this is where the real value is created. After it has been completed, the personal impact map will then be provided to the manager for review and approval. In the case of classroom training, we typically provide copies of personal impact maps from all attendees to the training facilitators, as they can use awareness of the key expectations of the attendees to guide discussions, application practices, and other learning activities.

Trainees are always advised to bring their personal impact maps with them to the training session. At the start of the session, we often have small groups of participants share and discuss their personal maps, noting similarities and differences, as well as the range of ways that this learning might be used to improve performance and impact the business. Occasionally during the training session, participants are referred to their maps and encouraged to make revisions and refinements as they identify better ways to leverage their new learning into valuable performance. Finally, they use the personal impact maps as the basis for a detailed plan of action.

In an e-learning setting, the personal impact map would be employed as the initial learning module, to be created during an on-line dialogue with the learner's manager. From that point, learners would be referred to the map as they completed learning interactions and activities. As in the classroom version, the personal impact map would form the basis for detailed action planning and further learning.

Linking Intentionality Dialogues to Development Planning

Thus far, the use of intentionality discussions and personal impact maps has been explained in the context of separate learning interventions and initiatives. We have explained, for example, how a personal impact map might be used as part of a person's involvement in emotional intelligence training. Intentionality discussions are a vital and integral part of any HIL initiative. In an organization that adheres to the high-impact learning philosophy across the board, however, it would be redundant to create separate personal impact maps for each and every learning intervention.

Therefore, in an organization that is seeking to broadly adopt the HIL approach, we suggest that the organization employ intentionality discussions on a regular cycle as a part of a systematic approach to development planning. One company with which we have worked, for example, encourages employees and managers to meet once every six months (in another company, the schedule is annual) and engage in the "front end" of an intentionality dialogue. During this semiannual meeting, they identify and clarify the business goals that are most important during the upcoming period (that is, the next six months) and formulate specific performance improvement targets that will best drive contributions to these goals. Then they jointly plan whatever learning might be needed to support this, creating a sort of "master" personal impact map that can then be used for any and all of the learning initiatives in which the employee will participate.

This embedding of intentionality discussions into the development planning system and process is, in our estimation, the ideal approach. (See Chapter 10 for a detailed treatment of using HIL in development planning.) We recognize, however, that readers who will be trying HIL for the first time are likely to employ it on a far more limited basis, possibly for only a specific training initiative. Regardless of the span of application of the notion of learner intentionality, be it with a single learning resource or across the organization's learning structure, both learners and the organization will realize the power and benefits that this insight brings.

Chapter Summary

High-impact learning is all about creating a direct line of sight between employee performance and how that performance supports the achievement of critical business goals. The way to make this line of sight explicit and obvious is through the notion of learner intentionality. Learner intentionality is best achieved through discussions between managers and their employees that explore the connections between business goals, employee performance, and learning opportunities. These connections, then, can be documented and illustrated for individual employees in "personal impact maps." Therefore, learner intentionality—a clear, individual, and personalized understanding of the linkage among learning, performance, and business results—lies at the heart of high-impact learning, and is a key to increasing the business impact of learning investments.

Effective Learning Interactions

Chapter Overview

For many educational and training professionals, designing and conducting learning initiatives is what we know and do best. When we consider learning interventions and solutions, the HIL approach does not differ greatly from what we already know about effective learning. To a large extent, what distinguishes the HIL approach and what makes it powerful is the blending of intentionality creation and performance support into the overall learning process. Thus, if readers were to dissect an HIL initiative to evaluate only the learning components (such as instructional modules or skill-building workshops) without considering the intentionality and performance support components, they would find that the learning elements were excellent but not radically different from non-HIL examples of good learning.

But there is a clear and distinct approach to the design and implementation of learning interactions and tools in HIL. That is, we are guided by and adhere to a consistent body of expertise and principles. These are the focus of this chapter.

First, we believe that the learning we provide should take into account and respect the experiences and needs of adult learners. In the first section of the chapter, we define and describe some of the particular tenets of adult learning theory and practice. The second section deals with our second guiding principle: We carefully and thoroughly match the learning media and methods we use to the particular learning and performance improvement objectives needed to achieve business impact. Our third principle, described and illustrated in the third section of the chapter, prescribes that best learning results from a carefully constructed balance among four key instructional building blocks: content, practice, feedback, and reflection. Finally, we review a detailed example of a blended solution to illustrate the rationale for the learning methods selected and to identify the appropriate balance among content, practice, feedback, and reflection.

Respecting Adult Learners

Although the technologies of our electronically enabled world change day by day, and almost minute by minute, the characteristics of good learning have not changed much since Dr. Malcolm Knowles described key principles of adult learning theory. In *The Adult Learner: A Neglected Species* (1990), Knowles describes research going back to the early 1950s that attempted to shed light on the special characteristics of adults in the learning process. This seminal work has been deepened and extended by others who have built on the groundbreaking Knowles research (see, for example, Brookfield, 1991; and Marrian and Caffarella, 1998). From this research and literature on adult learning, we have derived the following six guidelines that we believe are especially applicable to the HIL approach.

1. *Adults demand a clear and relevant "need to know."* The relevance of learning to workplace performance and objectives should be clearly explicated. Adults need to understand why their participation in a learning experience is required or suggested. In the HIL approach, we expend significant effort to clarify the "why" of learning as it pertains to performance objectives, and therefore to workplace and organizational goals. Many organizations have adopted "competency models" that provide lists of competencies and capabilities that have been ordained as required for each job. However, simply labeling a competency as being "required" does not meet the spirit of the need-to-know guideline. We believe that adult learners will be more responsive to a logical argument that demonstrates the linkage between the learning and a shared organizational goal.
2. *Adults need to be able to exert control over the learning experience.* Providing choices of learning methods, alternative learning schedules, options for soliciting feedback, and so forth, all help learners gain control over their own learning experiences. The learning experience that is mandatory, a "one-size-fits-all" approach, following the same lockstep process for all directly flies in the face of this guideline. The HIL approach always includes options for learners and further defines all learning at the individual level.

3. *Adults want their experience to be recognized and respected.* Adults bring a wealth of experience, knowledge, and expertise to every learning setting, and they want that expertise to be valued. Virtually always, regardless of the newness of the learning content, there are ways that the prior experience of learners can be brought to bear on the new learning. For example, employees learning to use a brand-new computer tool can reflect on other computer applications they know and apply this expertise to the new learning task. In the high-impact approach, we always recognize the value of experience and consistently build methods into the learning interaction to help each learner probe, reflect, relate, and understand how prior expertise can be leveraged into new learning and performance.

It is also wise to remember that experience is the best teacher. In the high-impact approach, we almost always sacrifice content to build in more opportunities to experience, apply, and practice. In other words, when designing an instructional intervention, we have to make choices as to how much content to provide and how much practice and application to facilitate. Typically, the best training shifts the balance heavily onto practice and feedback.

4. *Adults need to be ready to learn.* Recall that fully one-third of the HIL process is devoted to creating focus and "intentionality," building readiness to learn. A high-impact learning experience always contains opportunities for learners to identify and link their new learning outcomes to potential high-leverage applications that will be of value. In essence, this step helps learners to identify how they could use learning if they were to learn; it is action-planning *before* the fact. This is a very powerful process step in the high-impact approach. It serves to build readiness, something adults need in their busy world of competing demands for their time, and enables them to sharpen focus. In addition, it initiates the learning process, since learning why I might learn something is in fact already learning about it.

5. *Adults want to see the usefulness of learning.* This guideline is similar to the first guideline, which directs us to clarify the "why" of training. The "why" will make the most sense to adults when the purpose of the new learning has instrumentality, when it can be used to accomplish something that the learner cares about. Our assumption in the high-impact approach is that when we link training to performance goals and business results, we broaden the appeal of the value of training to include not only the learners themselves but also their managers and leaders throughout the organization. In essence, the HIL approach recognizes that there are many stakeholders for

learning in organizations beyond the targeted learning audience, and we include them in the value proposition of the training.

6. *Adults prefer learning to be connected with something that motivates them.* Employees are busy, with countless responsibilities and deadlines. Learning and personal development are only one among a multitude of ways that employees can choose to invest their time. If they choose to invest time in learning, then they must be able to clearly identify the "WIIFM," or "What's in it for me?" In the high-impact approach, we seek to build clear links between learning outcomes to performance objectives that are most likely to make a difference, to the learner's reward and incentive structure, and to the goals of the organization. We assume, of course, that there is indeed alignment among these factors. As we made clear in Chapter 4 ("Mapping Linkage to Business Goals"), this alignment must exist. If learning focuses on performance improvement that will not be recognized, then we know that we are in violation of this adult learning guideline, as well as the fundamental precepts of effective performance management.

Adult learners bring with them a significant set of experiences and skills, as well as a clear set of expectations to any learning they contact. If we want our learning to work, then it is smart to apply the best knowledge we can about how and why adults learn.

Matching Learning Methods with Desired Outcomes

What kind of instructional intervention should we build? Should we use a traditional approach to learning, such as an instructor-led workshop? Or is now the time to break with tradition and venture into the world of technology-enabled learning? What type of media should we select to create the best blended solution?

This choice of learning implementation methods *is* a critical decision that lies at the foundation of the overall learning and performance improvement solution. The solution must yield the business results that our organization requires, and it must do so with the most efficient use of learning resources. This selection process is difficult, given the ever-changing possibilities and capabilities of technology. It is further complicated by the fact that instructional designers and others responsible for creating learning solutions have inevitably been schooled in some subset of the available technologies. There is too much technology and too many methods for individual practitioners to become expert in all of them. Just as we become knowledgeable in a computer-based training authoring system, a new, more robust programming tool comes out. Just as we launch our first web-based training course, our organization begins looking at the possibility of satellite broadcasting. It is, of course, a natural tendency to use the tools we know best, and to some extent, this is good practice. Of course, we need expertise in design. On the other hand, we should not make media selection decisions with blinders on, deferring always to our most familiar and comfortable approaches.

The key to building effective HIL learning interactions and tools is to always seek the best possible match between potential and available methods and the learning and performance outcomes that are required to best drive business impact. This matching requires, of course, two critical elements of understanding: First, what are the learning requirements? Second, what available media and methods best suit those requirements?

Defining the Requirements of the Learning Solution

The decision surrounding the selection of learning media must begin with a clear understanding of the requirements of the learning solution. There are three sets of needs or requirements that shape any learning solution. These requirements stem from the content or the objectives of the learning itself, the needs and constraints of the organization, and the characteristics and capabilities of the learners.

Figure 6.1 graphically portrays these three sets of requirements and defines the "sweet spot" as the common overlap or intersection among the three different sources. That is, the final design of the learning solution should be determined by considering and analyzing the requirements from all three sources. It is our job as learning experts to assess the needs of these areas based on the skill and knowledge gap we are trying to address and to hit the sweet spot. Described below are the factors or the requirements that need to be considered in each of the areas.

Objectives/Content Considerations. The objectives and content upon which the learning is built should greatly influence the selection of the media used to communicate and teach it. Imagine, for example, that a company needed its salespeople to know how to complete an order on-line using a laptop computer. Given this skill-based performance objective, it is clear that the learning method must provide for skill practice, with performance assessment and feedback. On the other hand, imagine that a company needs to assure that all sales managers have read and understand a new legally required policy on nondiscrimination in hiring. In this case, a simple reading and self-assessment would work, as the learning method needs to convey information only in a format in which it can be understood and assimilated. Consider using the following questions to assess the needs of your content and objectives for learning. To what extent must your learning solution

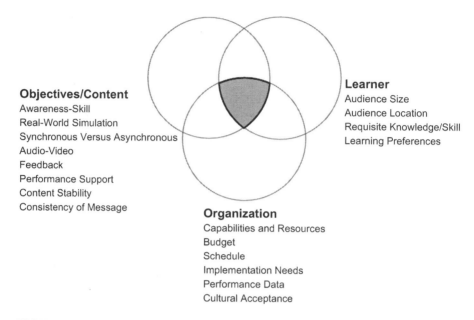

Objectives/Content
Awareness-Skill
Real-World Simulation
Synchronous Versus Asynchronous
Audio-Video
Feedback
Performance Support
Content Stability
Consistency of Message

Learner
Audience Size
Audience Location
Requisite Knowledge/Skill
Learning Preferences

Organization
Capabilities and Resources
Budget
Schedule
Implementation Needs
Performance Data
Cultural Acceptance

FIGURE 6.1   Learning Solution Design Considerations

- Achieve a general awareness and knowledge of content, versus a true understanding of content and acquisition of skills?
- Simulate real-world performance to achieve your learning objectives?
- Allow for synchronous versus asynchronous interaction to acquire skills and knowledge?
- Include audio, video, or both to support your learning tactics?
- Allow for contextual feedback?
- Provide on-the-job performance support?
- Allow for frequent revision?
- Ensure consistency of message across all learners?

We know that our goal is to design a solution that includes a blended mix of media. It is in your careful thought and analysis of the content here, and the way in which you answer the questions above, that will begin to lead you to the most appropriate mix of media. For example, it's likely that all of your content, objectives, or both would not benefit through the use of audio or video. However, it is possible that a slice of content or a specific learning objective could take great advantage of examples and nonexamples presented on audio- or videotape. In addition, it is likely that a portion of your content requires the synchronous interaction of practice and feedback that a group setting would provide, whereas other portions can be learned asynchronously, through print (either paper-based or electronically accessed).

Reflect on how you answer these questions differently depending on the content segment or the objective you consider. The differing needs of your content and objectives will drive you toward applying a variety of media within your learning, resulting in a blended solution.

Organizational Considerations. Once you have considered the nature of the content and objectives you are working with, review the requirements of your organization. Some learning solutions require extensive and complex organizational resources, whereas others require only the bare essentials. A large furniture company with which we worked, for instance, already had in place a strong and proprietary global computer network that could support the e-learning solution we designed. In many organizations, work requirements and schedules may prohibit certain kinds of learning solutions. The questions listed below will help you to identify the assets your organization can provide in the support of the creation of the solution, as well as the expectations and requirements surrounding the solution.

- Can your organization support the design, development, implementation, and maintenance of both traditional and e-enabled learning technologies with the human resources, systems, and facilities required? If not, what capabilities can you "buy" from the outside?
- What is your design, development, implementation, and maintenance budget?
- What is your time frame for design, development, and implementation?
- Must your solution minimize learners' time away from the job?
- Must your solution allow flexibility in scheduling learning into employees' work schedule?
- Must your solution provide for easy collection of performance data?
- Can your organizational culture accept or adapt to any or all learning strategies?

Your responses to the considerations above will provide significant insight into the blend of learning solutions that will be most effective. As you review the list of questions above, there are other issues you may need to address, ranging from practical considerations (such as time, budget, and the availability of internal resources) to cultural issues (such as the organization's openness to new learning approaches). Again, you may be able, through the creation of a blended solution, to minimize or completely resolve some of the constraints posed by the organization.

Learner Considerations.   Finally, the learners themselves place requirements and preferences on the selection of learning delivery methods. Some social learners prefer and gravitate toward the more synchronous forms of learning, such as workshops, structured meetings, chat rooms, and the like, whereas other learners prefer more asynchronous and technology-enabled forms of learning that allow them to control their access to learning. In addition, there are logistical considerations for the audience that need to be considered, such as size and geographic dispersion. Let us consider the following questions regarding the needs of learners. To what extent must our solution

- Be adaptable to large audiences?
- Be adaptable to geographically dispersed audiences?
- Be flexible to heterogeneous audiences with diverse knowledge and skill sets?
- Include experiential learning opportunities for learners who are concrete perceivers or active processors?
- Include analytical learning opportunities for learners who are abstract perceivers or reflective processors?

Obviously, a multitude of factors need to be considered in determining the best blend of methods for your learning solution. Making this decision even more complex is the broad array of methods that can be employed.

Learning Methods

As learning experts, we are not at a loss for "tools" in our toolkit when it comes to learning media. Technology continues to expand our toolkit with more trinkets and gadgets every day. Figure 6.2 provides a menu of learning methods generally in use today. Note that we have not attempted to include every version or type of method, especially within the technology-enabled list; the list would become outdated and inaccurate before this book ever hit the bookstores. We have, however, covered the broad range of methods typically employed by learning leaders in organizations today. Figure 6.2 illustrates these learning methods within a matrix that depicts the range of low tech to high tech along the horizontal axis. More important, the matrix associates all of the methods in relation to the vertical axis, which illustrates the continuum of asynchronous to synchronous delivery, which is a key design consideration relating to our content and objectives (see Figure 6.1).

Planning the learning methods that will be incorporated into a blended solution will be influenced as well by the learning objectives, a consideration we raised earlier in the chapter. Clearly, for instance, if trainees need only a fundamental familiarity with some content, then we can eliminate a number

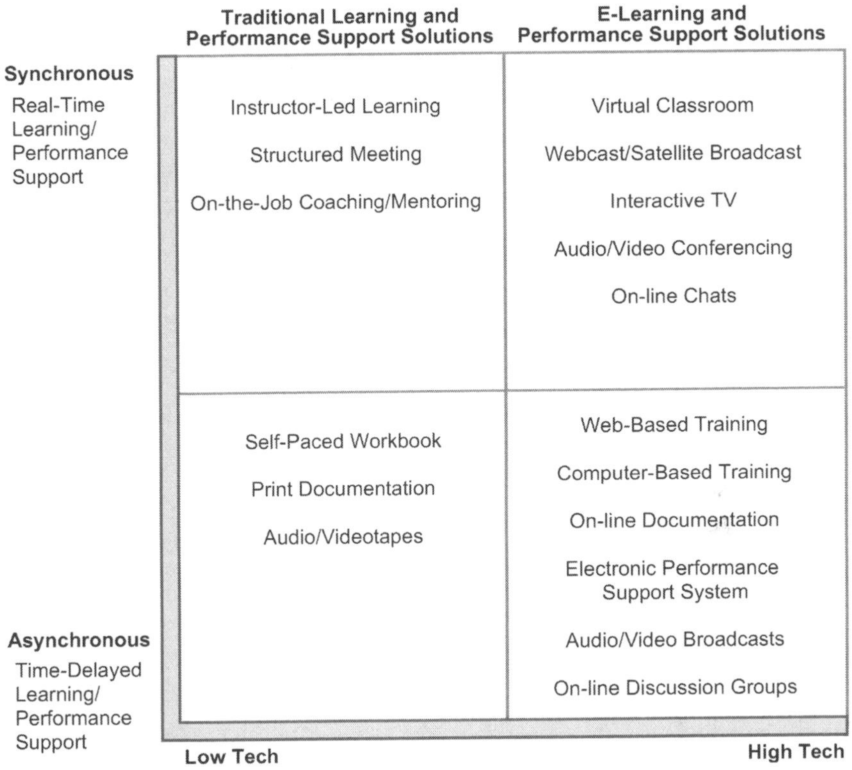

	Traditional Learning and Performance Support Solutions	E-Learning and Performance Support Solutions
Synchronous Real-Time Learning/ Performance Support	Instructor-Led Learning Structured Meeting On-the-Job Coaching/Mentoring	Virtual Classroom Webcast/Satellite Broadcast Interactive TV Audio/Video Conferencing On-line Chats
Asynchronous Time-Delayed Learning/ Performance Support	Self-Paced Workbook Print Documentation Audio/Videotapes	Web-Based Training Computer-Based Training On-line Documentation Electronic Performance Support System Audio/Video Broadcasts On-line Discussion Groups
	Low Tech	High Tech

FIGURE 6.2   High-Impact Learning Methods

of complex and highly interactive learning methods from our pool of choices. The key question we ask when considering the learning objectives required is: "To what level of expertise do we need learners to learn what we teach?" It may be that we need to simply reach a "knowledge" or "comprehension" level of understanding. If this is the case, it would be unnecessary and wasteful to build instruction that achieves much beyond these levels. However, if it is essential for our learners to be able to assess the values of hypothesis, for example, or to make a decision based on a persuasive argument, then our instruction must be rich enough to get the learner to the "evaluation" level.

We have adapted the well-known Bloom's taxonomy of learning objectives (Bloom, 1956) to a simpler set of four learning levels (awareness, knowledge, understanding, and skill) that are depicted on the vertical axis of Figure 6.3.

From this graphic, we can conclude that there are *inefficient* uses of our media, such as using classroom instruction or on-the-job mentoring to simply

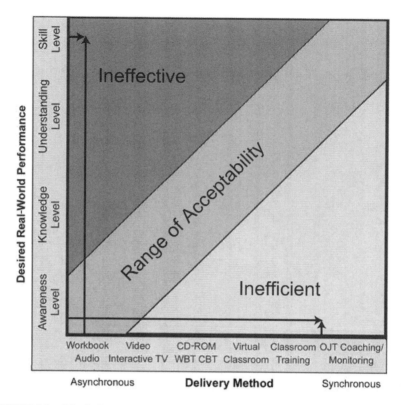

FIGURE 6.3   The Influence of Learning Levels on the Delivery of Learning

reach an awareness level of learning. We can also see that there are *ineffective* uses of our methods, such as attempting to reach an understanding or skill level of learning through asynchronous methods such as self-paced work-books or broadcast television. However, we see a band running diagonally through the matrix that identifies a range of acceptability. This band represents the best applications for our delivery technologies, based on the level of learning we are attempting to reach. In general, what this band of acceptability shows us is that as we aim to reach a higher level of learning, such as understanding or skill, we need to rely more heavily on synchronous methods of learning.

Again, as we consider this conceptual illustration, we see that it in fact completely supports the notion of a blended solution, in that most of the needs our learners have include a mixture of awareness, knowledge, understanding, and skill requirements. To most efficiently and effectively meet this range of needs, a blended solution is our best approach, as opposed to attempting to create a single learning event that "does it all." We might, for example, create a solution that blends low-tech, asynchronous methods such as self-paced workbooks or web-based training courses to build awareness and knowledge with synchronous methods, such as classroom instruction and on-the-job coaching and mentoring to build skills and enhance performance.

Four Key Dimensions of Powerful Learning Interactions

Ensuring that we have the most appropriate blend of methods is a major step toward building a learning solution that can and will achieve high impact. However, leveraging the medium to its best, most effective application also means looking within each learning and performance support component of the blended solution to ensure that the "right stuff" is there.

But what is the "right stuff"? What makes a computer-based or web-based training module "really good"? What makes one workshop stand apart from another? Don't be dazzled and fooled by the glitz and glimmer of the packaging. Good instruction is not defined by the production quality of its wrapper. All too often, we have seen highly produced, full-color, glossy learning materials that are completely lacking in the essentials of quality instruction.

Therefore, we need to apply some principles of sound instructional design to ensure that our learning experiences are meaningful, relevant, and rich so that our learners acquire the skills and knowledge they need. In creating high-impact learning solutions, we consistently incorporate four fundamental instructional building blocks.

- Content—the concepts, examples, principles, rules, formulas, guidelines, background information, and so forth, that form the knowledge base upon which effective competence is built.
- Practice—the opportunity to try out new behaviors and tools, to sharpen skills in an environment that supports experimentation and risk-taking.
- Feedback—the knowledge of results and information about reactions and results that helps learners understand how well they are doing, what they are accomplishing, and what effect they are having.
- Reflection—the opportunity to self-evaluate, to look back on experiences, to question assumptions, to reconsider goals, to ask "why?" and to reinvigorate and reenergize commitment.

As we noted, we always build our learning solutions to include these four basic components, although the balance among them will differ according to the nature of objectives to be mastered and the business requirements that drive a need for training. Before we discuss and define these four building blocks in more detail, it is useful to illustrate the variety of learning methods that can be used to implement each of them.

Table 6.1 summarizes some of the instructional strategies that can be used to build each of these elements into your overall learning solutions.

With these examples in mind, let's take a look at each of these dimensions of instruction and how you can best leverage their use within your high-impact learning solutions.

Content

Regardless of the type of learning we are attempting to achieve or the delivery mechanism we are employing, we will always have a message or specific content and information that must be communicated. This information may take many forms, ranging from a speech or lecture presented live or recorded on audio or video to textual or graphic material delivered in print or electronically.

No matter what form the content message takes, there are a few guidelines that the designers of learning should follow to ensure that their message is heard loud and clear

- Information should be broken into small, easy-to-reference chunks that are organized into a logical and straightforward sequence.
- Use graphic representations, photos, drawings, and animation to illustrate content as often as possible.
- Define concepts with a rich use of examples, nonexamples, stories, and analogies.
- Use memory aids, job aids, documentation, and checklists for content that does not need to be memorized.
- Shift the balance of learning time from the delivery of content to the other instructional components of practice, feedback, and reflection.

As we discuss the dimension of "content," we feel compelled to bring up a caution. It has been our observation through many decades of experience with corporate training that too many instructional solutions—particularly typical corporate training workshops—are drastically overloaded with content, whereas opportunities to apply the skills, receive relevant and rich feedback, and to reflect are scant, or artificial at best. There are probably many reasons for this. One reason we believe is that many designers of learning have a difficult time making the discrimination between need-to-know content, content that is simply nice to know, and content that is irrelevant. Think back to the last instructor-led workshop you attended. How much time was devoted to the practice/feedback/reflection elements of the instruction as compared with the content that was presented?

TABLE 6.1 Instructional Strategies for Powerful Learning Interactions

To Present Content, Use...	
Chunks and clusters	Examples and nonexamples
Advance organizers	Stories and analogies
Illustrations, tables, pictures, photos	Brainstorming
Memory aids/mnemonic devices/job aids	Field trips/tours
Rules	Panel/subject matter expert discussions
To Provide Practice, Use...	
Performance modeling and demonstration	Role-play exercises
Case studies	Games
Simulations	Oral and written questions
To Engineer Feedback, Use...	
Simple textual and oral interactions	Tests and quizzes
Mentoring and coaching	On-the-job observation
Buddy systems	Performance measurement and data
Video and audio recording/playback	
To Promote Reflection, Use...	
Debriefing sessions	Graphic recording
Follow-up meetings with manager	Assessment tools/surveys/questionnaires
Chat room discussions	Action planning
Network contacts	

If we are striving for an awareness level of learning, we may be safe in building in more content. However, we still need to provide some opportunity for practice, feedback, and reflection. Further, if we are aiming to achieve true understanding and skill, then there should be a significant shift in this balance toward a heavier investment in practice, feedback, and reflection.

Our advice is to be strategic and not comprehensive when it comes to including content in learning solutions. Do not include every nugget of information you have, but instead be selective. Only include the content that the learner can leverage on critical job tasks. If we cannot readily draw the connections between the content and key business results for learning audiences within our organization, then that content does not belong in the learning.

Practice

No matter what your learning outcomes are, no matter what your content is . . . practice is *the* essential learning strategy. It *must* be built into instruction for instruction to truly teach. Having said this, it is important to define what practice is and what it is *not*. Practice is not simple testing (as in lectures paired with quizzes and final exams). Instead, well-designed practice

- Is relevant. It reflects real-world performance as closely as possible.
- Breaks performance into component parts, so that each component can be mastered, then combined into complete performance.
- Does not penalize the learner for mistakes or for less-than-mastery performance; practice must occur in a safe, risk-free environment.

Practice opportunities can come in all shapes and sizes. As you can see from the table presented earlier, there are a multitude of strategies for incorporating practice into learning solutions. It is likely that the most creative, innovative, and memorable aspects of learning are actually opportunities to allow learners to practice their skills and knowledge. The challenge is to ensure that the practice strategies truly reflect the skills and job performance expected, as opposed to simply being entertaining and engaging.

The best practice conditions are those that are encountered on the job versus the artificial confines of the classroom. Whenever possible, employees' jobs and work environments should be rich with opportunities to practice new skills and knowledge. In fact, this is the approach used in the military, where the job is essentially defined as practice, explaining why sailors and soldiers seem to spend all of their time in drills and exercises. In many instances, the job environment cannot assure the safe and risk-free venue we need for practice. We would not, for example, want a bank officer in training to practice her newly acquired selling skills with a major client in a competitive loan environment, because it is likely that ineffective performance in this case would undermine a business goal. On the other hand, we are all familiar with the "trainee" nametag on our fast-food server, and most customers are willing to experience less than perfect service to help a new employee learn a job. In most instances, we aim to build practice into real-world job tasks, making exceptions and compromises when safety, performance, and other requirements must be met.

Feedback

Feedback that is immediate, accurate, and constructive works hand-in-hand with effective practice. Learners' first contact with any new knowledge or skill is tenuous and vulnerable. Think back to the first time you used a computer mouse to control the cursor on your personal computer. Can you recall how awkward it felt? How clumsy your movements were? How long it took to click and drag, or select items from a drop-down menu? But also recall how quickly you learned this skill, thanks to quick and relevant feedback. Your "mousing" performance was being shaped by the feedback you received directly from your computer screen . . . by watching the movements of the cursor based on your manipulation of the mouse. It's likely that you perfected your mouse-handling skills in a few short sessions. However, if you had not had the benefit of the visual feedback your computer screen provided, your mousing skills would have taken much longer to build.

The term "feedback" originates in the field of sound electronics, explaining the nasty screeching whistle you hear if you place a microphone too close to a loudspeaker. The feedback you hear is noise that is "fed back" into the microphone from the loudspeaker, then amplified and reamplified instantaneously and many times over, building to an ear-splitting crescendo. In the world of performance and learning, feedback means "knowledge of results", providing learners with knowledge that helps them see and understand the results of their learning. Learning is not possible without feedback, since it is knowledge of results that prompts learners to redirect their efforts and correct mistakes. When we learned to steer a bicycle, we quickly received feedback on the consequences of turning the handlebars too sharply, for example.

Feedback in learning takes many forms, depending on the subject matter and scenario. Customer service representatives learning how to assure a hesitant customer can receive feedback while practicing this skill from a third-party observer during a role-play exercise. X-ray technicians can receive feedback on their knowledge of exposure limits by taking a multiple-choice test. Electronic technicians can get feedback by working on a simulated piece of equipment that sends an audible signal or turns on a light when they misconnect a circuit. Nuclear power operators get feedback from a computer simulator that tells them if they properly opened or shut a valve during an emergency practice drill. Regardless of its form, verbal, written, electronic, test results, and so forth, feedback is an absolutely required part of all high-impact learning solutions.

Reflection

We believe that of the four dimensions for sound learning that we have presented, the dimension of "reflection" is probably the least understood and applied. As designers of learning attempt to pack more and more content into their learning solutions, the activities that provide opportunities to allow learners to reflect on the new skills and knowledge are the first to be neglected. Perhaps this is the case because as designers and facilitators of learning, we often cannot directly witness or measure the positive impact and output that this step in the learning process can have while it is occurring. All of the processing that occurs during reflection is experienced and internalized within each individual participant, most likely in a different way.

However, we know that much of what aids the application of new skills and knowledge to job performance is the learner's ability to connect this fragile new repertoire to existing skills and knowledge. So much more will be retained and applied when the learner can make a connection with earlier experience and say, "Oh, *now* I get it! This is just like . . ."

Although they may not have purposefully attempted to build reflection into their learning solutions before, many readers will recognize the common activities that provide opportunities for learners to reflect, such as action planning, follow-up meetings, and debriefing discussions. But too often, these instructional activities are treated superficially and given short shrift, since time is limited . . . and the need to move on to delivering more content is pressing.

As designers of learning, we should never short-change the investments we've made in content, practice, and feedback by not allowing sufficient opportunities for reflection. If time is the issue, consider reflection opportunities that occur following the formal opportunity to learn, such as live or on-line networking opportunities or meetings and discussions with managers or peers. Also, follow-up printed or on-line materials, such as newsletters or bulletins, and follow-up questionnaires or assessments can also prompt learners to reflect on their new skills and knowledge and consider novel ways in which they might apply it. People will naturally reflect on and reconsider their experience but may not invest much energy into it or take it seriously if they are pressed for time. One of our key tasks as high-impact learning architects is to promote and encourage reflection and help learners see that their experience and reactions are legitimate and authentic sources of knowledge and growth.

In summary, we must strive to build engaging, challenging, and relevant practice into our learning, to provide meaningful feedback mechanisms, and allow multiple opportunities to reflect on learning, at the same time keeping the delivery of content to the bare essentials.

Achieving Balance Among the Four Instructional Dimensions

As we noted, we always include all four of the basic instructional components (content, practice, feedback, and reflection) in any learning design. But the balance among these components may be drastically altered, swayed largely toward one or more of the components versus others, depending on the learning needs and methods. Consider, for example, one design that we created for a large sales organization that had grown rapidly, adding many new district managers.

Many of the new managers who had been selected for promotion into these positions had limited experience and expertise. The company had provided minimal training before they were placed in the management positions; business was growing so quickly, there was not time for an extensive management development initiative. The solution was to provide each manager with access to a coach, an expert in management who had also been trained in how to be an effective mentor. Each new manager used an impact map to identify a key and current business objective (such as penetrating a new account) and worked with the coach on-line and by telephone to create a development plan. The coach then guided the implementation of the plan and regularly discussed progress with the new manager along with some of the sales representatives who reported to the manager. In this way, the coach and manager worked together to keep the business moving ahead, at the same time assuring that the new manager got highly structured "practice" (actually, of course, it was real performance) that would provide highly meaningful and targeted learning for the manager. Each manager was required to keep a daily log of new learnings, reactions, and so forth, that formed the basis for weekly summary coaching sessions. Notice that this design is comprised almost entirely of practice, feedback, and reflection. There is virtually no prearranged "content," since the only content that is included is generated from the coaching sessions. Occasionally, a coach might recommend a particular reading or suggest that the manager complete an on-line instructional module.

In another instance, a learning design was comprised almost entirely of reflection. In this case, project management teams met at the conclusion of each project to complete a "postmortem" analysis of the project. These sessions, two days in duration, were highly structured group discussions and were facilitated by an expert group leader from the training department. Postmortem teams reviewed all phases of the project, noting especially what had worked well and what had not worked well. Each team was responsible for creating tools and methods that would improve practice on the company and for planning experiments with new techniques that could be tested in the next project.

These examples remind us of the age-old learning maxim that "experience is the best teacher." Although these examples are biased away from content loading, they are exemplars of the HIL approach in that they have embedded a high degree of intentionality and performance into the learning process. These learning approaches were based on the assumption that learning new content is often the least important element in a performance improvement initiative. Frequently, performance is hampered not because people do not have the ability to do something better but because conditions in the workplace have somehow kept them from performing as well as they are capable of. HIL learning designs can create conditions and tools (such as the project postmortems) that promote learning and performance improvement, allowing people to unlock their own learning capabilities, using reflection and feedback to guide practice that is tightly focused on key business and performance improvement objectives.

Blended Solutions: Revisited

Now that we have established the multitude of media we have at our disposal as designers of learning as well as the four dimensions of powerful instruction, let us take a look again at the notion of creating a blended solution.

We introduced the concept of the blended solution in Chapter 2, where we posed the question, "Does the e-world change everything?" Here, we stated that "a blended solution is simply a set of instructional components that combines e-learning with classroom learning, communication, and performance support tools. A blended solution affords the benefit of using the most appropriate mix or blend of instruction, performance aids, and communication to create the optimum learning experience."

Recall the blended solution from Chapter 3 that addressed the needs of Lynn and other financial advisors who needed to build skills around cold-calling and handling feelings of rejection. This blended solution included a variety of traditional and technology-enabled media.

1. The intervention began with a communication from Lynn's manager, in a staff meeting, announcing the new learning opportunities and connecting them to the new strategic direction of the company.
2. Lynn reviewed an impact map for financial advisors, then completed an electronic assessment tool to help identify her strengths and areas for improvement based on the most critical tasks for advisors.
3. Based on the results of the assessment and input from her manager, Lynn completed three web-based training modules on the basics of managing her feelings of personal rejection.
4. Lynn then enrolled in a workshop designed to practice her skills during role-play exercises and completed the necessary prework of documenting real-life scripts of the cold calls she currently makes.
5. Lynn participated in the workshop, along with all of its activities, and completed an assessment checklist at its conclusion.
6. She followed this up with several observation and feedback sessions with her manager and with other advisors to get valuable on-the-job feedback.
7. Finally, Lynn maintained constant communication with her manager throughout the process and continued to monitor and measure her performance, even posting her cold-calling success rate on an e-bulletin board.

First, from a blended media point of view, this example shows great diversity in delivery methods, including both traditional (such as structured meetings and classroom instruction) and technology-enabled approaches (including on-line assessment tools, web-based training modules, and electronic bulletin boards). We can also see how our four dimensions of content, practice, feedback, and reflection are imbedded within and across the solution components.

This blended solution illustrated a wise use of employing low-technology, low-cost methods to first teach content that could easily be communicated and learned in a self-paced, asynchronous manner through web-based training modules. Then, to begin to build true skills and fluency, participants attended classroom instruction where the environment for realistic practice using role-play exercises (supplied by the learners) and specific feedback was possible. We can also see how the solution reached beyond the "formal" opportunities to learn into the actual work environment. Opportunities to assess and reflect occurred throughout with assessment checklists and follow-up on-the-job performance observation sessions with her manager and other advisors.

What is striking about this example is that it is the combination of well-orchestrated learning media in conjunction with the support, coaching, and feedback from her manager, as well as the intentionality and focus that was built early on, that made Lynn's learning experience a success. Lynn's improved performance in booking more appointments did not simply result from her participation in learning or from only the one-on-one support from her manager or from her initial development planning activities. All the components were necessary, working hand-in-hand-in-hand, to achieve measurable business results from this high-impact learning solution.

Chapter Summary

The expectations that adult learners have regarding the learning and personal development activities they engage in are completely aligned with the philosophy of high-impact learning. The notions of relevancy, respect, readiness, and control, important needs to all adult learners, are also critical elements that can be found threaded throughout all high-impact learning initiatives.

Another defining characteristic of all high-impact learning initiatives is that they employ an array of media, with an explicit purpose and role in performance improvement. However, selecting the media wisely is an important decision since it can result in a huge commitment of an organization's resources. Therefore, determining the most appropriate delivery methods for building a blended high-impact learning solution takes into consideration the requirements of the content and objectives, of the organization and the learner. Hitting the sweet spot where the needs of these three sets of requirements converge is our aim.

High-impact learning solutions also apply four key building blocks for robust instruction. The four components that make up all good, sound, effective learning are

1. Content
2. Practice
3. Feedback
4. Reflection

Although all of these components are indeed necessary elements of robust instruction, we would urge the designers of learning to seek an appropriate balance of these elements in light of the level of learning that is to be achieved. As the level of learning increases from awareness and knowledge to understanding and skill, we must increase the opportunities to practice, receive feedback, and reflect proportionately. Remember that it is during the practice/feedback/reflection components that true learning-to-performance can occur.

Performance Support

Chapter Overview

It is a harsh maxim of learning and performance that the more an organization needs training, the less likely it is to be successful in improving performance. In other words, as the need for effective, powerful training increases—for example, during an organizational restructuring, the introduction of vital new technology, or a transition to a crucial new strategy—then the greater the resistance to change becomes. As the targeted performance becomes less like "business as usual," then it becomes more likely that existing job systems, culture, and other performance factors will not support new performance expectations and will be more difficult to achieve. This maxim of performance improvement is unfortunate, since its obverse tells us that it would be much easier to be successful when training was aimed at inconsequential and unimportant outcomes. But of course we want to make a difference when the stakes are high, and making a difference is important. Therefore, we need to help our clients create a positive performance support system and build constructive performance support tools and methods into our HIL solutions.

As we have seen throughout the second section of this book, the individual components of a high-impact learning solution become so intertwined that it is, at times, difficult to discern where one component ends and another begins. Creating learner intentionality, providing learning, and supporting performance, the three key elements in any HIL initiative, begin to lose their independent defining characteristics as they are woven together to create a unified and strong but flexible braided performance solution.

In this final chapter of Section 2, we will closely examine the third element of HIL initiatives, supporting performance improvement. With this chapter, we aim to fulfill two important objectives: First, we hope to broaden your view of

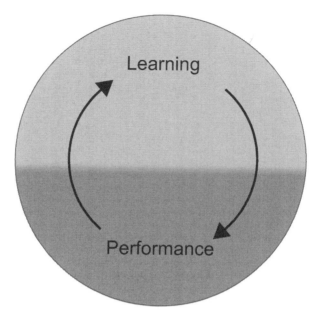

FIGURE 7.1   The Learning-to-Performance Process

what constitutes performance support in the HIL framework. You will find that performance support includes more than simple job aids and documented procedures. To help define the broad array of methods for supporting employee performance, we will review a performance systems model that illustrates a broad range of the factors that can influence employee performance. Second, we will urge you to thoughtfully consider the notion of integration . . . integrating and weaving elements of performance support throughout your HIL solution. Here we will revisit the learning-to-performance process. To help achieve both of these objectives, this chapter will be rich with examples.

What Is Performance?

Back in Chapter 3, we first introduced this simple model to help illustrate how learning leads to performance. (See Figure 7.1)

But what is performance? It seems like such a simple and obvious concept that one shouldn't even have to ask the question. However, the realities of the workaday workplace illustrate that the concept of "performance" may not be as well understood as we think. Just consider an example that is experienced by many employees every day: Let's imagine that Joe just arrived to work today at 9:15 A.M. (his normal work hours are from 8:30 to 5:30). Although Joe typically arrives to work on time, he commutes eighteen miles in heavy traffic to get to the office. And Joe's commute has been hampered lately because of construction and road closures, causing him to be late more often than usual. Further, let's say that Joe performs his job well, receiving better-than-average ratings on his performance reviews from his manager, Bob. Now Bob would say that he, as a manager, generally understands and knows how to manage employee performance. However, today he is particularly annoyed by Joe's tardiness and gives Joe an earful as soon as Joe arrives, telling him that he had better start getting to work on time or his pay will be docked.

Although Bob says he is focused on performance, this example would illustrate that, for at least this moment in time, he is focusing on Joe's behavior, the behavior of arriving to work (late, in this case). If Bob were truly focused on Joe's performance, he would instead begin to evaluate whether Joe's tardiness was affecting the completion of his job tasks and the achievement of his expected results. If, in fact, Joe was able to continue achieving the results expected of him in spite of his lateness, then Bob shouldn't concern himself about Joe's comings and goings. However, it is an unfortunate reality that many managers become fixated on employee behavior and lose sight of what's really important, which is performance that leads to positive business results. The good news is, though, that we see evidence in the workplace that this is slowly changing. Evidence such as flexible work hours, working at home, and even business casual dress and "jeans day" illustrate that managers and the HR function are beginning to understand that employees can still achieve measurable performance goals regardless of these other, mostly irrelevant workplace factors.

So we know that performance is not merely "behavior" on the employee's part. It's more than that. What converts simple behavior into performance is when that behavior leads to a valued consequence or an accomplishment of measurable worth (Gilbert, 1978). Clearly, this has been a key premise of this book: Traditionally, much of the "stuff" that went into the creation of learning solutions targeted changing employee behavior, without much attention or effort being paid to how that new capability could lead to improved performance and business results. Our objective with HIL initiatives is to simply focus on behaviors and the associated skills, knowledge, and competencies that can lead to valuable and worthy performance that will make a difference to business indicators.

Part of the challenge is in the transfer of new skills and capabilities to the workplace. In fact, the transition of skills from the learning environment to the work environment has been a perpetual "thorn in the side" of many learning and performance improvement practitioners. Further, learning transfer has been the topic of countless articles and textbooks that focus only on this particular aspect of human performance (see for example, *Transfer of Training*, Broad and Newstrom, 1992). There are several reasons why the transfer of learning to the workplace into valued performance is so difficult.

- Skills and capabilities are fragile—we have pointed out several times in earlier chapters that newly learned skills, knowledge, and capabilities are tenuous and can easily be abandoned when employees are faced with the demands that come with actual job tasks with real customers, deadlines, and expectations. One of the reasons for learners not building the confidence and fluency they need with their new capabilities stems from a lack of sufficient practice and feedback opportunities in a safe and nuturing environment.
- "Artificial" setting—even if learners have exposure to opportunities to practice and receive feedback on new skills and knowledge, it may be that these opportunities are too different from how it "really happens" in the workplace. A good example of this type of learning is intact work groups and teams attending an outdoor experiential event to help build teamwork and team effectiveness. As a part of these learning interventions, these groups of employees experience dramatic obstacles in the form of white-water rafting, mountain climbing, or some other outdoor challenge, and find that they must work together to succeed. Although these events are popular and provide participants with vivid memories of their experiences, participants often struggle with trying to regain that sense of team unity back in the conference room during routine team meetings.
- The "system" is broken—there is an old saying in the field of performance improvement, "If you pit a good performer against a bad system, the system will win almost every time" (Rummler and Brache, 1995). In other words, placing a talented and dedicated employee into a work environment with faulty processes and data, poor management, and a lack of incentives and rewards, just to name a few organizational obstacles, will almost guarantee marginal or unacceptable employee performance.

This final cause of poor transfer of learning to workplace performance is vast and deep with regard to analyzing and understanding employee performance and the remedies for poor performance. We will take a systematic look at the range of organizational obstacles to exemplary performance in the next section.

A Framework for Analyzing Performance

In this section, we present and discuss a performance analysis framework that we use in HIL approaches. The performance analysis framework identifies some of the critical performance environmental factors that influence performance, and as such are valuable for planning and implementing an HIL initiative. We use an analysis of performance factors in two ways. First, we use the framework to guide an analysis of the performance environment in which training will take place to identify performance factors and variables (measurement used for feedback and work incentives, for instance) that will impede or enhance the achievement of learning goals. We will then try to leverage the positive factors where we can and make recommendations to change the negative factors if that is possible. In any case, we will use our analysis of the performance environment to temper expectations and raise cautionary issues where appropriate. We might even suggest that the training initiative be aborted if we think the performance environment is such that it will overwhelm any improvement efforts that training could achieve.

The second way we use the performance environment analysis is to find opportunities and needs for building performance support tools into the HIL initiative. For example, if we determined that managers would not be able to effectively provide coaching to their employees, we might suggest adding specific skill-building activities for managers to the HIL solution. Readers will find several examples of these sorts of performance support tools as they are integrated into HIL solutions in the examples at the close of this chapter.

A widely accepted framework or model for analyzing employee performance that is used to identify causes for performance gaps is the Behavior Engineering Model, originally described by Dr. Thomas Gilbert in his groundbreaking book *Human Competence: Engineering Worthy Performance* (1978). This model, as well as Gilbert's book in general, is credited with the initial thinking and the articulation of what constitutes performance and how we can influence performance. Several writers have embellished and furthered this early thinking, including notable experts Geary Rummler and Alan Brache (1995), Bob Mager and Peter Pipe (1997), and Dale Brethower and Karolyn Smalley (1998), as well as many others.

The model we present below is not an original or novel model of performance analysis; instead, it represents a hybrid of the thinking that has been offered regarding the factors that influence and affect employee performance. We especially rely on our hybrid model because although it is simple, it provides a comprehensive checklist of the range of performance factors that should be considered when designing a HIL initiative.

As Figure 7.2 shows, performance can be affected by a number of factors that are represented by the outer circles. The factors noted inside each of the seven circles provide illustrations of the sorts of performance factors defined in each major category but are not a comprehensive list. Let us take a closer look at each of these categories of performance influencers, defining each in more detail and providing a brief discussion of how we use the factors to leverage solutions in for effective performance.

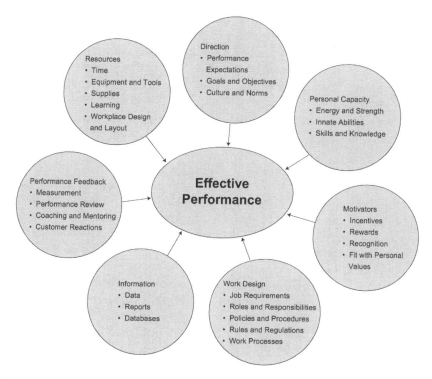

FIGURE 7.2   Performance System Elements

Direction

The direction factor represents the goals, objectives, supervisory influence, and other directives and cues (explicit and implicit) that people receive and that therefore direct their attention and performance. We have to be sure that the learning and performance outcomes posited in an HIL initiative are compatible with these direction factors. As we have already seen in the numerous examples outlined in the previous chapters, providing employees with direction related to their learning is precisely the purpose behind the "creating intentionality and focus" component of every HIL initiative. Prior to accessing any learning resource, we assure that employees and managers discuss performance expectations, goals, and objectives using impact maps as a basis during intentionality-building discussions. Although these discussions do not add a significant cost or time investment into the overall solution, they powerfully influence the intent, attention, and focus of the employee, allowing employees to customize and own the objectives of their learning.

An HIL initiative might include clarification of cultural expectations and norms or a discussion of these norms when we suspect there may be conflict between them and the performance outcomes of the HIL effort. Ensuring that employees understand the overall principles and values of the organization will help to guide their behavior and their performance daily, providing employees with the backdrop they need to always act and make decisions that are aligned with the organization's philosophy.

Personal Capability

This factor represents the innate ability—the sum of cognitive and physical skills and abilities—that people have to perform. Building capability is, of course, the intended outcome of a learning intervention, so this factor is always considered in an HIL initiative. Because many of the factors that influence performance in this category come as a result of selecting and hiring the right person for the job, we have to consider whether the training effort is sufficient to compensate for capabilities that may not be present in the workforce. In addition, most jobs require potential employees to have specific advanced degrees, certificates, or certifications. These sets of skills, knowledge, and capabilities are considered by the organization to be "givens" for the job, indicating that the organization is unwilling to provide this type of education for job incumbents. Further, the required skills, education, or certification for many positions are regulated by governmental agencies. Obvious examples of these professions include the medical and legal fields.

Motivators

Motivators are the internal value structures that provide incentives to people to perform in certain ways. A person who dislikes conflict, for example, will probably avoid confrontational interactions, since these are personally demotivating. A person who thrives on praise and recognition will often volunteer for extra assignments, since these often bring the praise that is sought. What is critical in this area of performance support is to ensure that the incentives, rewards, and recognition offered by the organization match what is valued by and motivating to employees. Incentives can come in many shapes and sizes. Typically, we think about incentives as falling into two categories: monetary and nonmonetary. Perhaps better terms might be tangible and intangible. In other words, organization can provide tangible rewards such as money, bonuses, stocks, trips, prizes, and the like, based on exemplary performance. Intangible or nonmonetary incentives are basically social recognition and praise of all forms. Although these forms of recognition are generally rewarding to everyone, most employees operate under their own personal set of values so that some rewards may be more powerful for them than others.

As we said, what is important here is that managers understand that all employees are not motivated by the same incentives. Managers must become acquainted with what makes their employees "tick" and attempt to match the incentives to employees' specific motivators. Often, helping managers meet this challenge may require extension of the learning intervention to include instruction and performance support tools for them to assure that they can be relied on to help motivate their employees.

In addition to matching the incentives to what motivates high levels of performance, it is important to ensure that the incentive is clearly and directly linked to the performance it is rewarding. The incentive must also follow soon after the desired performance outcome is achieved. The value of an incentive can drop to zero, or worse, even work as a "disincentive" if there is a huge disconnect or delay between the performance and the delivery of the reward. However, too often the chaos of the workplace and competing demands for their time distract managers and others from recognizing exceptional performance when it happens. They miss that magical moment and their efforts to follow up hours, days, or even weeks after the fact are clumsy and ineffective.

Work Design

The way in which work processes are conceived and designed within the organization has a direct and significant influence on employee performance. These work design issues include factors such as

- Work steps and procedures
- Job requirements
- Roles and responsibilities
- Policies and procedures
- Rules and regulations

Many organizations have processes, procedures, policies, and systems that are outdated or otherwise do not make sense in light of the goals of the learning initiative. When this is the case, of course, the work processes will stand in the way of employees' best efforts to put their learning to work and do a good job. Consider, for example, a sales organization that was training its field representatives to use a new strategic selling process. According to the new process, sales representatives were supposed to focus their efforts on only a few highly strategic accounts. Yet a review of the work procedures used in the field showed that several work steps, policies, and tools reflected a performance expectation that *every* account should be called upon. These existing work processes were in direct conflict with the new strategy and would clearly undermine the training investment being made. In this instance, we recommended an analysis and overhaul of field procedures to be conducted as part of the overall initiative.

It is good HIL practice to conduct a review of the performance environment in which trainees work in order to understand the work processes and tools in use, checking especially to be sure that these will be compatible with the goals of learning. This review of the work context will, at the same time, allow the critical incentive and reward variables to surface, as we discussed in the preceding factor.

Information

There is generally no lack of information in most of our work environments. It comes in the form of reports, databases, statistics, summaries, documents, checklists, guidelines, research reports, and so on. Now, with access to the Internet and the world wide web (not to mention our own organizations' intranets), most of us are constantly inundated with information. The challenge here is to do our best to match the informational needs of the employee's job tasks with the data and informational resources needed to perform those tasks, weeding out the irrelevant and unnecessary static.

As we discussed in the previous chapter, "Providing Effective Learning Interactions," much of traditional learning has been overloaded with information. What we advocated in Chapter 6 was to significantly pare back the content portion of the instructional design and dedicate more time and resources to building in opportunities for practice, feedback, and reflection. One simple way to do this without sacrificing truly essential content and information is to build reference and performance support tools that employees can access on the job. That is, much of the essential expertise, in the form of data, knowledge resources, and so forth, can be provided in external forms, such as in job aids and tools. These external information sources reduce the burden of information that employees have to internalize and memorize, letting them concentrate instead on skilled performance. At the same time, they allow training to be focused on practice with the tools and aids, developing truly proficient performance.

The HIL approach deals with the information in two essential ways. First, we try to reduce information contained in training interventions (content) to the minimum levels possible, relying instead on performance support tools such as job aids. Second, we again review the employee's performance environment to be sure that the information sources needed to support exemplary performance (the goal of training) are sufficient and effective.

Performance Feedback

This category is extremely vital and significant in an HIL initiative. Performance feedback refers to the several manners in which employees learn how well they are doing and what results they have accomplished. Performance feedback includes measurement, formal and informal performance reviews, coaching, even casual recognition, and other procedures and activities that provide employees with knowledge of results. Simply put, learning and performance improvement are not possible without comprehensive, accurate, and timely feedback.

Feedback typically comes from two primary sources: formal measurement and review systems and procedures, and supervisory guidance and interaction. In a call center, for example, the telephone system provides each customer service representative with a daily summary of the number of calls that were received, the time of each call, the waiting time for customers, and so forth. Representatives can then use this information to guide their performance, spending less time on breaks, for instance, if they need to respond to more calls. Supervisors, of course, provide feedback using both formal tools (performance checklists, for example) and in casual and perhaps even subconscious ways, such as smiling when they are told about specific behaviors or results. In an HIL initiative, we review the performance system to analyze the formal systems and procedures to be sure that they will be compatible with the learning goals. We also review supervisory capabilities and behaviors, often by talking with employees and supervisors in focus groups, visiting the workplace, and using other observation methods. Very often, we find that it is necessary to both develop new feedback tools and to train supervisors in their use. Because feedback is such a vital part of performance improvement, we almost always have to make efforts to strengthen the systems, methods, and capabilities in the organization with which we are working.

Resources

There are many opportunities to influence performance in this category of performance elements. There exists a huge array of resources that employees require to fulfill their job tasks and responsibilities. Among these are time, equipment and tools, supplies, workplace design and layout, and learning.

In fact, every work environment is rich with performance support in the form of resources and tools. We may never really think of them as supporting performance because they are so engrained in the job and work environment that they become "givens." Things like telephones, computers, work surfaces, and white boards are everyday work tools that we take for granted, that is, until we don't have access to them. Think about how a construction work crew taking down a power line and cutting your office off from electricity might affect your productivity. Or think about how difficult writing that next proposal would be without your computer or the use of software. Can you remember life without voicemail, without e-mail, without access to the Internet and the world wide web?

It is in this category of performance influencers that practitioners often look first if employee performance is not meeting expectations. The reason for this is that performance problems caused by a lack of resources and tools are typically easy to fix. For this same reason, we almost always have some recommendations to make about new tools and resources that could support an HIL initiative. In any HIL project, we typically uncover myriad causes across several of the categories of performance elements represented in Figure 7.2. Rarely do we find just one discrete factor that needs attention, and almost always it is the case that several factors interact. Employees may find it demotivating, for example, that informational resources are hard to access or are unavailable. Thus, when we create an information access tool that supports a new learning initiative, we might also discover that we have improved employees' motivation to use the learning in improved performance. We use the performance analysis framework both to analyze the existing performance environment to discover strengths and weaknesses and to build performance support into HIL products and processes.

Integrating Performance Support into a Blended Solution

As the examples in this section will show, a typical HIL initiative is a blended solution that combines e-learning and classroom methods with a variety of performance support tools that accommodate several of the factors shown in the analysis framework in Figure 7.2. At a simple level, integrating performance support into the learning process may only involve embedding job aids into instruction. In a more complex approach, we may employ a variety of performance support and integration strategies. We begin our discussion of integration of performance support with the more simple approach first.

In earlier years of the development of HIL, when we thought about performance support, we thought only of printed documentation and illustrated job aids of all shapes and sizes, from pocket cards to posters. In their most basic form, performance support referred to these simple information-bearing devices that we installed in the workplace. Further, any learning we built to support and help teach users how to use these performance aids often only provided a surface-level treatment of them, since these performance aids were designed to be as self-explanatory as possible.

The explosion of technology-enabled performance support tools and systems, however, has greatly altered our approach in recent years. For example, many performance support aids that function as informational reference tools today come in electronically accessed or on-line formats, with hyperlinks and extensive indexing. Although these electronic versions of documentation are not necessarily complex or even "high tech," they eliminate much of the inefficiency caused by reproducing and distributing paper versions. We also see a greater use of on-line help systems that support our use of software applications. But the ready availability of electronically enabled performance support methods and tools has more dramatically reshaped the conception and design of learning.

As we noted in Chapter 2, e-learning methods enable us to reduce the content load of traditional training, reserving classroom experiences for true skill practice and other highly socially interactive activities. Background information, content about principles and guidelines, and so forth, can be provided via Internet and other computer formats, reducing expensive classroom time and keeping it focused on high-return activities. It has also been helpful to replace the content and information that used to be loaded into lengthy classroom interventions with thoroughly documented reference material, so that the instruction simply helps users become familiar with its organization and applications. Electronic media have further allowed us to embed performance tools into the learning and performance process, so that they become the backbone and the focal point of the initiative, with extensive job-specific practice and feedback opportunities. These initiatives, in fact, become less and less "training" initiatives and more and more "performance support" initiatives.

Referring again to our HIL learning-performance model reminds us that an HIL initiative is comprised of four instructional elements: content, practice, feedback, and reflection. By creating information-oriented performance aids, we can greatly reduce the amount of content that we require learners to memorize or otherwise try to master. Our instruction becomes far more efficient and powerful because we can invest our efforts in building practice, feedback, and reflection opportunities to allow learners to apply the performance aids in ways that make sense for their job tasks. This shift in instructional strategy from content to practice/feedback/reflection also helps to ensure that the aids we build are more likely to be used on the job, improving performance on job tasks.

Applying this principle of reducing content and providing more information-oriented performance support is especially applicable to job tasks that involve information that is

- Complicated—the job task involves numerous steps that must be followed in a precise manner.

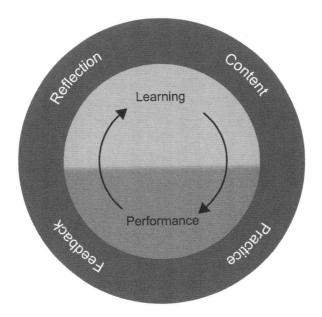

FIGURE 7.3   The Learning-to-Performance Process

- Infrequently accessed or applied—the job task is not one that the employee engages in often enough to warrant memorizing the procedures.

Frequently, our efforts to integrate performance go well beyond just the incorporation of information-based job aids, employing strategies based on combinations of the seven categories of performance factors illustrated in Figure 7.2.

We always build impact-mapping procedures, leveraging the "direction" factor to engage the attention and commitment of learners and their managers into our solution. We further employ the direction factor by building in recommendations, tools, and methods that will engage managers of learners in coaching, performance observations, objective setting, and so forth.

Performance feedback is also a readily available support strategy. In any HIL initiative, we investigate the performance environment and assess the adequacy of feedback that learners will have available as they try out new learning. Almost always, it is not as good as it should be. As a result, we frequently find ourselves building better checklists and measurement tools, then including these in training for managers of learners, so that they are proficient in providing accurate and timely feedback. When we are assured that feedback will indeed be readily provided, accurate, and timely, we can safely reduce up-front training investments, since we can rely on the power of high-quality feedback to improve performance. It is almost always cheaper and more effective to build learning into performance than it is to try to transfer learning (as in a separate workshop or module) into performance after the fact.

HIL solutions frequently include the introduction of new work tools that support and aid performance. Electronically enabled performance support system (EPSS) tools, for example, are powerful forms of performance support aids because they are built right into the performance of the task, such as accessing the help function while using a software application. These electronic support tools have become a more frequent inclusion in HIL solutions for two primary reasons: First, the technology and the skills needed to build them is increasingly more available and affordable, and second, so much of the capability we need to build regarding employees' skills sets revolve around using and applying technology, where EPSS tools are readily incorporated.

As a last resort, and in extreme cases, HIL solutions include recommendations for changes to employee compensation systems, as well as suggestions for the new or revised incentives and rewards in order to recognize exemplary performance and the achievement of goals. Frankly, however, we know that these nonlearning sorts of human resources systems are more resistant to change, and thus we more often try to work around them than to change them. Our first choice of integrating performance support into our HIL solutions is to make them as "learning like" as possible, since this is the arena in which we are most likely to be successful.

At this point, we will review several examples of HIL solutions. Each of these solutions has as its target a specific business goal, and each involves a considerable amount of performance support integrated into the overall HIL solution. In addition, all of these examples combine each of the HIL elements (intentionality, learning, and performance support) to form a strong, flexible, blended solution. Readers should understand as well that these examples are derived from some of our more complex work, since these instances offer the richest illustration of a variety of performance support strategies. It should not be implied that more simple solutions would not work. Simpler approaches do work, and we encourage readers to look for inspiration from these examples to try less complex approaches.

An Example—Building and Supporting a Better Sales Process

Our first example relates to work that focused on new salespeople at a global supplier of office furniture. Leaders in this company had long recognized the burden placed on newly hired salespeople as they struggled to learn about its complex dealership network and about the thousands of products and services they offered, as well as the many sales tools and methods they would apply as they began to work with their dealership's customers.

We worked closely with the company and its dealers to understand and document the sales process that exemplary, experienced salespeople followed, from the earliest stages of prospecting to closing the sale. This step of process clarification and documentation allowed us to help the company to articulate a single, comprehensive sales methodology, complete with sequenced phases and milestones.

To support this process, we crafted an Excel-based set of twenty-four linked tools that represented and operationalized all of the outputs, milestones, and phases of the sales methodology. For example, one of the tools allowed salespeople to create a call planning form that would guide the initial sales call with a potential customer.

Once the sales methodology and toolkit were designed, we then turned our attention to designing the most effective learning process for helping new salespeople master the steps and tools. To assure adequate skill building, the learning process was spread out over time with many opportunities for practice and feedback throughout. Outlined below are some of the key features of this learning approach.

- Working with their managers, salespeople completed a series of orientation activities and learning experiences aimed at getting them acclimated to the company, its products and services, and to their role. These activities included self-instructional video and print modules, broadcast television courses, and meetings and discussions with their managers and other salespeople within their dealership. Note that this process helped develop a good deal of "direction" as well as more general orientation.
- Once these salepeople had completed the required prerequisites, they began the exemplary sales curriculum. The curriculum consisted of four two-week instructor-led workshops held in a central location, spanning five months. Each workshop focused on different phases of the sales methodology, providing extensive opportunities to practice applying the tools to increasingly difficult sales scenarios. In addition, as learners progressed in the curriculum, practice expanded to allow for both focused practice and feedback on the new skills and tools that were taught, as well as opportunities to connect these skills with those already mastered through practice exercises.
- Between each two-week session, learners were expected to complete homework assignments and to work with their managers in applying the skills and tools they had learned in actual sales opportunities with dealership customers.

- The last session concluded with a two-and-a-half-day assessment center in which learners applied the entire sales methodology and toolkit in multiple sales opportunities, from developing account and opportunity strategies to closing the sale.
- We conducted follow-up telephone calls with each salesperson and his or her manager to discuss the learner's performance in the assessment center and to assist in the planning of future development activities for the salesperson.

This example illustrates how performance support tools can be embedded into an instructional process. When the learning process is spread out, as it was in this example, participants have the opportunity to practice skills in "bite-size" chunks, allowing incremental mastery. The process also allowed us to revisit intentionality at several key points, keeping learners focused on applications that were most significant to their particular performance improvement needs.

An Example—Improving Product Selection During the Sales Process

One of the universal challenges faced by salespeople, no matter what product or service they offer, is that what they offer is always changing. This is particularly true with product sales, where product specifications, features, benefits, applications, costs, and availability are rarely stable. Salespeople who sell products are constantly inundated with product updates, product launches, product knowledge literature and training, revised spec sheets, revised pricing sheets, and so forth.

Again, we refer to another example with the same office furniture client. One of the products they sell extensively is cubicle panels that define individual workspace. Panels are a critical element to the design of the space, having an impact on the work surfaces that can be applied, the selection of storage both under and over the work surface, the use of lighting, as well as many other design considerations. It is essential that dealer salespeople truly understand the features, benefits, and applications of every type of panel they offer, since much of the rest of the design specification depends on making the right choice of paneling. Fortunately for the customer, there are thousands of possible design combinations; this is unfortunate, however, for the sales representative; they cannot possibly memorize all of these changing specifications.

To assist salespeople in this important decision, we created an electronic decisionmaking tool. This tool prompted salespeople to respond to key questions regarding the use and application of panels in the client's space. The tool weighted the responses based on the best applications for each type of panel, then provided the salesperson with the best choices for panels for the particular application.

Although this decisionmaking tool itself does not necessarily represent cutting-edge thinking, the way in which salespeople access it is fairly novel. We found that salespeople were not traveling with their laptop computers much and had transitioned to using their palm pilots for much of their data exchange needs. Therefore, instead of packaging and delivering this decision-making tool for access on a computer, we configured it to be accessed on the salesperson's palm pilot.

In addition, we knew that we were making a substantial change in the sales process by introducing this tool, because in essence, we were mechanizing this decision regarding panel application. Introducing an electronic (objective and logical) decisionmaking tool into this process offended the aesthetic sensibilities of many salespeople and designers.

To reduce these issues, we conducted an instructor-led workshop *prior* to the introduction of this tool, to present the new concepts for the sales and design processes. During this workshop, we were able to get input from our audience regarding their needs surrounding the tool (for example, "Make the tool available on our palm pilots"), as well as help them internalize the advantages of new approaches to sales and design. Therefore, this workshop functioned as both an instructional event as well as a needs and audience analysis.

Following the workshop, salespeople and designers completed a web-based training module located on a sales learning and performance support web site, to learn how to access and use the new decisionmaking tool. The module presented numerous scenarios for various client workspace needs to allow users to try out the tool to see how it worked and to evaluate the product recommendations it offered. The module also reviewed the advantages of the new sales and design paradigm and encouraged salespeople to work with their sales and marketing managers to get comfortable using the new tool within the sales process.

This example illustrates the principle of reducing training content dramatically by employing a performance support tool that, in essence, replaces training. That is, the expertise is embedded in the tool learners' use, rather than the learners themselves. This allows performance improvement to proceed rapidly, and at the same time reduces instructional time and other costs. The training process is then oriented to usage of the tool and highlights practice and feedback as learners develop proficiency. This approach assures a high degree of business focus and linkage. Intentionality is reinforced each time learners practice, since they are practicing on scenarios that are derived from their own job and work issues.

An Example—Improving the Business Planning Process

For many organizations, business planning is the primary process used to prompt managers and leaders to pause and think about the possibilities that the future holds for the organization, to establish goals and objectives to realize those possibilities, and to build plans for achieving them.

Although the process of business planning is insightful and thoughtful, the act of creating the business plan itself can be labor and time intensive, as well as frustrating. Managers may not be familiar with the specific contents of a business plan, or what distinguishes a good business plan from a poor one. In addition, managers may feel that although their organization's business plan does not drastically vary from one year to the next, they are always "re-creating the wheel." Further, because the skill is used only once a year, there is no opportunity for recurring practice.

The leaders in this organization wanted to make their business plans more accurate and effective, so that managers actually used them to direct and manage the day-to-day operations of their functions (versus parking the plan on the shelf until the following year). This goal would be served by increasing expertise, but also by making the business planning process more pertinent and constructive, since it was meant to be more "real."

The initial solution the leaders considered was a plan to send all of their managers to a generic, publicly offered workshop on the principles and practices of business planning. Thinking about this need from a high-impact learning point of view, we recommended a different approach.

As we reviewed the many and complex requirements and specifications for the business plan, we determined that a performance support resource in the form of a set of electronic tools and templates would be the most effective approach to ensure that all business plans met. We crafted an on-line set of tools, templates, and wizards that provided the form and organization for the plan. These linked Word and Excel templates contained boilerplate text when appropriate and prompted managers for data and content as necessary. The tools also included completed models of business plans for managers to use as examples.

Managers then attended an instructor-led workshop that first introduced the new business planning process and the managers' role in the process. Much of the time during the workshop was invested in demonstrating the use of the business planning tools and providing significant opportunities to use them. The workshop also allowed managers to network with one another to discuss key issues and obstacles in their functions and solicit advice and counsel from one another.

A key component of this solution was the formation of a follow-up support network, assigning managers to small groups of like-minded managers and providing them with tools and methods for providing feedback and advice. After the workshop and during the business planning process, managers contacted others in their network to work through issues to create a workable plan. This included a peer review function, which served to upgrade the quality of the plans and to build a broader skill set among participants.

This example again demonstrates the use of a performance aid (the planning templates and steps) to shorten the path to competence. In fact, this is almost always a strategy in any HIL solution; it would be unusual not to include job aids and related practice opportunities in the learning process. More uniquely, this example shows how a simple follow-up process can support the continuation of skill development, allowing an incremental approach, and incorporating real-time practice and feedback. The peer review and support group process not only helped to upgrade performance but it served as a continuing check on intentionality, since participants discussed real business issues and goals during each interaction.

An Example—Improving Communication Effectiveness

This example took place in the laboratory division of a pharmaceutical company, where teams worked to produce assays and other analysis reports to internal customers. Initially, the training was a three-day workshop provided by a national vendor to teach communications skills for all laboratory technicians and supervisors. Although the training was quite popular, the client, the training director, was uncertain about business value, and senior leaders were skeptical of such "soft skill" training. On the other hand, the "success case" evaluation (see Chapter 9 for a detailed explanation of this method) showed that some learners were using the training to achieve significant business results. The problem was that not enough learners were achieving these results, so we were asked to strengthen the training process.

The revised training had these elements and methods:

1. The three-day event was broken into shorter segments and was rescheduled to occur for three hours once every two weeks, for a total of ten weeks.
2. An impact-mapping session was added as the first step in the training process. Learners analyzed their own job, then identified the key points where critical communication interactions could influence the achievement of a critical business objective, such as cycle time, report quality, rework, and so forth. For example, an analyst might identify that the order-taking process, a verbal interaction with a customer, could be improved to be more accurate. This accuracy would, in turn, reduce cycle time and rework.

3. Learners translated their individual impact map into a specific action plan to improve communications skills and effectiveness in at least one but not more than three critical interactions. This action plan was then, for them, the entire focus of their learning.

4. The generic practice sessions from the vendor were eliminated. Instead, learners wrote their own scripts to allow them to practice on a communications scenario that was keyed to their own impact map. The analyst who identified improving the order-taking interaction, for example, wrote several scripts depicting different customer types and needs. Then, in role-play practice, she practiced with a partner on these reality-based scenarios.

5. After each classroom session, learners had a "homework" assignment to try out some new communication skill in a real job interaction. One learner, for example, might try out the skill of using open-ended questions to confirm understanding. Each subsequent classroom session began with a brief report session, in which participants reported what they had tried and how well it had worked.

6. Participants created their own job aids (cue cards, for instance, to be used to prepare for a meeting with a key customer). As these aids proved valuable, we reproduced them and made them available to all participants.

7. Participants kept logs of their efforts and also tracked data about the success of their interactions. The analyst trying to improve order taking, for example, kept track of order fulfillment times and errors that stemmed from initial order inaccuracies.

8. We conducted a forty-five-minute lunch meeting for managers once every two weeks during which we reported our especially poignant examples of success among their employees. Although these were reported anonymously, they were credible and helped managers see the value of the training in helping them accomplish goals for which they were accountable.

9. After each ten-week session, we asked "graduates" who had accomplished especially noteworthy results to come back and help kick off the training for the next group of learners. These success stories helped motivate new learners and were especially useful in helping them to identify key applications they could aim for in their own impact-mapping intentions.

The revised training process was very successful. It raised training transfer rates to more than 80 percent and also produced many stories of validated success, where learners had used skills to accomplish noteworthy business results. Senior executives made a decision to extend the new process to all division employees and are following this learning-performance model even to-day in their learning initiatives.

This example shows how soft skill training can be made more real and business focused by creating a high degree of learner intentionality. It also shows how performance support—manager interactions, impact maps, practice and feedback on real scenarios, on-the-job practice and feedback, and so forth—can be integrated seamlessly into the learning process.

Chapter Summary

In our experiences of building and implementing HIL solutions, we have identified a corollary that pertains to the essential nature of performance support: The greater the need for learning and change in performance, then the greater resistance present in the actual work environment, ready to interfere with the new performance. This exacerbates, of course, the need for effective performance support tools and methods.

Our performance analysis framework is used in two essential ways: to identify performance obstacles and to plan and design helpful tools to be incorporated into the learning solution. Because learning is initially fragile, we can and must take every opportunity to evaluate the solutions we propose and find ways that we can support performance on the job, at the moment it happens. In more simple instances, this means crafting information in an easy-to-access manner or creating a tool that guides performance and includes these tools in the learning process. It also means embedding impact maps and other intentionality methods into learning. Almost always, we aim to involve and prepare managers for a more effective role in coaching and feedback. Where the performance environment poses more substantial obstacles, we might propose aligning rewards as a consequence for exemplary performance or redesigning the selection and hiring process so that the right people are hired from the start. We look at the entire array of possible factors and solutions, beyond just the learning interventions we build, to truly change performance in a meaningful way.

This chapter completes our review of the elements that make up high-impact learning. The final section of the book will help you to look forward and consider the possibilities and the issues that exist when transitioning to a high-impact learning approach.

Crafting High-Impact
Learning Initiatives

8

Chapter Overview

Much has been researched and documented on the topic of instructional systems design (ISD) and the processes that help to define and build truly powerful learning. We begin this chapter by taking a hard look at our traditional approach to training design and development and illustrate how this process falters in meeting the learning and performance needs of employees and businesses today.

We then present an altered design paradigm that weaves together a comprehensive analytical approach that works beyond the traditional process to craft solutions that will lead to consistent business impact. To a large extent, our design process mirrors the key elements of the more traditional ISD methods that have stood the test of time. It embeds these ISD methods, however, into the conceptual framework of the HIL approach, building on what we know about sound instructional design, adding new ideas and methods, and revising others to achieve HIL results. Readers already conversant with ISD approaches will find much in this chapter that is familiar. This familiarity will be partially helpful but may also pose problems, since such ISD-conversant readers will have to work hard to reframe their thinking. Readers with no background in ISD are encouraged to supplement reading this chapter with a reputable text in ISD (see, for example, Dick and Carey, 1990, a thorough source on which we often rely).

As we review the HIL design process, we will refer to a consistent example throughout the chapter to illustrate and dramatize the HIL design process. We also define and explain specific derailers, or situations and issues that exist within the organization that drive and shape our designs, sometimes indicating a need for nontraining and learning solutions. Despite their name, the derailers rarely actually derail our work; most often, they simply identify and highlight factors in the organization that must be attended to for any learning solution to be successful.

Traditional Instructional Systems Design

Instructional systems design, also referred to as instructional systems development, refers to a comprehensive, logical, step-by-step process for creating and implementing learning and training interventions and tools. ISD was originally developed for the military during World War II, when the need to train a vast number of soldiers and military personnel was great. The military needed to make the process of designing, developing, and delivering training as systematic and reliable as possible. From this need, the ADDIE (analysis, design, development, implementation, and evaluation) process was developed by Robert Gagne (1974) and his peers at Florida State University. The ADDIE model is still well accepted and followed and has been extended and amended by many others (Rossett, 1987; and Dick and Carey, 1990, among others).

The ADDIE model depicts the linear progress of the development of learning from its beginning, at analysis, through design, development, implementation, and finally, evaluation. This simple construct has functioned for decades as a tremendously useful organizer for designers and developers of training. Each of these ADDIE "process buckets" is deep and rich in methods, models, and tools that we can follow to ensure that the instruction we create will meet the needs of the learner. In fact, entire texts have been dedicated to a single component of this broad process, such as Allison Rossett's *Training Needs Assessment* (1987) and the popular text by Ron Zemke and Thomas Kramlinger, *Figuring Things Out* (1982), both with focus on the "analysis" element of ISD.

Problems with the ADDIE/ISD Approach

Although the ADDIE process has been a valuable construct for instructional designers, it has recently come under serious scrutiny. In fact, Ron Zemke and Jack Gordon published an article in *Training* magazine ("The Attack on ISD") in April 2000 specifically on this topic. Zemke, Gordon, and others, including Diane Gayeski ("Out of the Box Instructional Design," *Training and Development*, April 1998), present some compelling criticisms of this approach to the design of training. However, these experts are not the only ones in line to throws barbs at the ISD model. Significantly, we hear criticisms

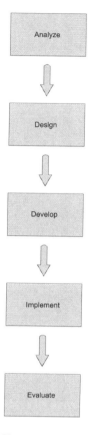

The ADDIE Model

FIGURE 8.1   Instructional Systems Design

most frequently and directly from our clients, who drive us to improve and streamline the processes we follow to fit the real-life business constraints they are challenged with. Here is a summary of the major criticisms of ISD we most often encounter.

The ISD Process Is Too Slow

Many learning and development functions, in an effort to standardize their own ISD methods, have articulated and documented detailed, cumbersome subprocesses using the ADDIE process as their backbone. These subprocesses typically call out numerous milestones, checkpoints, and approval requirements that all add time and cost to developing a learning intervention. In fact, we have seen the ADDIE/ISD process so bureaucratically exploded that it is next to impossible to develop even the most straightforward of instructional products in less than three months. We understand that much of good ISD is simply good project management. However, following the process to the letter without flexibility to the needs of the learner and the business requirements serves no one.

Increasingly, business demands call for far more rapid development and deployment of learning tools than ever before. Business leaders cannot wait for the designers of learning to follow their pet processes to produce effective learning. What they need is for designers to adjust their processes to work within the realities of the business and produce impactful learning solutions that can be implemented in weeks, sometimes even days or hours.

In other words, the design of learning solutions must be agile enough to respond to the need for learning when the need arises. Learning leaders will miss this window of opportunity by following every step and deliverable called for in the ADDIE process and subprocesses, and their learning solutions will be obsolete and outdated by the time they are finally ready to implement.

The Real Design Process Is Not Linear

You can see that the ADDIE process as shown in Figure 8.1 depicts a linear process, with a definite beginning and end. As a conceptual model that defines the activities necessary to build sound instruction, this is a valid construction. However, it does not illustrate the actual process that most instructional designers must follow on a day-to-day basis to build effective HIL learning.

The actual process that produces exceptional learning is instead and at once a dynamic, fast-paced, and iterative process. It is a process that uses rapid prototyping to get to an approximation of a solution quickly, then deploys it to its customers to both meet needs and to test it, revamp it, and deploy and test it again, repeatedly. It is a process that insists on new design ideas at any point. It is a process that uses evaluation constantly, continuously validating assumptions made during analysis and reality-testing proposed solutions against those assumptions. Tom Peters, in his energetic little handbook, *The Project 50* (1999), stresses the importance of quick prototyping to the success of any project, noting that it is possible to build and test some piece of *any project* within a few hours to two or three days.

The ADDIE Process Produces Overengineered Solutions

When it was first developed, the ADDIE/ISD approach was powerful and effective. Unfortunately, over the years, it has become contaminated by the current training paradigm that construes training as a "delivery of events" process, as we explained in Chapter 1. To a large extent, corporate training has become driven by needs to fill training classes, populate training delivery channels such as interactive TV networks and computer systems, and otherwise focus on satisfying and entertaining trainees, the mistaken customer of training services.

During the past twenty years, the toolbox for instructional designers has virtually exploded with new technology and approaches for delivering learning. Computer-based training, interactive video disk, multimedia, web-based training, virtual classrooms, satellite broadcasts, and other delivery methods have given the designers of learning a smorgasbord of delivery options from which to choose. Although all of these options provide us with excellent opportunities to build wonderfully blended learning solutions, they also provide the opportunity to become overly enamored with specific technologies, possibly misapplying them or overusing them. For example, the organization that installs the infrastructure necessary to offer web-based training (WBT) modules to its employees may initially rush to convert all of its existing learning resources over to WBT, regardless of performance needs, content, and learning objectives.

Also feeding this push toward the use of high-end, high-tech media are the expectations of the learners themselves, who have been raised on brilliant videographics and special effects in computer games, movies, and television shows. At the same time, there are huge armies of training vendors competing for attention and market share. All of these forces converge in a training paradigm and culture that keeps score by counting attendance and measuring trainee satisfaction scores on "smile sheet" surveys, and that purchases training packages based on the glossiness and "curb appeal" of training methods and materials. The net result is highly polished training methods and tools, engineered more to win rave reviews than to effectively and efficiently achieve business results.

Artificial Endpoint

The linear nature of the ADDIE process, as shown in Figure 8.1, implies a discrete beginning and ending, giving the designers of learning the false impression that once they get to "evaluation," they are done; they are there. However, we know that the true design process is not linear and that good instructional design requires an iterative process of design and development, try out and evaluate, then back to redesign again. Because of this, you're never really there, you're never really finished.

Bob Mager, popular and revered expert in learning and performance improvement and a longtime ISD proponent, puts forth the well-known trio of questions that lies at the heart of the most basic performance improvement efforts (Mager, *Analyzing Performance Problems*, 1997):

1. Where are we?
2. Where are we going?
3. How are we going to get there?

Even this simple construct alludes to a "final destination." But as the saying goes, "the only thing that we can be sure of is change." Everything within and outside of an organization is in a constant state of flux: competitive influences, characteristics of the marketplace, customer requirements and expectations, the organization's workforce, business processes, and tools. It would be far easier to list what's not changing. The notion that a learning initiative can ever be "done" is an artifact of the training as the delivery-of-events paradigm. When training and learning is seen mostly as an issue of creating rather than delivering a worthy program or product, then it is easy to conceive of an endpoint to the design process. When the mental model changes to an HIL-based process perspective, however, there is no such endpoint in the conceptual framework. A good HIL initiative is always a work in progress, an emergent process that accelerates toward increasingly effective and efficient performance improvement. In HIL thinking, a learning service is indeed provided to customers, but we would not think of the service as a static "event"; thus, from a pure HIL perspective, the same service is never provided twice. Components of an HIL initiative may be relatively stable, but as a whole, the process should be constantly refined and improved, using participant feedback and emerging customer requirements to drive continuing refinements.

The HIL Design Approach

Although we propose that the current view of ISD and the ADDIE model do not accurately describe the best way to design high-impact learning, we do not arbitrarily discard the ADDIE/ISD process, since many of the core elements of the traditional ISD process remain relevant and useful. We do think it is necessary, however, to change our paradigm, expectations, and values about the learning initiatives we create and the way that we go about their design and development. By adhering to the dominant ISD approach, we have unintentionally fostered standards and expectations within our organizations about how highly polished and produced our learning must appear to our audiences. Worse, we have engendered expectations that once our products are designed and delivered, they are "done," and that neither our customers nor we will have to do further work to continue to refine and change them.

The HIL design process that we present and explain in this section is not, then, a radical departure from the ADDIE/ISD approach that we have discussed. But we believe that the HIL design approach is different in some key respects, and some of these are differences in the spirit, rather than the letter, of the design process. Here are what we see as some key differences that the reader should no-tice and use as a conceptual frame for interpreting our HIL design process.

- The HIL initiative will always incorporate activities and products that integrate all three of the key HIL elements: focus and intentionality, learning new skills and knowledge, and assuring support for performance improvement, rather than myopically focusing only on designing and providing learning to build skills and knowledge.
- The HIL design goal is to initiate a performance improvement process, not "deliver" a finished learning solution. That is, we look to get something started, rather than to finish our design work. The design challenge is to get enough of a learning solution in place as quickly as possible, so that it can begin to drive meaningful performance improvement. At the same time, we will plan for the continued refinement of that solution so that it can be extended to additional customers in a form and manner that will be more useful and effective.
- The process for crafting an HIL initiative begins with an obsessive attention to the delineation of focus and intentionality. Before we lay design pencil to learning approach paper, we analyze, clarify, and document the linkage among the business needs and goals, role-by-role performance objectives, and potential learning needs and outcomes. The creation of intentionality (represented in the impact map format) is at the heart of any learning intervention. The impact map's expression of intentionality is not only the guiding focus of the learning initiative, it is a tool embedded at several points within the initiative.
- In the HIL approach, the HIL design process begins an engagement with the client that is, in itself, a learning process. As designers, we are learning more about how the client's organization works—what matters most, what are its strengths and weaknesses, and how learning can best be leveraged to drive individual and business performance improvement. At the same time, our client is gaining knowledge in how learning works to strengthen the organization, and what learning tools and methods will best accomplish performance improvement goals. The design process, then, is a consultative engagement that begins a technology transfer wherein the client develops an increased capacity for leveraging learning into business impact.
- The HIL design process requires and is characterized by deep client involvement and participation. Since performance improvement and support is an integral part of any HIL initiative, there are always key roles for clients to play. In a traditional ISD paradigm, we might see a learning solution as something the client is given, to then in turn

"administer" to someone else. But in an HIL solution, the client is always a part of the solution, with regular and continuing responsibilities. Further, the client will adopt increasing responsibility for the implementation and ongoing improvement of the learning initiatives. In the beginning phases of an HIL initiative, it is typical for the learning specialists to play a major role, but as time goes by and the initiative matures, the leadership and ownership role increasingly devolves to the client. Because the client is the ultimate owner and participant, deep involvement and ownership must be built from the very start, not only to build commitment but to assure that the HIL initiative is custom-tailored to all of the special needs and nuances of the organization.

Figure 8.2 graphically represents the HIL design process. First, notice that it has two major portions: the learning initiative itself, represented by the "braid" coiled in the center of the figure (we will explain the braid configuration soon), and the overall crafting process that forms the outer circle. Strictly speaking from a traditional ISD perspective, the learning initiative (the braid) is not a part of the design process but is the output of the design process. That is, in ISD the design process is done first, and its purpose is to produce the learning product, or event. But this is not true of the HIL approach, so we include both the "product" as well as the "process" in this figure. Remember that the HIL design process does not fit the old "event delivery" paradigm where we can clearly separate the product from the process that creates the product. Further, in the HIL design paradigm, the learning initiative is emergent and iterative, with design continuing through implementation in a successive and unending series of cycles. Thus, it is not possible to graphically represent the HIL design process without concurrently including the initiative that is being designed.

There are other key features of this graphic to notice.

- The process for crafting the initiative has three major phases: analyze, design, and create and try out.

In the analyze phase, we inquire about, define, and clarify the linkage among business goals, performer roles, performance improvement objectives, and learning outcomes. During this phase, we also seek critical information about the organization's key strengths, constraints, opportunities, culture, and other unique characteristics that will shape our HIL initiative. In the design phase, we envision and formulate the learning strategy—the braid of methods and tools—that will work best, given the special needs and constraints of the client's organization. In the create and try out phase, we build, review with the client, and quickly try out the first iterations of the actual tools, methods, and products that comprise the first iteration of the HIL initiative.

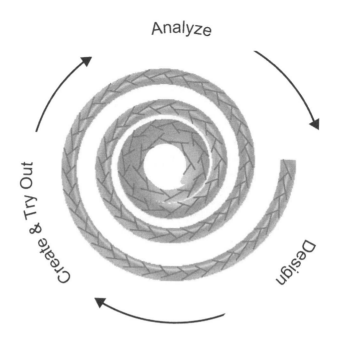

Analyze

Create & Try Out

Design

FIGURE 8.2   Process for Crafting HIL Initiatives

- The three phases are conducted in a cycle.

The crafting process is not linear but operates cyclically. We do enough analysis, for example, to design and create some tools and methods, then try out the first iteration of the HIL initiative. We do not show an endpoint to the cycle of phases, as they continue indefinitely. As we noted, we don't ever imagine that an HIL initiative is so good that it could not benefit from some improvements. On the other hand, we are very quick to assume that it is "good enough for now," so that we do not delay deployment until we have achieved some unnecessary level of polished perfection. Once we have tried out the initial versions of a solution, we may return to the analysis phase and begin the cycle anew.

- The learning initiative is a "braid."

We chose the image of a braid because it so aptly describes the concept of an HIL initiative. The braid has three strands: intentionality and focus, learning for skills and knowledge, and performance support. These three elements are always part of an HIL initiative. Further, like in a braid, they are knit together to form a single strand, each contiguous with the other, one sometimes "behind" another, but all three working together to add strength, as in a woven rope. Finally, a braid has successive segments where the three strands are rewoven again and again. These successive segments of the braid represent the iterative cycles of the HIL design process, where an initiative is repeatedly tried out, then redesigned, then tried out again, and so on.

- There are potential "derailers" within each phase.

Although we do not show them in Figure 8.2 (for the sake of simplicity), we noted earlier in the chapter that there are potential obstacles and issues that can "derail" the process of crafting an HIL initiative. We will explain and illustrate these derailers in later portions of the chapter.

- Each phase has substeps.

Though they are not shown in Figure 8.2, each phase has key substeps and elements.

In the remainder of this chapter, we will dig deeper into each of the three phases in Figure 8.2, one phase at a time. To illustrate work undertaken in each phase, we will revisit the Barking Frog Beer example presented in Chapter 4, using this example consistently throughout the remainder of the chapter. In addition, we will also highlight examples of derailers that can be identified at each phase.

A Deeper Look at Phase One: Analyze

This first phase of the HIL crafting process is dedicated to developing a complete understanding of the business and organization to begin to design a workable HIL initiative. There are four overall purposes for the work we do in this phase.

- Identify the critical business issues (CBI) that will be the target of the HIL initiative.
- Gain an understanding of the organizational context that will constrain and shape any solution that is to be pursued.
- Identify the linkage among the CBI, related work processes, the performance of employees, and possible learning needs and outcomes.
- Identify potential organizational barriers and derailers that stand in the way of success for any solution.

As most training and development practitioners know, we are not often invited into a client engagement to help address a major business issue. Much

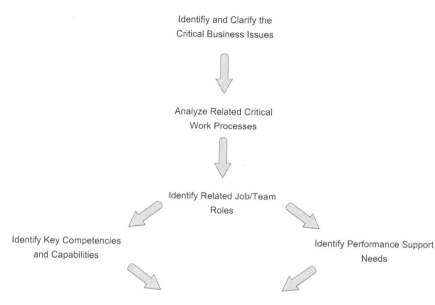

FIGURE 8.3   Phase One: Analyze

more typically, a manager might ask for specific training, even though that manager has not disclosed or may not have even identified a business goal that the training could help achieve. Or a manager may state the need in the context of a performance issue or gap, not necessarily linking the gap to a particular business goal. Thus, in the analysis phase we work in whatever order we can, depending on where and how we became invited to be involved, piecing together the hierarchy of information elements illustrated in Figure 8.3 as best we can.

Although the components in Figure 8.3 are graphically connected, we have not called them "steps." They are not steps because we may not necessarily pursue them in order, even though they are logically linked in a hierarchy, as shown in the graphic. That is, work processes achieve business goals, and performers work in job and team roles to implement work processes, learning outcomes (skills and knowledge) drive performance, and so forth.

The overall method for accomplishing the work of the analyze phase is to ask a lot of questions and gather a lot of information. Typically, higher-level information is gleaned during brief meetings with senior-level executives, both individually and as a group. If it is difficult to gain access to higher-level executives, then we start lower in the organization. Sometimes we may have to rely largely on the perspectives and observations of our immediate client, often a training director or a human resources manager. At some point, however, it is important that we confirm our understanding of business issues and goals with leaders at the highest level in the part of the organization where the initiative is to be pursued, even if our contact is limited to a brief memo rather than a face-to-face meeting. Whatever the case, it is important that we find agreement and alignment and that the CBI that is targeted is clearly connected to higher-order and current business goals and objectives.

At the same time that we are attempting to define the CBIs that exist, we are also asking questions about key organizational factors, opportunities, and obstacles that may shape our HIL initiative. We would ask, for example, how business goals are measured and how the measurement information is shared and communicated. We would also ask about the culture, how motivated and focused employees are, and what issues currently engage their fears and concerns. We would seek to identify and understand other organizational initiatives that are being implemented or considered, since these could interfere with what we might do. Many of the questions we use to learn more about organizational CBIs as well as general organizational factors are outlined in Chapter 4, "Mapping Linkage to Business Goals."

We also need to understand how learning influences key performer roles and how those roles connect to and drive business results. This understanding can then be documented and illustrated in the form of an impact map, again, discussed in Chapter 4.

The best sources for collecting the information required for the impact map are employees that hold the position being mapped, as well as their direct supervisors, managers, or leaders. This is not unlike the typical type of research an instructional designer would conduct with subject matter experts (SMEs) or exemplary performers in order to collect content for the design of learning. Thus, we might observe employees and ask questions, we might conduct small-group meetings, or we might meet individually with employees during breaks and slow work periods.

It is likely that your inquiry into job linkage will raise more questions about organizational goals and issues and that you may need to return to higher-level sources for clarification and resolution. Also, you will discover more information than is necessary to complete an impact map. You may wish to document this valuable data in a research or performance analysis report of some type; it will certainly feed later phases of your design process, such as how best to design, create, and try out solutions. You will also want to document and pursue further, if necessary, information about any critical derailers that you have identified during the analysis phase of the overall design process.

Let us now take a look at Phase One in action, at Barking Frog Beer.

Illustrating Phase One: Analyze at Barking Frog Beer

Barking Frog Beer is a national brewery that distributes its product through independently owned and operated wholesale distributors around the country. Occasionally, the corporation implements national marketing campaigns to strengthen its position and increase sales, at times providing training to support these campaigns and to strengthen distributor operations. Local distributors are required to participate in training and comply with corporate campaign requirements.

With the hopes of increasing their market share, Barking Frog Beer launched a new marketing campaign by introducing a "freshness date" printed on their product, on the assumption that consumers would be more likely to purchase beer that they could verify was "fresh." One of the requirements of the freshness date campaign is that the beer must remain refrigerated at all times. This posed a considerable problem for many wholesale distributors, since they were in the habit of simply parking delivery trucks overnight in their locked yards, even if the trucks contained cases of beer that had not yet been sold. Now, however, they would have to unload this inventory, put it in refrigerators, and reload the trucks the next day.

One large distributor with whom we worked was very unhappy about this new campaign. The owner of this distributorship (our client) feared additional loss of inventory through damage introduced by additional handling of unloading and reloading the product. A bigger concern was that the distributorship lacked sufficient refrigerator space. In fact, the distributor owner estimated that she would have to spend nearly $1 million to build the refrigeration they would need, along with an additional $4,000 per month in electrical costs to run the refrigerators.

Further, the corporate center at Barking Frog Beer was also requiring all distributor sales staff to attend a two-day workshop on selling skills to support the implementation of the freshness concept and methods. This two-day workshop would be conducted at the distributorship by a corporate trainer. This compounded the expressed unhappiness of our client, who felt that the campaign would significantly increase her operating costs, cutting into her profit margins.

Once she realized that she either would have to comply with the corporate campaign or lose her distributorship license, our client came to us for help. She was resigned to send her staff to the two-day sales training and hope for the best; after all, she told us, she was used to "wasting her employees' time on useless corporate training." What she wanted from us was a solution that would help her somehow lower her operating costs to help pay for increased refrigeration.

During our initial meeting with the distributor owner, we asked for permission to talk with a few of her key managers and made a promise to report back within two days. We then had brief meetings with the director of sales, who managed the delivery truck driver/salespeople, and the director of operations, who managed the warehousing and truck-loading function. A meeting with the director of distributor finance confirmed that the refrigeration capital and operating cost estimates of the owner were accurate. It was immediately clear from these meetings that the critical roles involved in the issues were the delivery truck drivers who returned each day with unsold product, and the warehouse employees who had to load, unload, and reload the product.

We also learned that the truck drivers distributed their product to retailers (such as grocery and party stores) through "peddle selling," meaning that the route drivers were also salespeople. That is, the product was not presold by internal salespeople over the phone, then simply delivered to retailers by truck drivers.

Route drivers were paid hourly, plus commission on all of the beer they sold each day. Warehouse employees filled all of the trucks each morning, based on the load sheets provided by the drivers. The load sheet provided warehouse loaders with an inventory of product and quantity that drivers wanted loaded on their trucks.

Drivers departed from the warehouse, followed their route selling beer to their retail accounts, then returned in the evening, leaving any unsold beer on their trucks. Prior to the institution of the freshness date, this unsold beer could remain on the truck until the next day, when warehouse loaders could then refill the truck to capacity.

While we were gathering this information, we also discovered some important performance issues and factors.

- Most drivers (but not all) did not "manage" the stocking of their trucks by warehouse loaders, nor did they want to manage this process or the loaders. They simply handed off their load sheets in the morning, then went and had coffee while the warehouse staff loaded the trucks. When they returned in the evening, they parked the truck and went home, leaving it to be unloaded.
- Drivers received data on a regular basis regarding their sales. However, they received no data regarding their return rate (that is, the amount of product they returned each evening). Although the warehouse director collected load and unload information, it was not communicated to the drivers.
- Warehouse loaders were paid by the hour and were not compensated in any way related to sales. The added responsibility of unloading trucks each evening to refrigerate the unsold beer, we were told, would not be an issue; the loaders would simply be paid for the time necessary to do this.
- "Shrinkage," the rate of damaged product that the distributor had to discard, was directly related to the amount of handling. That is, the more often beer had to be loaded and unloaded, the more often there was damage, such as a dropped and dented case. Of course, this directly affected profit, since the distributor bought the product from the brewery, and damaged cases could not be sold to retailers.

- We learned that the best return rate across drivers was about 9 percent and the worst return rate was close to 50 percent, with an average of 40 percent of the product being returned each night. That is, a few drivers came back regularly with almost their entire load sold—their load sheets closely matched exactly what they actually sold. However, most drivers returned their trucks nearly half full of unsold product.

This last bit of information was a vital clue, since it told us that the sort of performance that could reduce refrigeration costs already existed at the distributorship. That is, a few truck drivers seemed to do something different that resulted in little of their product being returned, and thus needing to be offloaded and refrigerated. We quickly asked to meet with these few exemplary drivers, and also a group of more typical drivers. At these meetings, we simply asked how they did their jobs, what information they used to project truckloads, and so forth. Here is what we learned.

Drivers who had the lowest return rate applied some very specific strategies for completing their load sheets and stocking their trucks. These drivers based their load on a systematic and detailed projection of sales for that particular day. They became familiar with the communities that their retailers served, reading local newspapers and watching for local events, such as softball tournaments and other occasions where large quantities of beer would be purchased. They also built strong relationships with the retailers, tracking sales trends and monitoring local preferences at the store level. By carefully monitoring all of these sources of information, these drivers could be far more accurate and precise in completing their load sheets and filling their trucks with the right quantities of the right product, thereby returning in the evening with a nearly empty truck and ensuring that their retailers never experienced an "out of stock" situation. Most drivers, on the other hand, simply asked for their trucks to be fully loaded with a mix of product that reflected the drivers' understanding of general and historical sales trends. This majority of drivers made no specific daily sales projections. Instead, they operated under the assumption that it was best to drive a full truck and to be prepared to sell most any mix and amount of product.

The few drivers with small return loads also worked differently with their warehouse loaders. They tended to spend more time on the loading dock and treated the loaders as if they were "partners." They talked with them about sales, welcomed their ideas about loading practices, and thanked them for especially good work. Most drivers, on the other hand, spent no time talking about business or operational issues with loaders. Relationships were not bad, they were simply not related to critical aspects of operations.

The last thing we did during the analyze phase was to inquire about the upcoming two-day corporate sales workshop. This workshop, we learned, dealt mostly with sales techniques for presenting the freshness campaign to retailers.

The session trainer was agreeable to modifying the content of the workshop, if this was something that we saw was important. With all of this information in hand, we felt we could move on quickly to suggest an HIL initiative.

Derailers for Phase One: Analyze

There are a host of possible barriers we may run up against during phase one, with many of the derailers being potential "show-stoppers," or issues that must be resolved before any meaningful effort should be invested in the creation of a learning and performance support solution.

- While interviewing senior-level managers and executives, you may discover that the functional areas within the organization are not aligned and working toward the same strategic end. Although their efforts and objectives seem sound individually, when evaluated as a whole, they may be following the wrong business strategy or working toward divergent business goals.
- As you begin to dive down into the work processes that most influence the CBI, it may become apparent that there are faulty processes in place, prohibiting effective and efficient performance. Evidence of this may be the mismatch between the outputs and the inputs of two linked and dependent processes. Or it may be as simple as employees following the wrong process, just because "this is the way we've always done it." Or it may be that the company is relying on obsolete methods and tools.
- We may identify poorly designed jobs or a poorly designed organizational structure.
- It may be that the people in job roles are incapable of performing the needed work because of poor selection and hiring processes, or because of poorly formed teams.
- If the performance management system within an organization is weak or ineffectively designed, then we will drastically weaken our HIL approach. Problems we have witnessed include issues such as performance expectations not being clearly communicated, a lack of performance feedback being provided, and a lack of appropriate consequences and compensation (both positive and negative) for performance. These derailers were clearly affecting performance at our distributor for Barking Frog Beer.
- Overall and more general organizational context factors can be incompatible with what we are trying to accomplish. It may be, for example, that we wish to implement our HIL initiative during a chaotic period of time for the organization, when there are other, competing initiatives vying for attention, commitment, and

resources. We also may have difficulty in rallying support and enthusiasm for our initiative from a senior-level executive, resulting in a lack of a sponsor or champion.

A Deeper Look at Phase Two: Design

Most designers of learning will find a comfortable familiarity with the activities that typically occur in the design phase. Design work for an HIL initiative requires a high degree of client involvement and participation. This allows us to take advantage of and leverage the clients' knowledge capital regarding the organization, the issue, the performance, and the audience. Too often, we have seen the unfortunate result of many learning initiatives that exclude the client from the design. These designers invest days and weeks inside an organization, conducting research and analysis activities, then they disappear for days or weeks as they work on their own, coming up with the "best" learning design. Not a peep is heard from the designers, until at last, they emerge with a full-blown learning design, complete with creative treatments, screen layouts, and so forth. Instead of leveraging the knowledge capital from those most familiar with the needs of the organization and the learner, designers create a solution on their own based on limited research, then toss it "over the wall" to the client, with the hope that their ideas will be fully accepted.

Involving clients throughout the design process will accomplish several things.

- It solicits their best ideas for the design and implementation of the solution.
- It obtains their input and feedback on your best ideas for the design and implementation of the solution.
- Generates buy-in to the overall design since they assisted in its conceptualization.
- Helps to identify and overcome possible barriers in the organization to getting the solution developed or implemented.

In the HIL design process, we broaden our view of the solution to the tools, resources, and possibilities to support all three components of an HIL solution: creating intentionality and focus, supporting learning of new skills and knowledge, and supporting performance improvement. We have to avoid a myopic view focused on just the learning tools and resources needed to teach the skills and knowledge we've identified during our analysis. Instead, we aim to build performance and intentionality into the learning process rather than "bolting them on" at the beginning and end.

The outcomes of the design phase typically include some type of a design document, which is the blueprint for the initiative, much like an architect and a builder create a blueprint to be followed during the construction of a house. In addition to the design document, there should also be a comprehensive project plan that will guide the development activities during the next phase. Effective project plans should include development schedules and milestones, listings of human and other resources needed for development, and budgets that itemize the costs associated with the development and implementation of the solution.

Let us illustrate Phase Two by revisiting our case example of Barking Frog Beer. We will then review common derailers that can occur during the design phase.

Illustrating Phase Two: Design at Barking Frog Beer

Based on the work we had done during Phase One: Analyze, we realized that decreasing the return rate of route drivers could lead to a number of very positive business results.

- Lower return rates meant that product would be handled less, resulting in reduced shrinkage and decreased costs.
- Lower return rates decreased the labor required from warehouse loaders in the evening to unload the unsold product from the trucks back into the warehouse, resulting in reduced labor costs.
- Finally, lower return rates also meant that less product would need to be stored and refrigerated. In fact, if we were able to attain an average return rate of 10 percent load returns across all route drivers, then the need for additional refrigerated warehouse space would be eliminated.

But we knew that it would take more than a simple workshop to ensure that these new skills converted to improved performance on the part of route drivers. Therefore, our HIL design, created during a series of collaborative group design meetings with the sales manager, warehouse manager, and groups of drivers and loaders, consisted of the following mix of solutions and strategies:

- All drivers would attend a brief meeting prior to their attendance at the corporate selling workshop. During this meeting, managers and drivers would review impact maps and discuss the connections between the objectives of the workshop, route driver performance, and key business goals of reducing return rate, capital investment costs, and shrinkage, as well as increasing sales volume.

- We recommended that warehouse loaders attend the first portion of the two-day workshop, instead of restricting it to only sales staff as originally intended. Loaders would thus become part of the "team" and would understand the overall business importance of reducing refrigeration needs. We also recommended revisions to make the sales examples more specific to reducing load return rates. Finally, we planned to include specific content and practice in the workshop related to the key skills that low load return drivers used to project sales and customize load sheets on a daily basis.
- Although route drivers had routinely received feedback on their sales, we recommended collecting and posting data regarding each driver's return rate in the lunchroom of the warehouse.
- We met with the sales manager and coached him on how to effectively conduct "ride-alongs" with drivers to observe and provide feedback on their new sales performance.
- We recommended changes to the compensation of both the warehouse loaders and the drivers, creating the notion of "team-based compensation." Specifically, we recommended that loaders receive a commission on all sales made by the drivers, as well as an incentive for reducing shrinkage. We also recommended incentives for drivers who met or beat the new return rate target, as well as a penalty for returning with too much product at the end of the day.

Derailers for Phase Two: Design

Based on the nature of the HIL design process, it is likely that we will identify our most challenging derailers during Phase One: Analyze. However, there are still a few issues that we might encounter during Phase Two: Design. These potential obstacles are listed below.

- *"Over-the-wall" design*—As we have mentioned, client input and involvement are essential both to the quality of the overall design of the solution as well as for acceptance and buy-in. This can be a significant obstacle, especially in organizations where the learning function is still viewed as the "fix-it shop," where all of the learning is designed and implemented without support or input from the "training customer." Fortunately, we did not experience this barrier with the distributors for Barking Frog Beer and benefited from extensive input from all areas within the distributor.
- *"Feed-the-machine" mentality*—Some organizations that invest in specific forms of learning delivery, such as broadcast satellite, web-

based training (WBT), or virtual classrooms, become overly enamored with the media so that every learning need turns into a new opportunity to apply new technology. We know that each type of media has modalities and characteristics of its own and should be applied based on what the media does best. Again, with the distributors for Barking Frog Beer and the solution proposed above, we did not run into this particular derailer.

• *"Locked-in-stone" solutions*—We often encounter existing or vendor-purchased training programs that take on a "do not touch" quality, so that our other HIL components must "work around" this given and fixed training. We have experienced many instances where our analysis uncovered additional or different content and practice requirements not currently reflected in the training offered. Designers have a couple of options here. First, you can augment the "fixed" training with other learning resources to deliver the missing content and improved practice and feedback. Or you can revise the existing training to better reflect and support the skills and performance you wish to build. This issue did arise in the case of Barking Frog Beer and the workshop selected for all route drivers. Although there was good correlation between the learning needs of the drivers and the objectives of the workshop, we had identified some missing content and wanted to make all of the practice opportunities more specific to our route drivers. Since the selected workshop was a generic program, purchased through a vendor, this created a bit of a hurdle for us. However, after some negotiation, we were allowed to make the changes necessary to customize the program.

• *Lack of organizational capabilities*—There are instances when the use of a particular type of medium is just the right tool to support learning or performance, but the organization does not have the infrastructure or capabilities to support that medium. Let's say, for example, that you would like to show some powerful video examples as a part of your WBT module, but you find out that your learners do not have the necessary video card installed in their computers to view video. These types of issues can be identified quickly during group design meetings as long as these meetings include clients who are familiar with the technical capabilities of the organization. If this is the case, then design work-arounds can be identified right there and then. This can become an issue, however, if the design for the solution is proposed without full knowledge of what the organization can and cannot support. With regard to the HIL solution we devised for Barking Frog Beer distributors, we were able to create a blend of solutions that were easily within the capability of distributors to implement.

- *"It's too hard" perception*—A serious obstacle that can be identified at this point in the process is that leadership, managers, and even members of the target audience perceive the proposed solution as being too complex, having too many steps, and too difficult to implement. The originally proposed solution for Barking Frog Beer distributors was for drivers to simply attend a two-day workshop. Now, with our HIL approach, we've built in additional steps and activities that make the solution seem longer and more complicated. This is a common "push-back" that we encounter often and is examined more closely in Chapter 11, "Making the Transition to High-Impact Learning." In fact, we did receive some push-back from the Barking Frog Beer distributors, notably from the sales managers who were now playing a key role in the performance improvement of both drivers and the warehouse loaders. We were able to manage their concerns through some informal meetings, as well as through the commitment and persistence of our champion, the owner of the company.

A Deeper Look at Phase Three: Create and Try Out

What is most noteworthy about this phase of the design process is the dynamic, iterative, rapid prototyping approach to the creation of all of the tools and resources we need to support our HIL solution (see Figure 8.4).

Rapid prototyping often means we conduct reviews and tests of pieces of the braided solution as we create them, rather than waiting until we have a finished and complete product. Rapid prototyping also means that materials are tried out on users in a rough form, rather than completely produced. And rapid prototyping means trying solutions out on users multiple times, not just once at the "pilot" test.

The success of this portion of the crafting process is critically dependent on a valid and comprehensive project plan. In addition, much of the success of this phase resides with a skillful project manager, along with a knowledgeable and skillful team of developers who are not only available and dedicated to the creation of this HIL solution but who fully understand the business linkage and importance of the initiative. Finally, it is imperative that this development group has the skills, tools, and resources they need to craft the solution proposed.

Illustrating Phase Three: Create and Try Out at Barking Frog Beer

The create and try out phase at Barking Frog Beer was fairly simple and straightforward. We were able to form a small development team, consisting

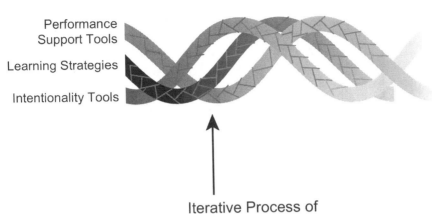

Performance
Support Tools

Learning Strategies

Intentionality Tools

Iterative Process of

- Develop Prototype
- Test
- Identify Design Changes
- Revise Prototype

FIGURE 8.4   Phase Three: Create and Try Out

of the corporate workshop leader and two of our staff members. We also got the sales manager to agree to talk by phone with the development team as the need arose. The following materials and tools were developed:

- Simple agendas and meeting outlines were created to guide the intentionality meetings between the sales manager and drivers. In addition, it was essential that the manager came to these meetings prepared with the impact maps we had created, as well as current data on sales, return rates, and shrinkage. One of us conducted the first meeting while the sales manager watched. The second meeting was coconducted by one of the sales manager and us. After that, and after we made changes to the agenda suggested by the sales manager or drivers, the sales manager took over this activity.
- The development team worked with the corporate sales workshop trainer to build in more relevant examples, practice, and feedback opportunities. We also built in opportunities during the workshop for drivers to work as teams to devise strategies for applying the selling ideas with their accounts. The workshop was conducted three separate times, with smaller groups of drivers. This was not only more convenient for drivers since it gave them choices, but it let us field-test a first version of the workshop. After we made changes, we conducted the second workshop and made more changes.

- Measurement tracking methods and procedures were created so that drivers and warehouse loaders could get data on return rates daily. We tried out the new procedures for the first week, then made changes. We continued to revise and try out these procedures until the drivers and loaders agreed that the feedback was both efficient and helpful. At this point, the system was officially installed.
- We provided job aids and performance observation checklists for the sales manager to assist him on driver "ride-alongs." One of our staff accompanied the sales manager on the first few ride-alongs to observe how well the tools worked and to debrief the sales manager afterward to identify needed improvements.
- We worked alongside warehouse loaders and their supervisors for the first few days after the workshop to see how well the new load procedures were working and to immediately get their feedback. This process suggested the creation of some job aids and revised load sheet formats. We made these and tried them out. As soon as it was clear that they worked and were helpful, we put them into final form.
- The changes we recommended in compensation were probably the most difficult component of the solution to manage and implement. Revising the compensation for drivers and loaders required numerous meetings with all of the managers and the owner. Although the intervention we had built was clearly working, a change in compensation was not agreed to. The HIL intervention was sufficient to help the distributor reduce load returns to the point where no additional refrigeration was needed, with a projected saving in excess of over one million dollars in the first year alone. The owner did agree to provide extra cash bonuses to all employees, and this seemed sufficient to enable the new approaches to be maintained without a fundamental change in compensation. However, it is likely that a change in compensation structure will be needed to assure long-term compliance and continued improvement.

Derailers for Phase Three: Create and Try Out

At this phase in the process, most potential issues and obstacles that could derail the project have been identified and resolved. There are, however, some lingering barriers that can still rise up and snag efforts to develop your solutions.

- *Resistance to a rapid prototyping approach*—The very nature of a rapid prototyping approach is that it is dynamic, fluid, and fast-paced. This process can also be described as chaotic, messy, and disorganized. Reviewers and others who are involved in the prototyping process may feel constantly pestered by designers who are looking for input and feedback. These reviewers may also be taken aback by the rudimentary and perhaps even inaccurate approximations that the prototypes may take, being more accustomed to materials that have a polished, "almost finished" look to them. Feelings of frustration may build with reviewers who might wish that designers invest more time and effort on pieces of the solution before coming for feedback.

- *Resistance to less-than-fancy solutions*—Similar to the first derailer described above, there may be a pervasive expectation throughout an organization regarding the face appearance and "curb appeal" of the solution. Keep in mind that the focus of an HIL initiative is that it achieves enhanced capability and performance that leads to true business impact. HIL initiatives are not defined by full-color, glossy participant materials, state-of-the-art animation, or WBT that is delivered on a palm pilot. HIL initiatives might have any or all of these high-tech characteristics, but these characteristics do not define high impact. Typically, it is more likely that an HIL initiative will lean toward simpler, low-tech, low-touch media and materials rather than solutions that have all the bells and whistles.

Chapter Summary

Our traditional ISD processes have come under great scrutiny and criticism over the past few years, and rightly so. Although processes like ADDIE helped us early on to streamline and standardize our efforts in the design of training, they are no longer valid constructs that accurately describe the way in which learning needs to happen in organizations today.

The approach to the design of HIL solutions that we have proposed in this chapter provides an alternative construct for the designers of learning and performance support tools and resources. It is a process that allows us to "connect the dots" between critical business issues and goals, to their related business processes, down to the specific job tasks and capabilities of individual employees. This design process guides us to use this organizational and performance context as the basis for constructing and implementing a complete and relevant solution. Finally, this design process highlights the notion of a blended, braided solution crafted as a result of an iterative and dynamic prototyping approach.

Using Evaluation to Build Organizational Performance and Learning Capability

Chapter Overview

It is almost a guarantee that no training initiative will achieve 100 percent impact. We always see variable results. More specifically, if we were to follow up a training initiative and assess the extent to which learning is being used in ways that impact business results, we will find that there are three categories of impact. Some extreme portion of the trainees is indeed using its training in highly effective ways. A similar but opposite extreme portion is not using any new learning at all. And everyone else is somewhere in between, trying out bits of the training here and there but with modest and variable success. Over years of evaluation studies, we invariably find these three degrees of impact. The proportions vary, of course. The more that the training is like the HIL approach, then the portion using its learning in highly impactful ways will be larger. But even in the very best HIL initiatives there will be variable success.

Another highly probable finding is that the causes of variability of impact have more to do with the performance system and organizational environment factors than they do with factors that are inherent in the training design and content itself. Though sometimes it is the training program itself that accounts for variable success, this is rarely so. Just consider the following example to illustrate this reality.

Imagine that one company purchases and implements a well-known and high-quality leadership skills training program. Further imagine that this company gets excellent results; many employees apply the skills in useful and impactful ways. Now imagine that another company buys and implements the same vendor-supplied program and achieves virtually no results at all. This example is a reality, of course, and is played out day after day, year after year, in organizations worldwide. And the same reality applies even within the same company. One business unit might use the program with great success, whereas another business unit has virtually no success. Clearly, the training program itself is not the major factor in success. What accounts for the difference is the manner in which the company (or business unit) uses the training, as well as the influence of the prevailing cultural and systemic factors (such as work habits, reward systems, preparedness of learners, measures, and feedback procedures, to name a few).

These systemic factors are "owned" by the management systems and leadership of the organization and cannot be directly manipulated by learning leaders or training departments. They can, however, be influenced by learning leaders. In fact, we posit that it is a direct and important role of learning leaders to do all that they can to influence these factors, since unless these systemic factors are identified and managed positively, organizations will continue to reap disappointing returns on learning investments.

We summarize these organizational cultural and systemic factors that influence training success into a single construct that we call the organization's "learning capability." We believe that it is a major mission of the learning function to develop the organization's learning capability. Finally, we see evaluation as the principal tool that learning leaders can use to accomplish this mission: building and strengthening learning capability, so that organizations reap continuously better results from their learning investments.

But traditional evaluation approaches can undermine training effectiveness and thwart efforts to achieve constructive organizational learning capability. Practitioners need a coherent evaluation strategy that builds lasting organizational capability to enhance business returns on training investments. In this chapter, we explain and describe an evaluation strategy and method that is aimed directly at this critical mission of building the organization's learning capability. We begin by reviewing the conceptual framework for a constructive evaluation strategy, also explaining how traditional approaches can be counterproductive. In the second section, we articulate and illustrate the HIL evaluation strategy. In the third and final section, we describe and illustrate the HIL "success case" evaluation method and tools, a highly practical, proven, and successful approach.

Evaluation and Organizational Learning Capability

In their continuing efforts to gain more leverage and credibility for their work, HRD professionals have perennially sought "bottom-line" impact evi-

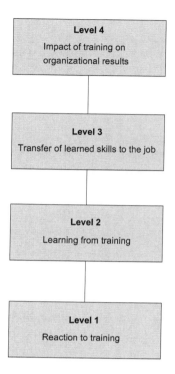

FIGURE 9.1   Four-Level Training Evaluation

dence. At the same time, the HRD profession has evolved away from training as a separate and independent transaction toward a more comprehensive framework that focuses on performance improvement. Both of these trends spring from the same impetus: Organizations expect and need value from training. Training professionals cannot afford to just deliver training; they must deliver results from training—results that produce improved individual and team performance that leads to worthwhile business impact.

The traditional four-level training evaluation framework was introduced by Don Kirkpatrick (1976) and more recently extended by Jack Phillips (1997) that includes an additional level focusing on return-on-investment, or ROI.

This model seems on the surface to mesh well with the push toward performance improvement. Increasingly, training practitioners view evaluation as a tool that can help them with their age-old struggle to prove their worth and compete more effectively in the ongoing battle for organizational resources and attention. "Impact," or level-four evaluation, and especially impact evaluation that produces estimates of ROI are typically seen as especially attractive. Because these methods focus on performance measures and business results, they are often seen as useful in influencing management to be more supportive of training and performance improvement efforts.

But traditional impact and ROI evaluation approaches can, in fact, undermine the effectiveness of training and impede the quest to transform training from a marginal intervention that produces slight gains in knowledge and competence to a fully effective performance improvement effort. Chances are many organizations are wasting time and money on evaluation activities that will not lead to strategically constructive results. To understand the role of evaluation in strengthening organizational learning capability, we need to dig deeper into evaluation purposes and strategy.

For years, the Kirkpatrick model for evaluation has been the primary driver of training evaluation in business and corporate settings. Evaluation at the first level (measuring participant reactions to training) has become so widespread as to be a standard element of almost every training initiative. In fact, it is often derogatorily referred to as a "smile sheet" evaluation, because it often seeks feedback on issues that are totally unrelated to the training, such as the quality of the food served or the temperature of the room.

But the higher levels of the Kirkpatrick approach, levels three (Do learners apply their new skills and knowledge on the job?) and four (Did this enhanced performance have an impact on business measures?) are far less applied, because they are viewed as being more difficult and more expensive to measure. Perhaps because of their perceived difficulty, and perhaps because Kirkpatrick called them "levels," which implies an ordinal relationship, the "higher" levels of the model have taken on the aura of a quest or goal unto themselves. Practitioners might state apologetically that they do "only" level one or two evaluations, but they are working toward doing "better" (beyond level one or two) evaluations. And ROI evaluation, posed as the next step beyond even the fourth level, is seen as a sort of holy grail to which those who seek the ultimate in evaluation results must aspire.

But evaluation is not some sort of categorical imperative, it is a tool. The purpose of evaluation is not to do it, or to get it done; it is to use evaluation to serve some larger goal. Evaluation is a means to an end. But what end? In the next section of this chapter, we articulate a comprehensive strategy for evaluation as an organizational learning process that can help organizations build increasingly greater capability to gain value from training investments. Before examining this strategy, however, it is useful to understand in detail just how the implicit strategy of continued pursuit of higher levels of evaluation is counterproductive.

Implicit Evaluation Strategy

In our experience, many training organizations and practitioners are pursuing evaluation blindly, as if it were an end in itself. Their strategy is not explicit but is taken more as an unexplored assumption that evaluation at the "higher" levels will lead to good things, that it might build credibility for training, earn support for training budgets, and so forth.

Much of the implicit strategy positions evaluation as essentially, though not intentionally, *defensive*. The common wisdom is that we should do evaluation proactively, since someday we might need it. Or if we do it now, we can preempt a budget strike, since we will be able to show that our training has indeed led to some worthwhile results. But a defensive strategy is not healthy for training in the long run. A defensive strategy presumes that a defense is needed and exacerbates suspicion. Worse, it will not lead to more constructive training practice, since the best that defense does is to protect the status quo. Worse yet, defensive evaluation diverts resources from investment in activities and procedures that do not serve customers or add value.

But avoiding a defensive posture is the least harmful result of an unarticulated or misguided evaluation strategy. The fact is that now, more than ever, organizations need the very best training and performance improvement that can possibly be achieved. Thoughtful, efficient, and constructive evaluation is at the heart of continuous improvement and is one of the vital keys to unlocking the desperately needed potential of learning for performance improvement. Today's global economy, accelerating technology, increasing demands for competitive advantage, and escalating struggle for capital demand a workforce that can not only learn quickly but that can rapidly and consistently transform new learning into enhanced individual, team, and organizational performance.

Meeting this challenge demands the very best world-class learning and performance capability. Evaluation is itself a learning tool that can be constructively applied to help organizations learn "on the job" how to leverage every last ounce of learning and performance improvement from their training investments. But this sort of return on evaluation investments will not happen automatically. Simply put, responsible training professionals cannot afford to conduct evaluation with any less care and thought than they can afford to conduct training and performance improvement without care and thought. ■

The Risks of an Implicit Evaluation Strategy

Pursuing the higher levels of Kirkpatrick's evaluation model without careful forethought poses three essential and significant risks.

1. It undermines performance partnerships with line management by misrepresenting the role and process of training in performance improvement.

2. It ignores the performance system factors that impinge on training impact.
3. It fails to provide accurate and relevant feedback that managers, the customers of training, need to guide performance improvement.

Let's take a closer look at each of these potential risks.

How Traditional Impact Evaluation Undermines Training-Performance Partnerships

The very notion of evaluating the impact of training begs some fundamental questions. Of greatest concern is that the pairing of the term "impact" with the term "training" implies that one should expect an impact from training, which leads one to jump to the next conclusion that training causes the impact that it is paired with. The quest for impact data and other "hard" measures of training value misleads training professionals and their customers as to the true nature and substance of training, and the process by which training leads to performance, and thence to organizational impact.

As training and performance improvement professionals, we frequently encounter line managers who "order" training as a solution for complex performance system issues. These managers' wishes for training as a magical "silver bullet" for performance impact are poignant and understandable but nonetheless pose significant problems for training professionals.

The reality is, of course, that training is not a magical silver bullet. As we have reiterated in earlier chapters, training produces only capability, not performance. People who acquire new capability must then transform their new learning into new behaviors, which can then lead to improved performance and finally to business impact, such as better quality products, improved customer satisfaction, reduced costs, and so forth. But any number of performance system factors can, and often do, derail the transformation of learning into performance results.

The many performance system factors that threaten results are owned by senior and supervisory management. Given this fact of performance life, training practitioners have worked hard to overcome the "silver bullet" myth, seeking to forge a partnership strategy with other key roles in the organization. Since these others hold the keys to the performance system, their active and cooperative participation is essential to make training work. The very essence of the partnership strategy is a clear message from training that "we cannot do this alone. Without you (the rest of the key players) training cannot succeed."

But the typical impact evaluation and ROI approaches send quite different messages. First, these approaches are inappropriately referred to as the evaluation of "training." When considering the Kirkpatrick model more closely, it becomes more apparent that the term "training" applies only at the first and second levels of evaluation. Therefore, at level three and beyond, when we evaluate whether trainees are using their learning, we are no longer evaluating "training"; we are evaluating the larger performance improvement process in which training plays only a small role.

This myopic focus on "training" during evaluation not only reinforces the popular (and dysfunctional) notion of training as just delivery of learning events, but it also looks suspiciously like seeking credit or blame. When evaluation reveals successful impact, the training function trumpets this success as a "training" success, sometimes even going so far as to produce an ROI case study that "isolates" the effect of the training, thereby seeking credit for the impact. On the other hand, of course, a training function that receives evaluation data that show little or no impact will be quick to point out that training alone cannot be held accountable, for after all, there are many other factors that bear on impact.

Second, because impact evaluation and ROI methods are rooted in the age-old research methods of quantitative analysis and experimental design, there is a methodological imperative to somehow tease out and "isolate" the effect of the training alone. But this methodological demand for the independent effect of training flies directly in the face of everything we know about performance improvement and systems thinking. On the one hand, we in the training practice are trying desperately to create a systems-based, partnership-focused approach to performance improvement that involves cross-functional networking with the many key players in the performance system. Why, then, on the other hand, would we want to turn this mental model upside down and invest evaluation energy to somehow isolate and "prove" just the part that training played? The training function has already been isolated for too long, both physically in the geography of the organization and conceptually in the minds of line management who have typically seen training as isolated from the mainstream of business performance.

Methods that seek to claim training "credit" for impact and not recognize the vital contributions of other players in the performance process are divisive and exacerbate political isolation of the training function. Improving individual, team, and business performance must remain the central focus of training practitioners, and we must work doggedly to create the internal alliances necessary to work systemically. We cannot afford to send mixed messages about what it takes to accomplish our mission, nor can we afford to divert resources into evaluation initiatives that are not aligned with it.

Lack of Focus on Performance System Factors

The effects of the prevailing performance system are consistently powerful and predictable. As we have already noted, the business impact that training leads to is more a factor of the performance system and organizational culture than it is the learning intervention alone. When we discover, as we inevitably do, that some people used their new learning in impactful ways, and others did not, the crucial question is *why*? Why, for example, were some trainees able to persevere despite performance system obstacles and make such good use of their training? What helped them do this? Why did some not try at all? What (or who) got in their way? What factors discouraged the large proportion of trainees and eventually forced their performance back to the pretraining levels?

Answers to these sorts of questions provide information that can be used to leverage training investments, helping shape the learning initiatives and the performance systems in which trainees work. For example, if a company has a valid need to improve the supervisory effectiveness of its managers, it does not matter very much what particular training program on that topic they create or purchase and implement. What makes a greater difference is how well they implement the initiative and whether the training they put in place is reinforced by the performance system in the organization. As we know from the comprehensive systems approach of the HIL model, the skills learned, for example, must be reinforced and modeled by senior managers, the performance reward system must require accountability, the trainees must receive coaching and feedback after training, and so forth.

Despite this truth about training—that the greatest determinant of impact is the performance system—the four-level framework does not guide inquiry directly to the performance environment, nor does it aim to identify and assess the most critical performance factors that make the difference between success and failure. The follow-up impact survey provided by a very well-known vendor of a popular training program on managerial practices and values, for example, contains dozens of questions that probe deeply into how much the training was used and in what ways. It enables a user to produce richly detailed graphs on levels of use and application. But there is virtually no mechanism to assess and discover the impediments to transfer and impact that represent the keys to leverage for increasing impact. In other words, this sort of evaluation can be used to defend and take credit for behavioral change but it provides no focused inquiry into what factors in the performance environment enabled or impeded that usage. Nor does it provide information that could be used to identify and recognize the key players in the performance environment who played the major role in the success, or failure, to achieve results.

Evaluation Feedback Goes to the Wrong People

Senior leadership and supervising managers are the "owners" of the performance environment. Senior management is responsible for the organizational structure, policies, and procedures that provide the overall performance system architecture. Supervising managers hold the keys to ongoing performance improvement, for it is they who are responsible for the day-to-day coaching and other performance management activities that most shape behavior. But the traditional four-level framework focuses on "training." It is conceived to provide feedback primarily to the training function as if it were alone responsible for performance improvement and essentially ignores the larger performance system.

If we want to evaluate transfer (behavioral change from training), we in essence must be evaluating the managerial and performance system, not "training." That is, the evaluation of training transfer should focus on managerial behaviors and the performance support environment that trainees encounter in their work, and the primary feedback channel should be to the "owners" of the performance system: line management and senior leadership. If we are really serious about improving the performance that training can contribute to, then we need to be equally serious about getting all of the players in the performance process involved. It makes no sense for the training function to implicitly accept responsibility for training transfer by creating and disseminating follow-up surveys that assess usage of learning when the principal feedback channel is to the training function.

Redefining an Evaluation Strategy for Performance Improvement

In today's globally competitive and constantly changing market and technological environment, training is a given. The pace of change is such that the "shelf life" of employee capability is ever more brief. Organizations must continuously reinvent themselves and find effective ways to rapidly help employees master new skills and capabilities. The central training challenge for organizations today is how to leverage learning—consistently, quickly, and effectively—into improved performance. Importantly, this is a whole organization challenge, not one that the training function can accomplish alone.

An evaluation framework that responds to this challenge must focus on three primary questions.

1. How well is our organization using learning to drive needed performance improvement?
2. What is our organization doing that facilitates performance improvement from learning that needs to be maintained and strengthened?
3. What is our organization doing, or not doing, that is impeding performance improvement from learning that needs to change?

These key questions are embedded in an evaluation strategy with the overall purpose of building organizational capability to increase the performance and business value of training investments. This strategy is essentially an organizational learning approach that is well aligned with the overall training mission, which is likewise to build organizational capability through learning. In other words, evaluation becomes an additional learning intervention that strengthens the training function's arsenal. Systematic evaluation of training serves as a sort of "on-the-job" training approach that is aimed at "teaching" managers in the organization how to leverage performance and business results from learning.

To implement this strategy, training practitioners design and conduct ongoing and systematic evaluation within their organization's training and performance improvement initiatives. These evaluation efforts are highly targeted and selective, focusing specific attention on particular aspects of selected learning programs and initiatives. Evaluation of this sort is conducted as action research; the aim is always to learn something related to one or more of the three critical questions listed earlier. We once, for instance, helped a major pharmaceutical company assess the impact of managerial involvement in preparing their employees for attending training. In this study (Brinkerhoff and Montesino, 1995), training managers tracked the training transfer rates of employees whose bosses met with them briefly before and after training. They discovered that this single factor alone dramatically increased the likelihood that trainees would apply their training in critical job performance. The conclusions of the study were reported to all managers, and the "lessons" from the study (how to assure that your employees provide your business unit with a return on training investments) were incorporated into management development courses, assuring that the feedback loop was completed.

In another case, trainees who had been especially successful in applying their learning to accomplish important business goals were interviewed. The interviews focused on two dimensions: First, evidence of the ways in which trainees had applied their learning and the business value that resulted from these applications was documented. Second, the interview probed for reasons as to why these trainees had been especially successful. This probing revealed that the process by which trainees were selected for training was a primary determinant of business value. In many cases, the timing of the training was wrong, such that work assignments and conflicting priorities precluded them from applying their new learning in ways that would be helpful to the business. As a result, the training department proposed new procedures for scheduling training and line managers revised their training selection processes. Notice that in each of these examples, evaluation information was used jointly by both the managerial and training functions.

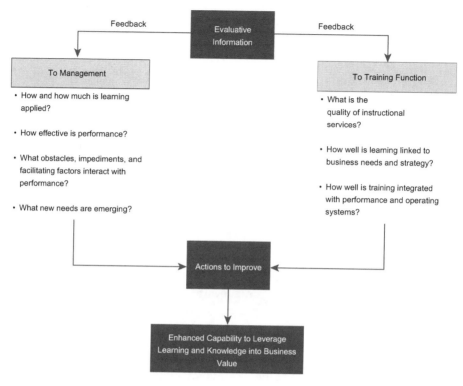

FIGURE 9.2   Evaluation as Capability Building

Figure 9.2 graphically represents this organizational capability-building evaluation strategy.

The box at the top of the figure represents evaluation inquiry focused on one or more of the three critical questions. The results of this evaluation then are communicated through two major channels. The left-hand channel represents the flow of information to the management of the organization. Since managers are the owners of the performance improvement process, the information to them focuses on application of learning by their direct reports and identification of performance system factors that impinge on training application. The purpose of this feedback is twofold. First, it indicates the sort of return that they, as customers of training, are realizing from their training investments. Second, it helps make them more aware of how well they are doing in helping employees transform learning into performance, what actions and policies are facilitating impact, what is impeding impact, and so forth.

The methods for providing this information are not limited to traditional reports, as these are unlikely to be read or heeded. Seek methods that will engage interest and participation; use presentations, stories in newsletters, discussions at management meetings, memos, briefings, "brown bag" seminars, recommendations for policy and procedures changes, and inclusion of relevant findings in management training courses and seminars.

The right-hand channel in the figure represents feedback to the owners of the organization's learning architecture and processes, typically the training department. These parties need information about characteristics of learning systems and initiatives that are successful, the clarity of linkage of learning goals and processes to business goals and needs, the effectiveness of instructional designs, the effectiveness of training management processes, the perceived quality of training and performance improvement services, and so forth. Evaluation information provided to the training function should pay special attention to cost factors, as it is the responsibility of this function to assure that learning and performance costs are continuously reduced and products and services made more efficient.

The channels converge in action to help the organization gain more business results from training. Actions include changes in managerial behavior, changes in performance systems structure (for example, measurement methods, rewards, incentives), changes in performance policies and procedures, changes in human resources initiatives, such as development planning, and other factors and processes that bear on performance improvement. Actions may also focus on the training function, such as improvements in instructional design, delivery systems, policies and procedures, needs analysis procedures, training administration, learning media, performance support tools, and so forth.

Actions based on evaluation results lead to improved organizational capability to leverage performance and business value from training, the ultimate goal of evaluation. This portion of the figure reminds us that evaluation has a clear and constructive purpose. It is not self-serving, it is not defensive, and it is not solely for the benefit of the training department. Like training and performance services themselves, evaluation is another tool to improve performance and business results. This also reminds us that management and the training function jointly share responsibility and leverage for this capability. Neither party alone can assure success, nor can either alone take credit. The performance improvement process has learning at its heart, but learning and performance are inseparable. Learning enables performance, and performance enables learning.

Everything that learning leaders do should drive the message of the inseparability of learning and performance and should support the shared ownership for the learning-performance process. Evaluation of training, when embedded in a coherent and constructive strategic framework like the one presented, is a powerful tool for organizational learning and capability building. It is not only consistent with the concept of shared ownership, it is a method for achieving and strengthening partnership. The struggle for effective partnerships of training with management is crucial for HIL approaches and the larger success of organizations.

Success Case Evaluation

We have developed a method for performance and impact evaluation that is uniquely responsive to both the capability-building strategy explained in the previous section and the HIL approach. We have found this evaluation approach highly effective in achieving HIL results, and it has been successfully implemented dozens of times in many major organizations and corporations worldwide. We call this the success case model (for reasons that will become apparent) and especially recommend its use to help organizations build the capability they need to drive performance improvement results from learning investments. We first outline and explain the success case evaluation method, then illustrate several strategic ways in which the method can be employed.

About the Success Case Method

We will first provide a general overview of the success case method, then provide more detail in a step-by-step explanation. The success case approach is deceptively simple and straightforward (see Figure 9.3).

It achieves evaluation efficiencies by purposive versus random sampling, focusing the bulk of inquiry on only a relative few trainees. The underlying notion is that we can learn best from the trainees who have been either exceptionally successful in applying their learning in their work and from trainees who have been the least successful. Thus, we use a two-step evaluation process.

First, we send a brief survey to all, or a large representative sample of all trainees who participated in training. In essence, this survey asks one root question (though we may use several items to ask the question): "To what extent have you used your recent training in a way that you believe has made a significant difference to the business?" From the survey, we identify a small group of exceptionally successful, and unsuccessful, trainees. Each of these small "core" samples is then probed in depth, through telephone interviews. In probing the successes, we want to document the nature and business value of their application of learning and identify and explain the performance context factors (for example, supervisory support, feedback) that enabled these few trainees to achieve the greatest possible results. With the unsuccessful trainees, we aim to identify and understand the performance system and other obstacles that kept them from using their learning. The success case study produces two immediate results.

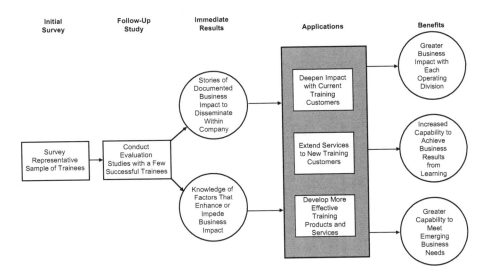

FIGURE 9.3   Success Case Approach

1. In-depth stories of documented business impact that can be disseminated to a variety of audiences within the company. These stories are credible and verifiable and dramatically illustrate the actual business-impact results that the training is capable of producing.
2. Knowledge of factors that enhance or impede the impact of training on business results. We identify the factors that seem to be associated with successful applications of the training and compare and contrast these with the factors that seemed to impede training application. For example, in a recent study, we found that in nearly all successful applications, the trainees' supervisors had also participated in the training and had used particular parts of the training to reinforce application on the part of the trainees. On the other hand, in most of the nonsuccesses, we found that their supervisors had either not participated in the training at all or if they had participated in the training, did not use any parts of the training to specifically support their employees' applications.

These two results can then be used as a basis for three different applications.

1. *Deepening the impact of training on business results for current customers.* The stories of business impact and knowledge of factors

that affect impact would be used to improve the way customers implement and support training to help achieve business impact. The primary customers for this deepening effort would be trainees and managers within business units that have completed training, or are preparing to participate in the training. Where we found, for example, that supervisory participation was a key success factor, we would make a recommendation that all supervisors participate prior to their employees' involvement.

2. *Extending services to new customers.* The results of the evaluation study are a highly effective means of discussing unique customer needs and how the training might meet those needs. The stories of business impact and knowledge of factors that affect impact would be used as the basis for recruiting new customers among business units not currently using training services.

3. *Creating organizational learning about training impact that builds training effectiveness capability.* The results of the evaluation studies would help management and learning leaders understand how they could improve both the delivery of specific courses and the overall learning architecture in the organization to achieve increasingly greater value from training investments. The success case studies always suggest improvements that could be made in the training processes or materials, and also in the process by which the training is implemented. We might add procedures into the training administration system, for example, to track the extent to which supervisors of trainees who register for training had themselves already received the training. In cases where they had not, we could also include a procedure to inform them of the benefits that prior trainees have experienced and encourage them to likewise participate so that they could expect similar positive results when their employees engage in the training. The idea here is to leverage data about the successes and failures of the organization's training experience into "lessons" that the organization can use to redefine how it organizes and manages its training operations. Because these lessons are based on real and documented experience, they are perceived to be credible and actionable.

Implementing a Success Case Evaluation

Prior to planning a success case evaluation, readers should have chosen the training initiative that they wish to evaluate and should have determined that conducting a success case study will accomplish some worthwhile results. In

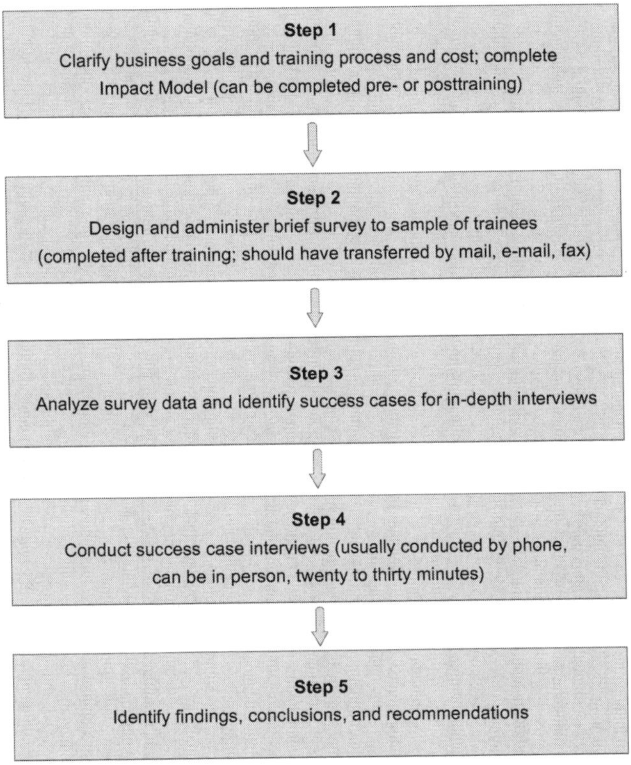

| **Step 1** |
| Clarify business goals and training process and cost; complete Impact Model (can be completed pre- or posttraining) |

| **Step 2** |
| Design and administer brief survey to sample of trainees (completed after training; should have transferred by mail, e-mail, fax) |

| **Step 3** |
| Analyze survey data and identify success cases for in-depth interviews |

| **Step 4** |
| Conduct success case interviews (usually conducted by phone, can be in person, twenty to thirty minutes) |

| **Step 5** |
| Identify findings, conclusions, and recommendations |

FIGURE 9.4   Success Case Evaluation Process Overview

the final section of the chapter, we present and explain some success case application opportunities and explain the benefits that a particular success case application might achieve. Figure 9.4 provides an outline of the five major steps in planning and conducting a success case evaluation.

Step 1: Construct the Impact Model.   The intended or probable business impact is the focus of this step. In some cases, the intent of the evaluation is to determine the extent to which the training is leading to some intended or "promised" business impact. In other cases, the evaluation is more open-ended and seeks to find what, if any, business impact the training is helping to achieve. In either of these scenarios, we construct an "impact model," which uses the familiar impact-mapping approach presented in Chapter 4. The impact model explains for each job role category (for example, a manufacturing supervisor or a sales representative) how a person in that role might have used the training and what results and subsequent business impact that

TABLE 9.1   Impact Model for New Supervisors

Application of Supervisory Training	Business Impact
Identify and rescue employees' issues and problems with workplace conditions and culture	Avoidance of grievances; improved satisfaction and retention of employees
Constructively promote and support productive performance (setting objectives, providing encouragement and recognition, and so on)	Improved productivity; achievement of production targets
Constructively promote and support positive and appropriate diversity and gender relationships	Avoidance of problems and complaints; limitation of legal liability
Support and encourage employee development	Improved performance and achievement of production targets; improved employee satisfaction and retention

usage of training would have led to. Consider, for example, some supervisory training we recently evaluated. The client determined that the training was intended to target four valuable supervisory behaviors for new supervisors, which are outlined in Table 9.1.

The impact model is then reviewed with key stakeholders to assure that it is complete and accurate. Again, we want the impact model to reflect what, if the training is working as hoped for, it should be accomplishing. Once it is confirmed, the impact model will serve as the basis for the survey.

Step 2: Design and Administer Survey.   The purpose of the survey is twofold. First, we use the survey to identify the most successful and least successful users of training (where success is defined by the behaviors identified in the impact model). The second purpose of the survey is to assess the extent of success. That is, we want to gauge the breadth of usage of the training, determining the probable extent of successful applications and successful users of training. How many trainees, for example, fit into a category of "highly successful"? How many are not at all successful?

To estimate these proportions, it is helpful that the survey also assess some key demographic characteristics of the respondents. These characteristics might include their functional area or the number of years that they had been in a supervisory position. This demographic data will help us later in estimating where in the organization impact occurred and what sorts of employees were most and least successful. If, for example, we found that 80 percent of our success cases came from one specific business unit, it will be important to probe the performance factors that differentiate that unit from the others.

The survey itself should be brief and ask the fewest questions needed to gauge who is most likely and least likely to have used the training in the way the impact model illustrates. The survey for the supervisory training program, for example, had four major items, plus five demographic items, for a total of nine items in all. Brevity is vital, as we want a high return rate. To increase the response rate, we almost always use an e-mail or web-based survey, unless the organization does not support such technology. In any case, a hard copy written survey is usually the least favorite alternative.

A final survey design issue is the sampling approach. Usually, you want to send a survey to all of the trainees from a recent time period (usually no more than one year after training). If surveying the total training population is unmanageable, then a large sample is usually sufficient. Survey design and implementation is a rigorous science requiring specialized expertise. Readers who are not familiar with survey methods or do not have access to expertise are referred to the abundant survey methods literature; a book we particularly recommend is *Survey Research Methods* (Babbie, 1990).

Step 3: Analyze Survey Data and Identify Success Cases. The survey analysis will likewise focus on two purposes. First, we want to sort the respondents into three groups. We are most interested in two of these three groups: the small extreme (usually the top 10–15 percent) reporting the greatest degree of usage and claimed impact, and the small extreme reporting the very least impact. Everyone else who lies between these extreme groups comprises the third group. We use the actual data distribution to formulate the size and parameters of the extreme groups. For example, in one study, we found that over 60 percent fit into the group that claimed the highest impact, which was an unusually large proportion. In this same case, there was only 6 percent in the lowest extreme of no impact claimed and a very small middle group. In another case, only 3 percent fit into a highest usage and impact group, and the "no impact" group represented almost 40 percent. Each case is different, though it is best to define the parameters of "high impact" so that you skim only the very highest claims of impact, since we want to study and document the very best impact that the training seems to be producing.

We also use the survey data to get an idea of demographic differences, if any, in the distribution of high, and low, success cases. If, as we noted, all successes came from one part of the organization, and all low success cases from another, then we have probably discovered an important clue as to factors that are influencing impact. In studying the impact of sales training provided by interactive television to automobile dealerships, we found, for example, that no dealerships smaller than a certain level of gross sales reported high impact. When we explored further during the interview portion of the study, we found that small dealerships did not release people from the sales floor to attend training. That is, in these smaller dealerships, salespeople had to "duck out" of the showroom briefly to participate in the training, and they would just as quickly jump out of the training if a customer came into the showroom. Larger dealerships, on the other hand, provided "training releases" and used accounting procedures so that salespeople who took time out for training were not punished by receiving negative adjustments to their commissions.

Step 4: Conduct Success Case Interviews.   Success case interviews are nearly always conducted by telephone, for the obvious reasons of convenience and cost. It is a good idea to begin the interviews with the strongest "successes" as these will help you put reported performance system factors into context and get hunches about how they bear on successful applications. Early in the interview, you need to "qualify" the success case. That is, you want to be sure that the person you are interviewing did indeed use some part of the training, and especially that the use of the training led to a clear, documentable, and verifiable result of value to the business. If the person just really liked the training and thinks it was good but cannot relate a specific and concrete application of significance, then you terminate the call at that point.

If your interviewee is a verified "success case," then you direct the conversation to address the following questions:

- Exactly how, when, and where did they use their training?
- What specific parts of the training did they use?
- What results did this application help them achieve?
- What value did these results have? (We ask this, unless it is already clear and obvious.)
- How do they know that it was the training that helped them achieve these results? (Did they already know how to do this?)
- What helped them use the training and get these results? (Here, you are looking for key performance system factors.)

If the sort of success you are documenting would be more credible if it were verified, ask for a source for corroboration. For instance, one success case interviewee gave total credit for her successful results to her supervisor. We followed up with the supervisor to discuss and confirm her role and contribution. In another case, a financial planner told us that his use of training had enabled him to move up to the second-place ranking in sales productivity. We confirmed this status with his supervisor. Remember that the quality of the data collected should be able to "stand up in court."

When we conduct the interview, we always have the interviewee's survey results in hand and have studied them prior to the interview. This enables us to make specific reference to the survey responses and to be more efficient. We might say, for instance, "You noted that you used your supervisory training in a way that really helped an employee solve a problem that otherwise would have led to a grievance. Can you tell me more about that?"

With nonsuccesses, the interview is more simple, since there is no success to probe and document. Here, the purpose is to find out *why* the person was unable to use the training. To make interviewees comfortable, it is always good to let them know that not applying skills learned in training is not uncommon and that they are like many other people who were likewise, for one reason or another, unable to find a way to put their training to work. As you probe for systemic factors that got in the way, it is good to use the ideas and hunches you already gleaned from your success case interviews and refer to the performance system factors discussed in detail in Chapter 7.

Step 5: Identify Findings, Conclusions, and Recommendations.   In this final step, you put together all of the information from the survey and the interviews. Findings are listed as the "facts" of the study. For instance, it is a finding that "32 percent of the trainees reported to have used their training in ways that led to significant impact." Another example might be, "Of the successful instances of impact, 80 percent were cases in which the supervisory training was used to promote performance improvement, whereas only 5 percent of the successful instances of training related to avoidance of grievance or legal issues."

Only conclusions that can be clearly and directly linked to the data can be presented. We might conclude, for example, that "nearly one-half of all the trainees used their training in ways that led to significant business impact." This conclusion would be based on our extrapolation of kinds of usage we discover in the success cases interviews and our estimate of the breadth of such usage from the survey results. Imagine, for example, that the survey data showed that sixty respondents, or 49 percent, reported usage of training that we classified as "likely high impact." Then, imagine we selected from that group of survey respondents a random sample of ten people to interview. Imagine further that each of the ten we interviewed was indeed confirmed a verifiable success case, evidencing a valuable application of the training. Since we randomly sampled from among the potential success cases, we can reasonably extrapolate an estimate of 49 percent of the trainees experienceing a successful application of the training. That is, it is probable that any of the people from that group of 49 percent would have reported an equally believable successful application of the training. In this way, and using the demographic information we also discover, we combine survey and interview data to arrive at likely conclusions. In a similar way, we might conclude, "Supervisory support was a key factor in successful application of the training."

Finally, we will make recommendations. In the case of the automobile sales training, we might suggest, for example, that small dealerships be provided with an alternative training plan, since local organizational practices are interfering with impact. Or in the case of the financial planners where supervisory support played such a key role in impact, we recommended that training be provided to all employees' supervisors first. We also suggested that since supervisory support was so important, supervisors who did not practice the training applications themselves think twice before they sent their own employees to be trained, as they were likely to be wasting valuable time and money.

Success case studies do not need to be as formal or as thorough as suggested by the steps above. It may not be important, for example, to extrapolate estimates of the breadth of impact achieved. In a preliminary training initiative, for instance, it may simply be helpful to use the success case interview method to discover some successful applications of training. These successful applications can then be built into the content and materials that future trainees will use, helping them more quickly apply their training by using the experience of those who were trained earlier.

Opportunities for Using the Success Case Approach

We have found a number of highly strategic opportunities to use the success case method in promoting HIL. Its principal value is that it helps to quickly identify how well a training initiative is working and what critical performance factors are impinging on impact. In this closing section of the chapter, we briefly outline some more specific and typical applications that readers may find valuable.

Supporting "Rapid Prototyping." Rapid prototyping is a term used to describe an iterative approach to development of products and services. Rapid prototyping is a strategy used by a service or product provider to meet a quickly emerging market need even though little may be known about that need, or there is not enough time to provide a complete solution, or both. Rapid prototyping enables a provider to meet the need quickly, before the opportunity passes, and use the resulting market experience to shape and refine future iterations of the product.

Although the term is usually applied to the development of technical hardware and software, rapid prototyping applies equally well to the training arena. Given the pace of change, technological advances, and global market forces, training needs are likely to emerge more quickly than ever. Using a rapid prototype approach, a training department can quickly design and provide a rough and admittedly incomplete solution by compressing the normal needs analysis and development time line. Soon after the training is provided, a success case study could be conducted, using the resulting data to revise and refine the training solution. Several cycles of design, delivery, and evaluation would allow quickly changing and emerging needs to be met, but at the same time, later iterations of the training would be improved based on the real experience of previous trainees.

Supporting Experiential "Discovery" Learning.   We have used the success case approach in a way similar to rapid prototyping, but for a slightly different purpose and context. In some cases, it is clear that an organization must improve on one dimension or another, but there is a lack of knowledge or agreement as to exactly how this improvement should be addressed. In a large public agency that serves war veterans, for example, it was very clear that new organization and cost-reduction changes would require more effective supervisory performance and behaviors. At the same time, the agency had been required to improve on some key organizational performance and client service factors, such as improving service quality, reducing service time, and so forth. There was little time, however, to conduct the sort of research and development that would pinpoint the specific supervisory behaviors that would drive improvement.

Using a success case approach, the agency provided brief, nondirective supervisory training to a group of volunteer supervisors in a specific geographic region. The training was loosely structured and consisted only of an introduction to some relatively generic and broadly applicable tools—a brief guidebook for improving employee communication and a job aid for conducting "on the fly" staff meetings. The initial training, a group meeting, consisted only of two parts: a discussion to reconfirm overall agency improvement goals (such as to improve service) and a brief introduction to each tool, lasting only about ten to fifteen minutes per tool. The participating supervisors were then asked to go back to their agencies and try out whatever they thought would make sense, using the tools in ways that struck them as valuable. They then met a month later and shared notes on the successful applications they had had and the unsuccessful applications. These discussions were essentially success case interviews, though they were conducted in a group setting, where everyone was a potential success and nonsuccess case. Following these meetings, they then refined their applications of the tools and again collected and shared information about their success. After several months, they arrived at a few promising applications of the tools that consistently led to success. These applications were then built into more traditional training for larger groups.

Supporting Pilot Tests.   We have often helped clients conduct a success case study after a pilot test of a new training initiative. The success case study is then used to refine and improve the training prior to a more extensive roll-out. The success case study is also used to determine where and how to conduct the next phase of the training, based on the knowledge of performance system factors that played a role in impact. Finally, the success case information is used to generate a list of helpful suggestions for customers of the training that they can use to get the best results the training has to offer. In one case, for example, the pilot tests had showed that training was most successful when it was used within two weeks of completion of the training. In this case, managers were advised to review their employees' work schedules and determine the best time for scheduling each employee for training. In the past, managers scheduled training according to holiday and vacation schedules. Based on the success case data, they were able to see that the best results could be achieved by using a different set of scheduling criteria and constraints.

Selling "Performance Consulting." Training leaders have often and long recognized that performance system factors in their customer's work settings get in the way of training impact. But they have had little success in getting their training customers to allow them to work with them on refining and improving the performance context. Success studies provide compelling evidence of the effects of performance system factors on training impact. They also provide compelling stories of what business impact and value training is capable of achieving when it works. When combined with data about what managers are spending on training, even when they get no results, the success case information can be used to make powerful arguments to training customers about the sorts of changes they could make and the benefits they would receive if they were to make them. In organizations where we have collected success case data, we have experienced the rare phenomenon of being asked for performance system help. That is, when managers who are not getting results such as those they hear about from their fellow managers who did achieve them, they want to know what they can do to catch up.

Marketing Training. By its very nature, the success case approach to evaluation yields incredible and exciting stories of performance by employees in organizations around the world. We all clamor to hear or read of these accomplishments and results, wishing that we could boast of our training solutions in the same fashion. Success case evidence demonstrates the power of training, and that training can achieve real and valuable business results. These stories of documented results make powerful marketing stories that show potential customers the potential value that they, like others have, can achieve.

Chapter Summary

Sifting out the positive impact that training may have had on performance has unfortunately been the misguided goal of many evaluation tools and methods. Traditional approaches to evaluation often attempt to isolate the effects that training produced, ignoring the larger performance improvement solution and process. As a result of this inappropriate focus on training, these methods cast the relative credit (or blame) for impact directly on the training component of the solution.

Evaluation with an HIL solution takes an entirely different approach, both strategically and practically. Because every HIL initiative begins with the identification of and focus on specific critical business issues and key business goals, we have clearly established the objectives and improvement targets for our solution. By defining the clear line of sight between employees, performance, and business goals through impact maps, we have from the start outlined the broad parameters for our evaluation strategy.

A straightforward but powerful method to measure the impact of any performance improvement initiative is the success case method. Through the success case method, we can identify, document, and quantify specific instances of positive performance impact as a result of our HIL solution. We can also, through this evaluation method, identify factors within the environment that enhance performance, as well as barriers that impede performance. This valuable knowledge helps us to diagnose issues of transfer and work to improve our HIL solutions. When viewed and applied in this manner, evaluation then becomes a vital tool to help us improve the value of our performance solutions, as opposed to a report card that validates the worth of the training department.

High-Impact Employee Development Planning

Chapter Overview

Most organizations have some sort of formal system for employee development planning (which, to be brief, we'll refer to as EDP). These systems vary tremendously from organization to organization. Some are highly structured and systematic, including a high degree of managerial involvement and accountability, employee assessment, and formal learning plans. Others are more loosely defined, and yet others barely exist beyond a pro-forma requirement to create a plan and file it. The spirit of an EDP system, regardless of its formality and sophistication, is to guide the learning and development of individual employees, helping them to identify learning goals and then create a plan to achieve those learning goals. HIL, of course, shares a common purpose with EDP, since HIL aims to guide and direct learning investments and initiatives so that they achieve the greatest business impact and value. Given this common purpose, it is imperative that EDP approaches be aligned with HIL, both conceptually and procedurally.

In this chapter, we explain how development planning is a key tool for implementing HIL in an organization. We also provide clear and practical guidance for readers to bring their organization's EDP approach into alignment with HIL—a must for readers who will use HIL with an internal training department or function. We start with a discussion of the conceptual commonalties of HIL and EDP and include an explanation of how a high-impact EDP approach can help create high-impact learning throughout an organization.

Why HIL and Employee Development Planning Must Be Aligned

To this point in the book, we have explained and described HIL in the context of single and separate learning initiatives. We have illustrated, for example, how HIL might be applied in a learning initiative to help financial advisors use emotional skills training to achieve performance improvement and business results. We encourage readers to do as we have done in many settings: Adopt and apply the HIL methods and tools with a single learning initiative, to help that initiative achieve business impact. But HIL has its greatest benefits when it is implemented as a holistic approach to learning and training in an organization; on a long-term basis, it should not be used solely with separate training programs or initiatives.

Multiple Intentionality Dialogues

Recall that the HIL approach devotes a good deal of energy to creating and sharpening learner intentionality. As a first step in a learning program, for example, we would engage learners and their managers in an impact-mapping dialogue, to identify the key and optimum linkage among individual learning objectives, performance improvement results, and business goals and needs. Recall, for instance, in the example of the financial planning training in Chapter 3, that Lynn (the HIL exemplar) met with her manager to discuss how she might use emotional skills to make more phone calls and book more appointments, driving their office's key business goal of increasing sales and market share. A major portion of their dialogue dealt with the question of business goals and issues and also focused especially on how Lynn's performance could be improved to address those business goals.

In essence, the impact-mapping dialogues we have illustrated in the book so far have been in the context of a single training program or initiative. In other words, the context of the impact mapping interaction has been constructed around a single-program focus, where the participants in the dialogue have been aimed at connecting this single learning opportunity to performance and business goals. Consider, however, that an employee might be involved in more than one learning opportunity in a given time period, such as the span of a year. For purposes of illustration, we will create Fred, a supervisor in a medical laboratory that provides diagnostic tests and reports to hospitals. During the next year, Fred is planning to participate in a project management growth assignment, assay equipment troubleshooting training, a college course in management theory, and a series of e-learning modules in

TABLE 10.1 Four Hypothetical Impact Maps for a Single Employee

Trainee	Key Skills	Critical Action	Key Results	Business Unit Goal	Company Goal
Fred	Project management theory, methods, and tools	Plan and lead effective process improvement projects	Effective and constructive improvements to lab processes	Reduce cycle time Improve customer service	Reduce drug development time
Fred	Assay equipment troubleshooting	Provide timely and constructive coaching to equipment maintenance teams	Equipment maintenance teams achieve downtime objectives	Reduce cycle time Improve customer service	Reduce drug development time
Fred	Management theory	Help develop project management procedures and tools as part of Project Capability Team	Effective project management tools and methods suitable for adoption by lab division	Reduce cycle time Improve customer service	Reduce drug development time
Fred	Interpersonal communications	Provide constructive and persuasive advice input at Project Capability Team meetings	Effective and constructive suggestions and proposals provided to Project Capability Team	Reduce cycle time Improve customer service	Reduce drug development time

communications skills. Now, imagine that we wanted to create a high degree of intentionality for each of these learning initiatives, using the HIL approach. Imagine further that we had done so (Fred has met with his manager, discussed business goals, and so on) and had created the impact maps portrayed in Table 10.1.

Notice that the far right-hand portion of each of the impact maps in Table 10.1 is the same. That is, the business and company goals to which Fred's performance contributes are identical. This is, of course, the way it should be, since these elements are the relative "constants" in an impact map, that is, performance results and the business goals to which they contribute change over longer periods of time but are relatively constant over a year or so. When they do change, it is because market or organizational changes demand changes in business goals, and these changes are then reflected in job performance requirements.

What is different in each map in Table 10.1 is the way in which each of the learning opportunities will be used in Fred's job. Again, this is as it should be and is in fact why different learning opportunities are included in the map. The learning needs are driven by the performance needs, and more than one learning opportunity is often desirable or required to achieve sufficient performance results. In our example of Fred, the right-hand portion of the map is what will guide his learning, as it specifies the results, for both his performance and the organization, that Fred's learning activities are expected to facilitate. But given that the unit level and overall business goals to which they are linked are common, it would be redundant and a waste of time for Fred and his manager to meet for separate dialogues for each learning initiative. In other words, just one dialogue could have created and confirmed the information necessary to complete the right-hand portion of each impact map. This "one dialogue" is what we would include in an HIL-based approach to development planning. That is, from our point of view, the intentionality dialogue should be conducted in the context of EDP, versus a special and additional "add-on" to each and every training opportunity that an organization might provide.

Individual Versus Organizational Focus

As we noted in the chapter overview, employee development planning is a procedure in which learning goals for employees are identified on some sort of recurring cycle, typically annually. We also noted that EDP as it is defined in organizations ranges from very informal and ill defined to highly structured and carefully elaborated systems. Regardless of its degree of structure and formality, the intention of an EDP system is to define learning outcomes for employees. Further, almost all EDP approaches entail some degree of interaction between individual employees and their managers. In this way, as we have noted, EDP is essentially the same as the intentionality dialogues described in Chapter 5; each creates learning outcomes and plans, and each includes interaction between employees and managers.

Despite this similarity of EDP approaches and HIL, EDP and HIL come at the issue of learning goals from two very different perspectives. In most popular usage contexts, EDP is viewed as an individual-oriented process. That is, the purpose of the process is to arrive at an individual development plan that meets individual needs and interests. Certainly, the overall and long-range purpose is to promote organizational interests, such as employee retention, worker satisfaction, and so forth; organizations rarely act on anything that does not serve some sort of larger organizational purpose. But the fact remains that the EDP process starts and ends with individuals and in most common usage is viewed as a means to serve the specific interests of individual employees.

But the purpose of the HIL intentionality dialogue is very clearly to forge a connection—a clear and logical linkage—between particular individual learning outcomes and specific business goals. In this respect, the HIL approach goes beyond typical EDP. The common EDP system creates a learning plan and learning outcomes for individuals but does not entail an explicit analysis of linkage to specific business goals, nor does it document any such linkage. HIL, on the other hand, identifies individual learning objectives but goes on to link these to specific business goals.

There are two important reasons to integrate an organization's HIL and EDP approaches. First, as we have already discussed, if an organization is going to adopt the HIL approach in more than one learning initiative or program, then the issue of managing multiple intentionality dialogues is raised. It would be best if there was one discussion about the linkage of performance objectives and business goals and how these drive learning needs and outcomes. Clearly, when we specify "one discussion," we are not at all promoting the notion that the issue of performance improvement should be talked about once, and only once, and never raised again. A healthy and constructive performance management culture will be characterized by many informal, impromptu interactions between employees and managers. We are simply noting that the formal system should require only one such structured exchange per development cycle (for example, each half-year) but would also encourage that this formal discussion be referred to and built on in continuing dialogue and interaction.

Second, if the HIL and EDP processes were not linked, then there is a risk that the organization engenders two conflicting approaches to employee learning. On the one hand, the HIL approach is creating a system and culture for learning that is oriented to the business value and instrumentality of training. On the other, an unlinked and unintegrated EDP approach would appear to promote another sort of learning culture that positions employee learning as solely an individual benefit. Here again, we must add an important caveat. We do not suggest that business linkage and the HIL approach be promoted to the extent that the organization embraces a "hard line" sort of perspective on learning. We would not want to create a cultural belief that training is a part of a larger system to exploit employee talent and that the only reason we train someone is so that we can then get our money back in performance. As will be very clear in later sections of this chapter when we illustrate an HIL-based approach to EDP, such is not at all our belief. Quite to the contrary, we strongly believe in the intrinsic value of learning and see learning as good in itself. Further, not all learning is intended to be HIL oriented, and the organization needs to invest in learning opportunities that serve individual growth and development purposes.

But we also know that the learning systems in organizations will be greatly strengthened when they provide a means to clearly link learning to business needs and outcomes when that learning is driven by and intended to serve explicit business goals. What is most important is that the organization adopt an integrated approach to training and learning that is consistent and unified under a common conceptual framework. The employee development planning process is the "front line" through which all employees and their managers interface with the learning function of the organization, and as such it should present a strong and clear message about the business value of learning.

Before we begin to describe and define the HIL approach to EDP, it is useful to reflect on and discuss some of the common issues and weaknesses of typical EDP approaches and systems. Unfortunately, development planning is not a strength of most organizations and is not characterized by a robust, committed to, and effective system. Indeed, research on employee development systems has shown that it is more often implemented poorly and sometimes almost totally ignored. A recent study conducted jointly by the Society for Human Resource Management and Personnel Decisions International (PDI) revealed that more than one-third of human resources professionals were quite dissatisfied with their organizations' performance management systems, and most of the dissatisfaction derived from specific weaknesses in development planning (*HR Magazine*, 2001). Further, in a related study, fewer than 30 percent of employees actually had any sort of documented development plan, though their company's policies and procedures mandated such a plan. Readers who elect to pursue the development of an HIL-based EDP approach or who simply want to modify their organization's current approach would be well advised to work hard to avoid the weaknesses of typical systems noted in the next section.

Weaknesses of Typical EDP Systems

Employee development efforts are frequently viewed with a great degree of skepticism and pessimism in most organizations—and often with good reason. These systems do not provide the value they should either to the people who participate in them or to the organizations that sponsor them. Managers and employees are too busy and pressured to spend their time in nonproductive activities, and if they see their development planning system largely as a pro-forma exercise with little value or consequence, they will rightfully avoid it. It will do little or no good to build HIL concepts and tools into a system that is already broken. Following are some of the typical and major flaws that we have encountered and that must be offset with an HIL-based approach.

Perception That Development Is Just Another Employee Benefit

Training that is available through the EDP system is often considered something that the organization is willing to "give away" to employees, just as it is willing to provide them with health insurance and a parking permit. It is true, of course, that training and learning opportunities are indeed valued by employees and are a key determinant in employee satisfaction, and therefore related to retention. But there is greater value to training than just its meaning as an employee benefit. Further, when it is viewed only as a benefit, then learning loses its function as a tool for human and organizational performance and improvement. When EDP is seen as simply a means to distribute an employee benefit, it is driven by the wrong sorts of influences, such as fairness, equitable allotment of resources, rewarding longevity, and so forth. Although all of these values may be important, they overlook the strategic value of learning and undermine the efforts of the training function to establish itself as a valued business partner and resource.

Lack of Management Support and Accountability

A manager's participation is necessary to provide performance feedback, suggest goals, interpret organizational needs, assist employees in assessing their current capabilities, and in authorizing time and resources for development. In our experience, managers in typical organizations view EDP as an administrative burden rather than a useful performance improvement and planning tool and thus give it only the most cursory attention. They have rarely been required by their own managers to invest time in the EDP procedures and typically would receive no feedback on how well they support the process. When the managers do not fully and thoughtfully participate in the development of learning plans for their employees, it is likely that neither party will take the resultant plan seriously or have many expectations for it. This creates a sort of vicious cycle, as expectations are low to begin with, thus creating low commitment and involvement. When low commitment and involvement lead to meager, if any, outcomes of consequence, then expectations are rightfully lowered even more.

In many organizations, there is virtually no accountability for adhering to the EDP requirements and no consequence for failure to participate. Almost never is adherence to the process measured, and almost never is a manager rewarded for involvement, or chastised for lack of it. If organizations do not hold both managers and employees accountable for thorough and thoughtful development planning, then the plan will languish. Further, it is unlikely that specifications for development plans exist, and thus it is hard for anyone to tell if there is a good plan, a bad plan, or even no plan in place.

Focus on Competency Gaps Versus Performance Improvement Needs

Many organizations have subscribed to the popular "competency movement," in which exhaustive competency models have been developed for job roles and categories. In this system, for example, there will be a list of competencies that are required for each job, such as the skills and knowledge one needs to be a sales representative, or an information system technician, or a project manager. In many organizations, it is not unusual to find that there are long "laundry lists" of competencies that have been defined for each job position in the organization, sometimes delineating dozens of competencies (skill definitions) for each job. Clearly, these models have value and can be useful in selection, promotion, and even development planning. The problem is that when they are applied in EDP, they are not strategically used.

In a typical EDP application, for example, these competency lists often serve as the basis for the employee development assessment, wherein employees are rated on each specific competency. The competency gaps, where one's current capabilities are most discrepant from gold-standard levels, become the highest priority targets for development. Because competency models are almost always accompanied by related assessment scales that yield quantitative ratings, they take on a quasi-scientific aura that leads to unwarranted actions. Although this approach is seemingly scientific and attractive in its simplicity, it rests on the false and nonstrategic assumption that all competencies, and thus the gaps that assessment identifies, are of equal value. If, for instance, an assessment shows that a person has a large gap between the current level of ability on "ability to resolve misunderstandings," then that gap becomes a high-probability target for development. Typically, the list of learning needs is the same as the list of competency gaps, the highest-priority learning need being the largest gap, the second-highest learning need being the next largest gap, and so on.

But according to an HIL perspective, needs for development should be driven by the demands of the business context as it is projected to exist when the developed skills will become available for deployment. It is fully possible, for example, that an employee should develop a skill that is already rated as "adequate," because the particular business needs in that employee's work area will require an extraordinary degree of capability in the near future. Or a current strength of an employee may even be a target for development, if an even greater strength in that competency would drive some valuable result. In other words, it is not strategic to simply aim the development system at filling gaps and deficits. A development system that aims only to fill gaps and deficits is based on "one-size-fits-all" thinking and will not leverage each individual's development and capability for the greatest possible impact. Even when the assessment system requires raters to include some sort of weighting based on their assessment of the "importance" of the competency, there is no process for or assurance that this judgment is based on a strategic understanding of performance improvement needs and business issues.

Exclusive Focus on Current Context

Every organization is under pressure to meet the obligations that confront it on a daily basis. Further, each organization is working with systems and tools (assessment checklists, and so on) that have been developed, approved, and installed sometime, often a long time, previous to their use. Further, individuals who are participating in the development planning system are basing their career advancement hopes and interests on already existing career "road maps," competency models, and so forth. All of these factors conspire to bring a form of myopia that prevents the identification of capabilities needed for future growth and competitiveness. In most EDP systems, there is not an adequate, well-developed process that provides the time and space for managers and employees to plan against a thoughtful projection of future business needs and market conditions. The risk, of course, is that all development only prepares an organization to be especially good at tasks that are needed for today but may be obsolete tomorrow.

Unfocused Development Targets

EDP systems in most organizations are not designed to be strategic or to produce anything more than the sum of all of the individual plans. Typically, development targets are driven by individual interests or that person's manager's idiosyncratic perceptions of what might be useful for that person in the future. One manager might view the EDP system as a means to give employees what they want and focus the development dialogue simply on helping the employee be clear and certain. Another manager might see the development planning role as to shape and influence and thus might be quite directive in suggesting development targets. Yet another manager might see the proper role as being the steward of the organization's tight learning resources and require employees to elaborate punishingly detailed rationales for learning opportunities. Yet another manager may see the development process as a career counseling session, and so forth, with almost as many perceptions of the proper role as there are managers.

Employees, likewise, may view the EDP system from a variety of perspectives. Some may see it as a performance review and feel that it is best to hide weaknesses and misrepresent themselves to avoid being "branded" as a person needing development. These people are most likely to identify easy-to-reach learning goals of little real significance. In contrast, another employee may see the EDP system as a route to develop the skills needed to get out of a dissatisfying job, and others yet may have unrealistic expectations and understanding of their own capabilities and career goals. Again, there may be many different views of the EDP system's requirements, purposes, and value.

But based on our experience with many EDP systems, few are likely to be based on a systematic reflection and analysis of strategic business needs. As a result, the development needs and resultant learning outcomes are usually diffuse, highly variable in scope and quality of definition, and not integrated with an informed business analysis. In many cases, they will be viewed as "wish lists" by managers, who will then be driven by their responsibility to control costs to pare these wish lists down to reasonable levels.

In sum, common EDP systems are fraught with weaknesses and potential problems. In contrast, given today's fast-moving and ever-changing business context, there is more need than ever for effective approaches that can lead to real impact and value. In the next section, we outline and explain the overall purposes that an effective EDP system should fulfill. Then we turn to a description of the HIL-based approach that supports these purposes and addresses the weaknesses presented here.

Key Purposes for Development Planning

A comprehensive and effective employee development system should be more than just an employee benefit or a bureaucratic channel through which employees choose from and enroll in a cafeteria of diffuse training opportunities. We list five key purposes for EDP that balance the needs of the organization and its employees and serve the larger purpose of building organizational strength and business results. The order in which we list these purposes is not intentional, as their relative importance will vary according to the needs of an organization. A growing organization, for instance, might need an EDP system to focus on filling emerging leadership positions, whereas an organization that is having difficulty recruiting and retaining talented people might need the system to focus on meeting employee aspirations for personal and career growth. Overall, the larger HIL purpose of leveraging learning investments to serve organizational and business needs prevails, but these more specific purposes will help readers understand the value that an effective EDP process can achieve.

1. Improve Performance in Current Roles

Emerging business needs and inevitable pressures for constantly increasing productivity require continuously improved performance from employees. Providing learning and development resources that are focused on critical performance improvement needs is one of the methods by which organizations develop constantly improving results and efficiencies. No competitive organization can afford to rest on the laurels of today's good performance. Constant learning, constantly improved performance, and constantly increased productivity are demanded by a competitive environment. In this respect, the HIL approach provides its strongest contribution to EDP systems, since it is driven by and specifically linked to business goals.

2. Stimulate Individual Development and Career Growth

A good EDP system will provide meaningful opportunities and effective development for employees to learn skills that will enhance their promotion (or make them attractive to new employers). The system should systematically help employees define career opportunities, assess career choices, and clarify career paths and milestones to help them plan their advancement. Providing career growth opportunities is a key component of a strong organization and enhances recruiting, retention, and overall employee satisfaction. By providing learning linked to career growth, organizations increase the likelihood that employees will remain satisfied and that competent people will be available to fill new openings, reducing the costs of external recruitment and selection. Career growth also provides a valuable service to individuals and will increase their loyalty and commitment, which are likely to increase the energy they devote to their work.

3. Develop "Bench Strength" for Succession Planning and Strategic Staffing

The overall aim of this purpose is to enable an organization to deploy its human capabilities in the ways that best serve business and organization needs. One key manifestation of this aim is succession planning. Ideally, an organization would have a backup person ready to replace each person in a key role in that organization, should the current role-holder suddenly depart or be indisposed. An effective EDP system provides the training and education that prepares people for these new roles. The contribution of EDP in this respect is that it enables the organization to move people quickly and confidently into vacant or new positions, with the assurance that the new inductee is indeed capable of performing at the same level of competence of the person being replaced, if not more capably.

A strong EDP process also provides the basis for forming ad hoc teams of employees to meet emerging business needs and opportunities. At IBM and other companies, for example, competencies are tracked as they are developed and are entered into a database. That database can then be queried to match competency profiles needed to form capable teams of people to address sales and other opportunities. The EDP process should be responsive in that it provides a knowledge base from which to deploy competencies into business processes, and it needs to be proactive in that it assures that competencies needed to meet emerging needs are already developed.

4. Build Organizational Capability for Future Success

The rapid pace of change in global market conditions, technology, demographics, and other similar variables will almost certainly demand new competencies and capabilities. Many organizations, for example, will face global competition and will expand to serve global markets. Even though these needs may not be present in the current context, forecasts suggest that such capabilities may be demanded in the future. Successful organizations will be those with readiness to perform effectively in new situations. EDP systems need to look beyond skills needed for today's workplace and focus in part on a longer-term horizon. This means that an EDP system needs a strong analytic basis in today's performance improvement requirements and a forecasting component that identifies probable future scenarios and their competency implications. In this respect, EDP is a form of "insurance" that employees will possess the knowledge and skills to best leverage the opportunities that the future will surely present.

5. Satisfy Individual Needs for Growth and Feeling "Invested In"

More than ever, employees expect that their employer will provide them with growth opportunities and invest in them as individuals. This is true for current employees, impacting retention, and it is true for prospective employees, impacting recruitment and hiring. It is not uncommon for recruits to inquire about development opportunities, and opportunities for development may sometimes be a key factor in choosing an employer. Organizations have many means by which they can show their concern for the personal health and welfare of their employees. Systematic, effective, and constructive EDP sends a message that each employee's learning and growth is important and that the organization is willing to invest in its people.

People in today's chaotic business environment know that a corporate downsizing, reorganization, merger, or acquisition is as close as tomorrow morning's news. In the face of this uncertainty, employees are compelled to continuously upgrade their skills and knowledge, so that they are ready to move to a new job if and when the opportunity is provided or circumstances dictate that they must.

An effective EDP system, even if all employees do not use it equally at any given time, provides all employees with a feeling of confidence and satisfaction, key elements in forging positive morale. Employee morale is known to be an important part of an overall effective organization and is clearly related to performance effectiveness and achievement of business goals.

Balancing Individual and Organizational Needs

Although it is not an explicit purpose of an EDP system, it is important that an EDP system be constructed to provide a proper balance between individual and organizational needs and interests. We characterize this balance as a compromise between "getting" and "giving." On the one hand, organizations must be structured and managed to get the best performance from people. That is, the organization has hired and developed its people to acquire the optimum capabilities needed for an effective and competitive business. The organization will not achieve its goals if people do not give the best performance they can, so that the organization gets a performance return on its investment. At the same time, people are not resources to be consumed but are a unique individual capacity, capable of nearly infinite development and ongoing renewal. Any organization must also "give," to nurture the health and well-being of employees. To remain effective in employment roles, people must be healthy in the other roles of their lives, as parents, caretakers, and social and spiritual entities. They likewise expect any organization to which they give their time and energy to respect these needs and to give back ample opportunities for growth, social expansion, and capability development. Figure 10.1 portrays this give-get balance and tension.

This balance is crucial and must be maintained; imbalance puts the organization and the people in it at risk. For brief periods, an organization may be able to get more than it gives, but it cannot do this for long. If the organization expects people to work too hard for too long, they burn out, become less effective over time, and eventually perform well below their capability. Likewise, in an organization that errs on the side of giving and relaxes its expectations for superior performance, people will perform below their capability, eventually fatally crippling the organization.

At any given time, needs for give and get will vary, from work unit to work unit, from individual to individual, and from one business scenario to another. Almost always, needs for "give" and "get" will be, to some extent, in conflict. Managers are the focal point for this conflict. The EDP system must give them the tools and the capabilities to manage this continuing tension and effectively balance the task-versus-people conflicts inherent in their role.

Integrating EDP with Other HR Systems

In a large organization, there are other human resources systems and policies that serve similar purposes to EDP, or are otherwise related to EDP purposes and procedures. Most organizations, for example, implement some sort of formal performance appraisal and review process at least annually. Performance reviews are intended primarily to result in ratings (judgments) of an employee's performance to aid in decisions about whether to retain, promote, or place the employee on the "fast track." Many organizations also use systems for administering training and development activities and for keeping track of and filing data on the training records and competency profiles of employees.

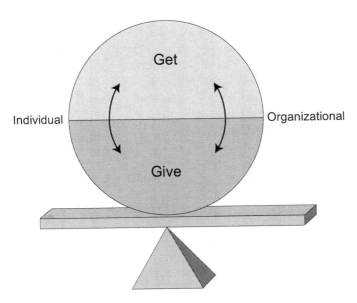

FIGURE 10.1   Balancing Individual and Organizational Needs

Likewise, many organizations offer a tuition reimbursement program that supports employees who are pursuing higher education opportunities from colleges and universities. These sorts of systems and procedures that are related to assessment, providing learning opportunities, or keeping track of employees' growth and capabilities should all be integrated and made to work compatibly, without redundancies and overlapping requirements.

It is especially important to integrate the systems the organization uses for performance appraisal and review with EDP, as these two systems almost always share a similar assessment component. That is, an EDP system will typically include some way to assess an employee's capabilities to help determine learning goals. Of course, we have already pointed out that a common flaw in such assessment methods is to assume that a "gap" is equivalent to a need for development, versus the HIL approach that always considers business goals in the identification of learning needs. Performance review systems also include assessment, as decisions about adequacy of performance for promotion and retention must be based on demonstrated capabilities. EDP systems likewise need to consider demonstrated capabilities, since the best indication of a person's capabilities is almost always to see whether and how well they have actually performed.

But even though they share a common process of assessment, EDP and performance review have fundamentally different purposes. The purpose of a formal performance review is to render summative judgments about employee performance that will guide future employment status. The purpose of EDP is to guide future learning to provide the greatest possible opportunity for employees to succeed. These two different purposes require complete, accurate, and reliable assessment information. To assure accuracy and fairness, it is wise to gather the opinions and perspectives of the person who is being assessed. That is, people should have an opportunity to provide their own assessments of what they see as their essential capabilities, strengths, and weaknesses. But we have to also recognize that people approaching a self-assessment may likely adopt a fundamentally different internal framework, depending on whether the assessment is for a performance review or development planning.

In approaching and preparing for a performance review, employees will adopt a "selling" mentality, since they know that the outcome of the decision-making process is a summative judgment that will affect vitally important factors, such as promotion and compensation, even the ability to hold the job itself. They will thus be led to present their capabilities in the most positive, even exaggerated manner. In a development review, on the other hand, the job itself is not at stake. What is at stake is the opportunity to build capability, to better oneself, and to have the chance to grow and overcome the weaknesses that may eventually be revealed in a summative performance review judgment. Thus, if the purpose is to argue that one is not very capable in some areas in order to get access to learning resources, the proper stance is to underestimate one's capabilities.

Managers and employees must be helped, with clear policies, sound procedures, and effective tools, to recognize the potentially conflicting purposes inherent in the EDP and performance review systems, and cope with them constructively. Confusion about the two systems or simply lumping them together (which is common in many organizations) can allow each purpose to subvert the other and weaken both systems. For these reasons, it is wise to clearly separate the purposes of performance review and development planning and to provide separate tools to accomplish each.

The HIL Development Planning Approach

In this section, we outline the framework and methods for an HIL approach to development planning. We do this in two basic segments, first by explaining the three fundamental factors that shape a learning need as we define it in an HIL/EDP approach. We then briefly describe the critical components of the HIL/EDP process that assure that the three fundamental factors are accurately identified and fully considered in completing development plans for employees. At the same time, we discuss how the proposed HIL/EDP process components overcome the weaknesses explained earlier in this chapter.

The Development Plan Drivers

The HIL development planning approach is built around the integration of three key "drivers" listed below and graphically portrayed in Figure 10.2.

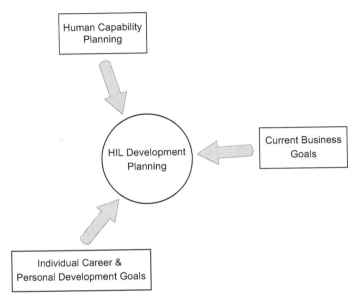

FIGURE 10.2 Three Key EDP Drivers

1. The future market context and competitive environment determine the overall capabilities that an organization must maintain or develop if it is to be successful in the future. One of the most significant threats to continuing growth and competitive strength is the lack of motivated, trained, and focused talent. Strategic human capability planning is as important to an organization's success as financial and capital planning. Effective human capability planning starts from the outside in. Leaders of an organization must scrutinize the likely future marketplace and competitive environment and analyze these scenarios to anticipate what competencies (knowledge, skills, and personal attributes) the organization will require to implement its strategy in the future marketplace. In the pharmaceutical industry, for example, it is likely that government agencies will continue to enforce greater cost controls and pressures to reduce prices. A development planning system would need to raise and address the question of how this future trend might impact competencies needed in different roles. What additional capabilities might be needed, for

example, by production managers if cost reduction becomes a future imperative?

2. Current business goals and related performance improvement needs, of course, continuously demand enhanced and new capabilities. An effective development planning process should regularly review the business goals and challenges that are impending, then analyze the related job and team roles that need to drive improved business performance. This analysis then leads to the identification of performance improvement needs, and thence to needed improvements in capabilities that are the basis of learning needs. When development planning focuses on performance improvement needs, several benefits are realized. First, managers are more likely to support development when it is keyed to business goals and objectives for which they are accountable. Second, improving employee capability in areas of key business improvement needs helps the organization perform more effectively, which benefits the organization and also highlights the role of training and development as a vital business contributor. Finally, employees who demonstrably help the business succeed are better positioned for career success and promotion. They can readily see how their investment in learning will not only help them in longer-term career development but will also assist them in performing their current role more effectively, likewise contributing to their success.

3. The individual's career and personal development goals are also a key driver of EDP needs and will often be at the center of the employee's interest in development planning. The relative influence of this driver has increased significantly over the last decade with a rash of corporate downsizing and reorganizations and the legacy of distrust and abandoned loyalties these upheavals create. One constructive result of these disruptions is that individuals are assuming more responsibility for their careers and their employability. With or without the support of their organizations, employees are more determined than ever to add valuable knowledge and skills to their personal repertoire. In this sort of environment, employees increasingly expect and deserve EDP systems that will help them chart a course and develop the competencies for future success, regardless of where and by whom they may be employed.

Individual interests and goals will vary, of course, and so this individual aspect of the EDP process needs to be flexible. At the same time, the EDP process should provide forthright guidance and opportunities for self-appraisal and reflection. Organizations should not just randomly "give away" development opportunities for the asking, since these may not serve the employee's or the organization's best interests in the long run. Realistic assessment, honest feedback, and thoughtfully considered advice are needed to help employees interpret their interests in the larger context of the organization and market and to help them accurately appraise their capabilities and aspirations so that they set meaningful and realistic goals.

Figure 10.2 shows that a development learning need is driven by and shaped by any one, or a combination, of the three fundamental drivers. Any driver alone can create a learning need. Consider, for example, that a company is going to launch an entirely new line of products based on a new technology. A sales representative whose job it will be to sell that product would have need to learn about the product, its benefits, how to sell it, and so forth. Or consider the case of a senior manager in a company that is facing an impending merger with a foreign business, who will therefore need to sharpen skills in providing leadership to a blended group of highly diverse employees. Some other development needs will be driven by a combination of the three drivers, where consideration among all the drivers will help determine the learning needs with the highest priority and urgency. Further, of course, the relative influence of each driver will vary from time to time depending on the specific dynamics of the organization, each employee, and the environment in which each must perform. As will be clear in the next section, the suggested HIL/EDP process assures the optimum opportunity to fully and accurately consider each of the three key drivers.

The HIL/EDP Process Components

The EDP process we have developed and recommend (see Brinkerhoff and Messinger, 1999, for a more detailed description) can be configured into a variety of steps, reflecting a range of bureaucratic constraints and opportunities. The specific steps are not so important as being sure that the EDP process includes some particular vital components, regardless of the configuration of steps. We know of successful and HIL-based EDP processes that have assessment as the first step, for example. Yet another company with an equally effective and successful HIL-based EDP process includes assessment as the third step. Further, we believe that the process must be characterized by ample dialogue and interaction between managers and their employees and that managers and employees should collaborate at all stages of the process. EDP done in this joint dialogue aligns the strategic planning and goal-setting processes with the three key drivers and promotes the cohesion and interdependence among participants that help establish a more mature and productive professional relationship. Continuous dialogue is an essential ingredient to this form of EDP planning, with each round of discussion sharpening the focus of development plans and improving the likelihood that organizational and personal resources are used efficiently.

The key components we promote are as follows:

- *Use employee/manager dialogue to align development targets.* This component is characterized by information sharing and discussion intended to clarify the meaning, significance, and relative importance among the three key drivers. No one driver should be permitted to take unwarranted precedence over another, and employees should always have the opportunity to present a case for their own individual interests and aspirations.

- *Include a process that gathers information about future needs.* There must be a process to identify and interpret impending and forecasted market trends and pressures that shape future capabilities that the organization and its individuals will require. This process should be systematic and should also include a procedure whereby the information is openly shared with and discussed with employees. In one company that has adopted an HIL/EDP approach, for instance, the senior management team meets annually to discuss this topic in a one-day workshop. Previous to the workshop, the HR leader has provided all participants with a number of readings including expert projections, industry trend reports, competitive analyses, and so forth. The senior team creates a "white paper" that is then distributed to managers on the company's secure intranet. Managers then discuss the paper and its implications in their staff meetings.

- *Create and share information about business goals and their associated employee development implications.* Recall that the HIL approach to EDP seeks to avoid a development planning process that is "gap driven," where static competency models and capability assessment drive learning needs in the absence of reflection on strategic business needs. An impact map is the perfect medium for implementing this component and assuring a strategic focus. One company with which we work provides an excellent illustration. In previous meetings, managers had created a high-level impact map for all the major job and team roles in the manager's unit. Then groups representing each team and/or job role met to create job- and team-level impact maps. Following this, and at the beginning of the development planning cycle (annually, in this case), each individual employee created an impact map for his or her own role, showing how they individually defined and characterized their role and its connection to their performance objectives and the unit's business goals. Then when employees and their managers conducted individual meetings to begin their joint development planning, they discussed and compared notes on the impact maps to reach a mutual understanding and agreement.

- *Use accurate and valid assessment data.* Employees and their managers need to base development decisions on solid assessment data. Although we do not want assessment data to drive development targets, good information about current strengths and weaknesses is vital for consideration. Multiple perspectives (for example, 360-degree feedback methods) are always preferred, and assessment data should always allow incorporate self-assessment. The process must likewise allow for thorough review, discussion, and comparison among the several assessment perspectives.

- *Review and discuss the employee's individual career and personal interests and goals.* The matter of identifying employee goals and aspirations should not be spontaneous or ad hoc. Rather, there should be a process and tools that help the employee reflect on and think these through prior to the meeting, so that the discussion is based on a thoughtful and careful consideration.

- *Set a small number of focused development targets.* It is our experience that trying to develop more than three or four new skills per year diffuses energy and attention and produces a diminishing return on time and money.

The planning process should settle on a limited scope—no more than two or three—of highest-priority targets, again being sure that all three drivers have been adequately considered. Where more than this small number of targets are identified, a prioritizing step is necessary to arrive at a workably small scope.

- *Develop a thorough and detailed learning plan.* A complete learning plan should include specific development targets, learning methods and resources to be employed for each target, application objectives defined in performance behaviors, managerial support and resources needed for implementation, and measures by which the acquisition and application of learning will be assessed.

- *Consider a broad range of learning opportunities and methods.* Too often, development plans are limited to narrow options for methods constrained by consideration of only classroom and other traditional training tools. Development plans should consider nonclassroom and noninstructional methods, such as mentoring, apprenticeships, job rotations, special assignments, and so forth. EDP systems should include assistance from the training and development function (many use on-line resource systems), since there may be a large number of options for learning, and professional assistance can be very helpful.

- *Development plans should include joint approval processes.* Managers, and sometimes even the manager of the employee's manager, should cooperate in and approve the final development plan. The employee and manager should jointly review the plan, revise it if necessary, and ultimately each make a formal commitment to its implementation.

Chapter Summary

Most training and development professionals intuitively believe that investing time, money, and energy in the process of strategic employee development is worthwhile. The HIL approach attempts to formalize and institutionalize that belief and bring an HIL framework and perspective to all of the organization's learning investments and operations. HIL promotes a partnership between learning experts, managers, and employees that can drive not only continuous learning but continuously improved job, team, and business performance.

An HIL approach to EDP assures that there is clear business linkage in the development plans that are created for individuals in the organization. This business focus helps assure manager involvement and commitment and builds credibility for the process throughout the organization. The HIL approach to EDP also includes a balance among business, future, and individual interest perspectives, thus producing a development plan that results in the highest possible business value.

Making the Transition
to High-Impact Learning

Chapter Overview

Training leaders from hundreds of organizations have participated in HIL workshops and presentations over the past several years. Many of these people have been inspired by the HIL approach and want to begin using HIL in their training initiatives and projects. They ask the good question: "So . . . how do we start?" This chapter is a response to that question and reflects the experience we have built in helping and working alongside training leaders in several dozen organizations—corporations and companies large and small, government departments, and nonprofit agencies. Although each experience has been different, with a variety of challenges and issues, our work together has been based on and has contributed to a consistent set of principles and strategies that we review and explain.

We start this chapter with a reminder that a transition to an HIL approach is likely to involve a considerable amount of change. The bulk of the chapter addresses a set of guidelines and principles on which we rely to guide our work. In the final few paragraphs, we step back from the HIL approach and offer some closing thoughts on the relationship between learning and performance improvement and the larger mission of helping to build effective organizations.

HIL and Change

Our first words of advice relate to change and recognition that beginning to use the HIL approach constitutes, in most instances, a relatively major change from "business as usual." Most organizational training operations and policies are based on the fundamental mental model of training as "delivery of events." As we noted in the first chapter, this mental model runs deep and colors the way that training is perceived, organized, and conducted throughout the organization. Transition to an HIL approach will involve a number of changes, some overt and immediate, others more subtle and systemic.

We have learned from our work that HIL is based on a very different set of ground rules and assumptions about training and learning. A poignant experience we had will help illustrate this. We noted the circumstance earlier in this book where a large Fortune 100 client had been providing, for several years, a moderately popular three-day leadership skills workshop for senior managers. Although the workshop did not earn rave reviews or extraordinary attendance, it did earn acceptable end-of-session evaluation scores. Even though it enjoyed a moderate level of popularity and participation (perhaps because it was also the only training opportunity for midlevel managers), the leadership in the training department knew, from informal follow-up studies, that it had virtually no impact.

In a transition to an HIL approach, some sessions of this workshop were redesigned to include a learner intentionality intervention prior to the workshop. Attendees and their bosses (senior vice presidents) had a conversation about performance improvement needs and had completed personal impact maps. Further modifications were made to the workshop design to include ample opportunities for participants to discuss their impact maps and attempt on their own to individualize their learning.

Their discussions were models of good learner intentionality building and resulted in clearly articulated performance objectives and linked business goals to guide postworkshop application of learning. However, through an administrative oversight, two sessions of this workshop were provided *without* including the activities to process the impact maps and work on individual performance improvement objectives. Interestingly, these sessions were delivered in exactly the same way that they had been previously, by a seasoned facilitator who had previously also earned high end-of-session scores for the very same workshop.

In essence, a fortunate error created an "experiment," where we found out what happens when you provide good HIL-based intentionality but make no changes in the instructional delivery itself. The result was dramatic: End-of-session scores from the two sessions were dismally low. Follow-up interviews made it clear that attendees came to the workshop with a very different set of expectations and then found them unmet.

This experience made it clear to us that HIL is based on a different set of fundamental ground rules and expectations. In the traditional, events-delivery paradigm, expectations are generally low; learners and their managers do not really expect that training will result in much change, nor do they hold it accountable for such results. Typically, it is expected that the training will be entertaining and lively, that it will be a positive change from dreary work routines, and that it will offer at least mild inspiration and opportunity for reflection. Trainer accountabilities are to put on a good experience, trainees are expected to participate with at least mild vigor, but no one expects to be challenged too deeply. Further, when it is over, it is over, and no one should be expected to really change or do anything differently.

The HIL approach is much the opposite of this, as we learned in our unplanned experiment. Senior leaders were surprised to be involved in the intentionality dialogues, but once involved, they voiced enthusiasm and gratitude that "things were going to be different" and were pleased to learn that they could expect some business-related results from their and their employees' involvement. Trainees likewise felt challenged to put their learning to use and knew that there were clear accountabilities for applying what they were going to learn. Both parties felt that something worthwhile and new would come from this and entered into the training with an implicit contract for change and performance.

When the session failed to deliver on this promise, they were demonstrably disappointed and vocally upset. It was clear to us that the ground rules had changed, and we were working under a new value premise for the results of training. The training session was fully acceptable under the old paradigm rules and assumptions. But once the same session was replayed under a new set of assumptions and rules, it failed miserably—even though the training had not changed at all.

This experience has led us to work carefully and systematically when helping organizations adopt the HIL approach. We recognize the magnitude and depth of the change involved and respect the responsibilities that any change initiative involves. You must help people through the change process, to effectively cope with all the challenges that change entails. In the following pages, we highlight and discuss some of the more specific changes that a transition to HIL involves. We believe it is helpful for readers to consider and understand the potential threats and challenges that HIL can involve. In the following section, we provide specific guidance on strategies and methods for changing to an HIL perspective.

Manager Involvement and Responsibilities

In most organizations, it is standard practice for managers of employees to play only a minimal role, if any at all, in the training of their employees. Typically, manager "support" for training is operationalized as giving permission for employees to attend training, perhaps paying their costs and approving a budget expenditure. Beyond this, managers take little responsibility for participating in the learning activities of their employees. In the HIL approach, as we have seen, things are expected to be quite different. HIL recognizes learning as a performance improvement process where the person most important to the learning is, next to the learner him- or herself, that person's manager.

At a minimum, managers in HIL initiatives will be expected to think about and discuss business goals and related performance with their employees. Although they may already be used to doing this in their role of performance management and appraisal, they may not be used to considering goals and performance in a learning and training context. They will also be required to think through how different learning options and opportunities apply to performance improvement objectives. Again, this may be somewhat familiar, depending on roles managers are expected to play in development planning, but chances are HIL requires more careful and systematic thought and analysis.

Managers in HIL initiatives also get involved to a considerable degree in following up their employees' learning participation and are asked to provide feedback and coaching. Sometimes, this might entail that managers require some new learning; at a minimum, this will be familiarization with the content and objectives of their employees' learning participation. But sometimes their expected role in coaching and providing feedback may demand more skill and knowledge in how to assess and coach for new and different performance behaviors and objectives. It is not unusual that an HIL blended solution will contain one or more learning modules and activities for the managers of primary participants.

Time Span and Commitments

We have also noted that HIL conceives of learning as a process that spans longer periods of calendar time. In a traditional approach, for example, employees might attend a three-day workshop. In an HIL variant, this training might be reformulated to engage the learner (and manager) over a three- to six-month period of time. Over this period, learners and managers will participate in iterative cycles of instruction, practice, feedback, and reflection, all woven together into a carefully crafted structure blending e-learning, self-instruction, classroom group experience, and performance support tools. In sum, this HIL version of training might consume no more total time than its traditional counterpart, but the process will stretch out considerably across the calendar.

Even though total time commitments might not be expanded, it will not always look this way to training participants and customers. A major vendor of leadership training who has adopted the HIL approach, for example, has discovered that their salespeople encounter resistance in selling the new HIL version of training. Previously, customers could readily define and think about a simple and single time commitment (for example, a two-day workshop), but now they are asked to plan for a series of events and interactions. This appears more complex and may require a more complicated planning process to identify optimal implementation schedules and coordination. The traditional "events" way of thinking about training, although it may not have led to much impact, was at least easier to implement. Customers, managers, and learners could "see" training more easily and simply, because it was just one, single intervention, with a clear-cut start and finish point.

Focus on Performance Versus Training

In HIL, the focus is on performance, not just new learning. This requires some different thinking and action on the part of both learners and their managers. Managers, for instance, will need to think about and discuss the ways in which current performance is or is not sufficient to meet expectations and objectives. Learners, likewise, will need to reflect on how well they are doing, their strengths, and their weaknesses. Further, the HIL approach is quite clear that the goal of learning is performance improvement that will lead to business impact.

Although this notion is conceptually appealing, it is certainly less "safe" than the traditional way of thinking about training. A learner in an HIL approach has to make a commitment to actually do something with the learning, and it is also clear that the learner will be accountable for performance. In the traditional approach, all one had to do was to attend the training and at minimum just be a good "training citizen"—participating with enthusiasm, asking questions, and so forth. Although the learner may have had to act engaged, he didn't really have to do anything concrete afterward. In the HIL approach, the learning interaction itself is just a part, perhaps even a small part, of the larger process, and there are clear expectations for applying learning in new and improved behavior.

All of this focus on performance, with its concomitant commitments, measurement, accountability, and feedback, may be less comfortable than the old training paradigm. When learners and managers begin to catch on to what is expected and the expanded requirements for action, they may balk.

Different Roles for Trainers

The performance and business focus also has implications for training facilitators and instructors. In the traditional training paradigm, the focus is solely on the learning event itself. In this respect, trainers were "done" when they finished delivering a good session. They could bask in the applause and praise of trainees (assuming they "put on a good show"), and although they may have been exhausted, they were at least satisfied with a job well done. Training facilitation is still likely to be part of an HIL initiative, but it is almost certainly never all of it. And it is clear that a good learning interaction (for example, a workshop or seminar) is just a stepping-stone to a larger and more important goal. This may prove unsettling to trainers and others whose conceptual and goal horizon was no farther away than the exit door of the training room.

Additionally, in the traditional paradigm, trainers could mostly be just content experts whose primary job responsibility was to learn how to do a good job of putting on a workshop or leading a seminar. They were expected to be experts in the content of what they taught, but beyond that, were not expected to know much about the business of the organization in which they led sessions. It is not uncommon, in the traditional approach, to have a facilitator hired simply to deliver the session, which will be attended by a range of people throughout an organization. True, some familiarity with the roles and responsibilities of these attendees might be helpful, and good trainers would seek to know something about them. Trainers and the sessions they led were expected to have pertinent content, but translation into application behaviors and specific business examples was left to (usually unnamed) others.

In an HIL approach, on the other hand, learners are each entering with a clear focus on a performance objective linked to a business need. We saw this poignantly illustrated in our example of the failed leadership training at the opening of this section. Further, they expect that the learning interaction will provide them with an opportunity to think about and discuss exactly what they need to improve learning and performance. In reality, even in the HIL approach, trainers are not expected to be an expert performance consultant for each and every individual learner or team. The designers of the learning event must accommodate for individualization in the event itself, as well as before and after the event, thereby reducing the potential burden on training session facilitators. Nonetheless, trainers may feel threatened by the HIL approach and will need careful attention to help them understand and accept their role and its responsibilities.

Different Measures of Success

In most organizations, the training function is budgeted and monitored according to the amount of activity it generates. Most often, this activity is defined as the number of hours that are delivered or the number of seats that are filled. In other words, the measurement system focuses on activity versus results. Or put another way, the "results" that training is accountable for producing are defined, implicitly, as participation in training. Enrollments in training are carefully monitored and become a surrogate indicator for success. This makes some sense. If a training offering does not attract participants, there is something wrong. No training department will last long if it creates workshops and other training resources that in turn are never attended or accessed. Conversely, if a training department provides a workshop or other service that is broadly subscribed, with participation bulging at the seams, this intervention will be considered, at least initially, successful.

But when training is conceived as an event to be delivered rather than a process to achieve a result, the application of misleading measures of success becomes rampant. As we know, what we measure in organizations gets managed. Thus, if we measure trainee satisfaction, trainers will work hard to drive scores of satisfaction (level 1 evaluation) upward. Likewise, if we measure enrollment, trying to fill seats in workshops (or fill hours of on-line participation), then training designers will work hard to design and schedule training activities that will lure participants.

The HIL approach puts the emphasis on results of learning and training, rather than mere participation or engagement. The HIL practitioner will need to find alternative measures and indicators of success, such as achievement of learning outcomes and changes in performance, to properly report on the progress of HIL initiatives. As long as training is accountable for and counted by event-based measures, there will be a difference between what really needs to happen in training and what appears to be happening according to reported measures. Unfortunately, the cards are stacked against the transition to an HIL approach, since there is no traditional and standard approach to measuring and accounting for the results of training. Virtually all training departments and operations are accountable for producing hours of training or filling training seats in events.

In sum, a transition to HIL entails change in many aspects of training organization, perceptions, and operations. The learning leader should be aware of the implicit threat and disruption that any such change involves and be prepared to manage the HIL transition as a change initiative. Many people in the organization, especially trainees and their managers, will need to be patiently coached and assisted through the transition. Once success begins to be apparent, the approach will win devotees on its own. But getting started and being successful through the initial fragile stages of change is difficult and needs to be managed accordingly.

Strategies for Making the HIL Transition

Our overarching advice to those wishing to begin to implement HIL initiatives and start their organization on the road to more impactful training investments is to go slowly. A recent experience we have had will support this advice. There has been a popular professional movement in the past few years in the training industry to convert from a "training" to a "performance" perspective (see, for example, Robinson and Robinson, 1996). Although this call for a focus on performance was, and is, a right-minded notion, it has gone off the rails in a number of organizations, and not because the concept is faulty. Training does need to build a greater focus on performance; indeed, that is the major premise of this book. But the popular wisdom began to interpret this call as a mandate that put training and learning in the backseat, whereas "performance consulting" became the right thing to do.

We have had considerable experience over the past few years with companies that were trying to make a transition from training to performance consulting and had called on us because they were having little success. In some cases, in fact, their transition efforts led to the downfall of the training department, causing it to lose its budgetary support and be formally decommissioned as an internal function. As we saw it, the fatal error was that these departments began first to change the way in which they were organized and viewed in their companies, rather than starting first to change the nature of the work they did. Some of these departments spent a lot of time changing the name of the department and renaming titles for staff. For instance, someone who used to be called an "instructional designer" was now a "performance solutions engineer." The result was typically that their customers were confused by the new jargon and didn't understand efforts to explain new procedures. They also saw no change in the results being achieved but rightfully deduced that this was still the same old training department, just flying a new title flag.

In our work with these companies, we first advised them to stick with their core mission of learning and training. Then we recommended that they incrementally leverage their opportunities and requests for training services into work that would lead to worthwhile business results for their customers. The first thing to do, we said, was to accomplish good results that their customers would value. Then, as they built a track record, they could begin to try out new roles for some training staff who had demonstrated new capabilities. The last thing to change, if at all, would be titles and policies, and these only if they were necessary to maintaining the new success.

This experience forms the basis for our advice in transitioning to an HIL approach. Above all, we recommend a patient, incremental, and iterative strategy. This means that we don't try to change too much too fast, but look for smaller wins that can be recognized and applauded. This overall strategy breaks down into more specific approaches that we list and explain further.

Proceed on a Project-by-Project Basis

The HIL approach is adaptable to a project basis, since it can be applied to a number of training projects, large or small. It is far easier to manage and control a single, project-based initiative than it is a more broad and amorphous effort, such as a training department reorganization. Further, a project typically has only one, or a few, distinct objective providing a clear target to aim for and a relatively contained and manageable set of conditions. A project is also relatively small in scope and provides a better opportunity to succeed. Projects also provide excellent hands-on, action-learning experiences that give designers rich opportunities to practice their HIL skills.

We have identified two major types of HIL projects that present excellent opportunities to develop, demonstrate, and refine HIL capabilities. The first sort of project, represented in Figure 11.1, is referred to as a "fixed training intervention" project.

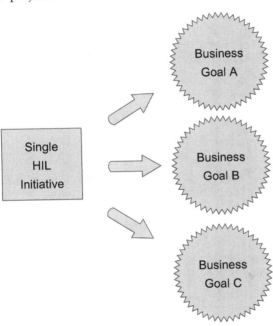

FIGURE 11.1   Fixed HIL Learning Intervention Project

As shown in the figure, the training intervention is a given, in that it already exists and is currently being implemented, or is about to be implemented. The challenge, in this setting, is to build HIL tools and methods into the implementation plan so that participants in the training are more likely to apply their learning, regardless of their work setting, in ways that will produce business impact. Because it is possible, in this "training as a given" scenario, that trainees may come to training from different work units, the figure shows a range of business goals and impact.

Consider an organization that has been implementing a leadership development seminar for a number of months. Imagine that this seminar is relatively popular, such that drawing attendees is not an issue, and that the seminar also has a strong skills focus and a solid instructional design. Given these conditions for success, we can build some HIL-based intentionality building processes and some performance support tools and methods onto this already strong instructional foundation. This organization, a company that operates a nationwide chain of clothing stores, makes the leadership skills course available to all of its management personnel. These managers could represent several different roles, such as small store managers, assistant managers in a larger store, a manager in a central shipping facility, and so forth. We augmented the workshop design by adding a component whereby the training participants engaged in one or two teleconferences with their managers a week or so prior to the training workshop. In this conversation, they identified a key business issue, such as reducing theft from the store, increasing customer satisfaction, reducing shipping times, and so on. Then they created an impact map representing their agreed-on learning focus. Participants brought their impact maps to the workshop, where the training facilitator formed them into small groups according to the nature of the business issues on which they were focused. During the training, they shared ideas and strategies for applying their learning and worked to create action plans, getting peer reviews and feedback. Also, their skill practice session incorporated their own particular action outcomes. Following the session, their action plans were provided to their managers, and they conducted an application planning session.

In this approach, very little was done to change the basic content or design of the training session itself. But the "wrap-around" HIL tactics helped to individualize learning for participants, giving them each an opportunity to leverage their learning into business-focused action. The organization was able to use this HIL approach to sharpen the business focus of the training, pinpointing this generic session on a range of specific and measurable business objectives.

Figure 11.2 represents the mirror image of an HIL project, in which a single business goal is fixed and there may be more than one training intervention. In this sort of project, there is a single business customer with a particular business goal, such as a sales manager wanting to increase market share or a production manager wanting to reduce order fulfillment time. In this case, the business customer and goal are a "given," and the HIL project will plan and implement the several learning and performance support interventions that are needed to accomplish the business goal. We helped the R&D division of a cereal company, for example, increase the number of acceptable new product ideas that are generated. Our intervention plan consisted of several components. There was, for example, a team leadership training effort for R&D managers. A reduction in staff had led to a reorganization into research teams, and it was evident that managers did not have the skills needed to lead teams. There was also

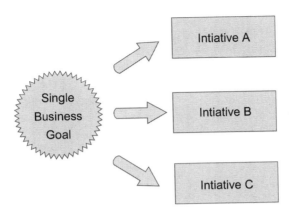

FIGURE 11.2   Fixed Business Goal Project

poor articulation of the process for coordinating a new R&D effort among the many food developers, nutritionists, manufacturing operators, packaging professionals, and so forth. We helped this group meet on a regular basis, to refine and document their total R&D process steps and milestones. Finally, we helped the product team leaders develop their project management skills by participating in a vendor-provided workshop. This was supplemented by tools for monitoring projects and an on-line project progress checklist that we developed for their use. Together, these interventions, methods, and tools helped the R&D division almost double the number of acceptable new product ideas that they brought forward in a six-month time period.

The "business goal as given" sort of HIL project is typically more ambitious and complex than when the training intervention is a given. In this respect, working on a single business goal can be more challenging, since it will stretch the design and development capability of the training function. The advantage is that the project has a single, clear, and committed customer and a distinct and important business goal.

In any case, proceeding on a project-by-project basis is an excellent way to build staff capability and earn respect from customers. Limiting HIL adoption to projects one at a time keeps efforts manageable and keeps risks to a minimum.

Aim for Early Wins

Building expertise to successfully plan, design, implement, and manage HIL initiatives is a learned skill. It is wise to keep this learning manageably contained, with relatively low risk. This means that given a choice of projects, it is probably best to choose the simplest option, the project most likely to succeed. Although learning will certainly be derived from failed efforts, this is not the best way to begin. Remember that the learning challenge extends beyond just the training staff who will be involved in designing and implementing the HIL effort. Other stakeholders, including managerial customers, trainees, and senior management, will also be learning. Scoring a "win" for your customers will help convert them over to an HIL philosophy and will also be most rewarding for all involved.

On the other side of this admonition to go for a winning initiative are two competing criteria. First, it is good to apply HIL to projects and efforts that are important, capable of making a significant contribution. That is, you do not want to waste your HIL resources on an inconsequential initiative. Thus, you should choose an HIL project that, if it does succeed, will be recognized as a valuable contribution to the business. Unfortunately, it is often the case that the more significant an effort is, the more complex and difficult it is as well. Thus, you must seek a balance of likelihood for success in relation to business significance.

The second competing criterion has to do with the complexity of the initiative. There must be some level of challenge and complexity for good learning to occur. That is, you don't want to try out the HIL approach on an effort that poses virtually no challenge at all, since without some level of challenge and stress there is unlikely to be much learning and capability building. So some degree of "stretch" is desirable, because this will motivate people to learn and lead to a feeling of honest accomplishment. On the other hand, keep in mind that there must be a high degree of potential for success. When considering likelihood for success, these are some of the questions we raise.

- Is there sufficient organizational stability among the key players that they will likely stay employed and involved throughout the HIL effort?
- Are there sufficiently few competing priorities and distractions to assure that key players can remain focused and attentive throughout the effort?
- Is the business goal significant enough to warrant time and attention and to justify the investment of resources?
- Are the budgetary resources needed likely to remain committed throughout the life of the initiative?
- Is the performance environment of the key players (especially the trainees) sufficiently supportive to enable them to stay focused, committed, and involved?
- Is the political agenda relatively "pure" such that there are no hidden agendas, private missions, or other unclarified issues and obstacles that could derail the project prior to its completion?

- Do the key players have the respect and commitment of their senior managers?

Partner with a Champion

Nothing can die on the vine more quickly than a project without a strong champion. One of the first things we look for when implementing an HIL initiative is a strong and committed champion in the organization. Further, this has to be a champion with enough organizational respect and position power to facilitate the acquisition of resources and involvement from key roles. When implementing an evaluation study, for example, we know that we need a readily recognizable and respected top manager to issue a cover letter to survey recipients, urging them to cooperate and respond.

Ideally, the champion for a project is also the sponsor and customer for the project, so that the champion has a vested interest in success. This is important, as any project, particularly a new sort of project like an HIL initiative, will encounter obstacles and unplanned diversions. At such times of stress, it is especially important to have a champion who is committed to success and who will intervene when the going gets tough to solve problems, smooth ruffled feathers, and commit additional resources if need be.

A champion needs to have bilateral influence. On the one hand, a successful project needs cooperation and support lower in the organization, to provide leadership and influence to help get things done. The HIL initiative, for example, may require extra time commitments or attention from lower-level supervisors. Here, it is helpful to have someone in the direct chain of command who supports and endorses the effort. The champion also needs to have respect and influence upward in the organization, winning attention and commitment when it is needed from other parts of the organization. The HIL initiative might, for example, need special permission from a leader in human resources or computer support from an information technology department. In one instance, we needed a special dispensation from a union official to allow a testing program to be embedded in a learning project, since the local contract did not allow for testing.

Use HIL Projects for Staff Development

Transitioning to an HIL approach will inevitably require new or refined skills for some training staff. Learning in situ, in action on real projects, is usually the most powerful and effective learning. One of our HIL clients who has been very successful has made a special effort in her training department to use a "buddy" system. Whenever a new HIL project initiative is undertaken, this training director assigns a newer, less experienced person to team with a more seasoned person. She has found that not only does the new person learn but the person in the lead role has to think more carefully, justifying actions and reflecting on ideas and decisions. Further, there are many times where the simple questions and observations of the less experienced person have caused the two to arrive at ideas and decisions that neither would have thought of alone. In this way, she continuously builds and deepens her staff's expertise and at the same time accomplishes valuable work for her customers. This example supports the age-old adage that the true test of knowledge is teaching it to someone else.

Staff can also leverage the learning opportunities available in projects by working in a "group practice" environment, much like many medical offices today. A peer review process can be very instructive, where all plans, materials, tools, and so forth, are reviewed internally by the group before they are shown to clients. Another learning practice that leverages staff development is regular and structured "postmortems" on projects. The staff from one training department with whom we work, for example, dedicates one Friday afternoon each month to formally debrief a project. Each staff member is required to write a brief reflection as part of this process and identify at least one strength of the project and one recommendation for revised approaches or tools for future projects.

Building HIL capability is a long-term, ongoing process. In our own practice, we find that we have grown and refined our HIL approach continuously over time. Clients with whom we have worked earlier are surprised, for instance, when we return for later work and have made a change in our tools or methods. Clients have also pioneered and suggested new approaches and applications. For example, Canadian Tire Acceptance, Limited, a successful provider of credit and financial products and services, was the first organization to apply the impact-mapping tool as an integral part of an individual development planning process. They have since moved this work ahead and are now using impact maps as a fundamental HR systems tool for job descriptions, workforce planning, hiring, performance review and promotion, and so forth. In the process of writing this book, as well, we have yet again changed and added to our HIL tools and methods.

In sum, we see HIL practice as synonymous with learning. We approach every engagement as a learning and development process, both transferring capability to our clients and refining our own expertise.

Earn the Right ·

We sometimes construe this admonition in this way: Let your actions and methods speak for themselves. A concrete example can help bring this advice to life: We have sometimes watched a person new to HIL try to explain the impact-mapping process to a potential client. This person would try to tell the client all about an impact map, explaining what it looked like, what it did, and how it was developed. Typically, we would see the client's eyes glaze over after twenty seconds, or they became confused, distracted, and impatient. On the other hand, we have many times just talked with a client about their business, listening actively, and asking clarifying questions. Then we'd bring a completed impact map to our next meeting with that client. We simply show it to them and ask if the map reflected the business challenges and linkages we heard them speak about. Immediately, the client "gets" it and sees intuitively what an impact map is. In fact, it is not unusual for a client to correct our draft, making it more clear and accurate. From that point on, that client knows what an impact map is, what it does, and what value it has. We never need to "explain" it or otherwise talk about it in the abstract.

As we noted in reviewing the negative experience some companies have had in trying to make a wholesale changeover to performance consulting from training, we think it is most important to first achieve better results for clients, building a track record of capability and success. Training departments that have tried to propose new ways of working, with new methods and tools, have often met with frustration and resistance; it can sometimes sound too complex and abstract. Our advice is to find a small project with a strong champion, then do whatever it takes to make that project work, using HIL methods and tools as you can. When that project is over, you have won a supporter who will plead your case and verify your good work. Then, identify and complete another such project, again doing what it takes to make it succeed. Only after several of these have been conducted do you begin to emerge and talk about change, introducing suggestions for new methods, processes, tools, and so forth. Let the track record precede you, earning the right to seek out new customers and supporters.

Ride a Trojan Horse

This suggestion is similar to the preceding one and can be used in conjunction with efforts to "earn the right." Many times, learning leaders with whom we've worked feel caught in a bit of a "catch-22." They know much more about how to work in an HIL mode than they are given leeway to within their organization. They have a lot of performance technology capability and expertise, but no one is asking for that kind of help. These beleaguered practitioners will note, for example, that they know exactly how to do a better needs and performance analysis, but their manager customers call them and order training, much as they might order a pizza. They think they know what they want (a training session), and they simply want it delivered. And they make it clear that they will go elsewhere to fill their order if the training department cannot deliver.

In these cases, where there is an honest request for help, even though it may be somewhat misguided and confused, our advice is to see this as a "Trojan Horse" opportunity. Recall that the Trojan Horse of mythical lore was used to get an invitation to proceed through the palace gates. Only after they were inside the kingdom did the soldiers hiding in the secret compartments of the horse emerge. In the same way, we recommend viewing a request for "training" as an opportunity to do something worthwhile for a needy client.

Rather than reject their request because it isn't built upon a thorough needs analysis, or rather than trying to get your client to agree to a different approach, we suggest that you simply say, "Yes. We can help!" Then, listen carefully to their request, ask questions to clarify where you can, and reconfirm your willingness to assist. Build in just enough HIL technology to assure improved results, but not enough to alarm your client and reject you altogether. Blend in the tools and methods where you can, "hiding" them in your client's terminology and suggestions. Increase your use of HIL methods and tools as you go, remembering that it is sometimes easier to ask forgiveness than it is to get permission. Again, do what you can to help your clients get successful results from "their" ideas and suggestions, and let success win you the right to ask to work differently.

Use Evaluation Strategically

Recall that in an earlier chapter we described a strategic evaluation method and approach. An evaluation effort makes an excellent entry-level HIL project. A large financial services company, for example, had for years been implementing an innovative and far-reaching training program in emotional intelligence (see Golman, 1998). Although there was a good deal of support for the program among participants, there was also considerable skepticism among senior executives regarding the business value of this large investment. At the same time, the leaders in the training department knew that they could make revisions to the program that would make it more effective and efficient, but it was difficult to get support to revise an initiative that was already under scrutiny. The training leaders decided to evaluate the business impact of the program, using the success case method described in Chapter 9.

The evaluation accomplished two significant results. First, it convincingly demonstrated the business impact and value of the training. It showed, clearly and unequivocally, that the training was learned and used by employees at several levels in the organization to achieve worthwhile business results. This finding was sufficient to sway the belief of a number of skeptics. As a result of the evaluation, it was fair and reasonable to conclude that the training, when it was used and supported, could and did lead to a range of significant business results.

However, the evaluation also showed that the training was not used and supported throughout all parts of the organization, and, therefore, it did not lead consistently to valuable impact. This second major finding of the evaluation quite convincingly demonstrated that there was unrealized business value yet to be achieved from the training. That is, there was a significant proportion of the training population for whom the training did not lead to worthwhile business results, but that it probably *could* have done so. The potential value of the training was, then, significantly greater than the realized value.

This finding lent justification to proposed efforts to revise the training so that it would indeed produce more value. Because the evaluation also helped identify the systemic factors that impeded value, there was clear direction as to the specific improvements that should be made. It was clear, for example, that manager involvement in the training consistently added value. This finding supported a proposal to create and provide a truncated version of the training so that busy managers could participate, thus helping them directly support their employees' use of the training. It was also clear from the evaluation that, in many cases, the training could be dissected into shorter modules to target more specific segments of the training population. New financial advisors, for instance, could clearly benefit from a highly targeted version of the training with a focused skill practice component that would help them conduct successful meetings with prospective clients.

In sum, an evaluation project can be a useful initial HIL project, since it will stimulate further interest and support for improved training. In many cases, our first engagement with a client has been to conduct an evaluation study. In almost all of these cases, the client has gone on to revise the training, adding more HIL-like elements and procedures to achieve greater business impact.

Tell Your Story

If readers were to follow most of these recommendations, they would be planning and implementing HIL projects that began to make a difference with their most important customers. The "tell your story" advice springs from the value of these initial wins. As key customers experience the added value of HIL initiatives, they can become the strongest and most credible advocates for this new way of doing training business. In one large organization, for example, we found ourselves in a room full of skeptical and jaded middle-level managers who were strongly resisting and rejecting our findings that suggested that managers like themselves needed to provide more active and sustained performance support to their employees after training. The meeting was unplanned, but it quickly became an opportunity to recruit another small group of managers to partner with us in HIL training for their support and technical staff. We had already conducted a few such projects in the organization but needed to extend our reach and influence. In the midst of the meeting, and at its lowest point, a manager with whom we had worked a few months earlier arrived and took the floor. She told a story of how her work unit was now operating more effectively than ever and had in fact recently won several lucrative contracts. In closing, she noted that she could not have accomplished these results without the close work we had done together with her. When asked if her work with us hadn't involved more time and effort on her part, she readily admitted that it had indeed imposed additional effort. But, she quickly added, the work had been worth it (evidenced by her new contracts), and by this point in time, she had figured out ways to reduce her additional commitments. This was a key turning point in the meeting, and within minutes, we had several managers queued up waiting to volunteer their departments for the next round of initiatives.

We hope the point here is clear: Good HIL work gets results, and a few words about these results from your customers will speak loud and clear to your prospects. The first mission is to work, quietly and in the margins if necessary, to achieve results and earn a story to tell. But when the results have been achieved, break the silence and tell the story. Ask your satisfied HIL customers to lead meetings, write articles for company newsletters, support an evaluation project, speak at company forums, and so forth. These satisfied customers are the most credible and persuasive sources of evidence that training can make a difference. Help them tell the story, suggesting approaches they can use and helping them prepare presentation materials and notes. Success breeds success, but only if it is recognized.

Beyond HIL: Influencing Organizational Effectiveness

The thrust of this book has been, of course, to help readers understand and apply the concepts, methods, and tools of the high-impact learning (HIL) approach that we have developed and refined over the past several years. We would consider the book a great success if readers were motivated and able to use only some of this advice, as long as this led to helpful and constructive results, however modest. We understand that many readers work in extremely challenging organizational environments where only small gains will be possible. Others, we know, are well advanced in theory and practice and are fortunate enough to work in (or have created through heroic efforts) progressive and supportive training organizations. For the latter readers especially, we note that the mission goes beyond just doing training and learning well and improving employee performance. In fact, HIL is really just the starting point.

A Framework for Organizational Effectiveness

Although there are many definitions and models for organizational effectiveness (OE), they are largely similar in that they recognize that people and performance are only a part of the larger picture of OE. Figure 11.3 provides a graphic representation of the hierarchical structure of organizational effectiveness that readily portrays the relatively minor role of people and performer capability in the OE framework.

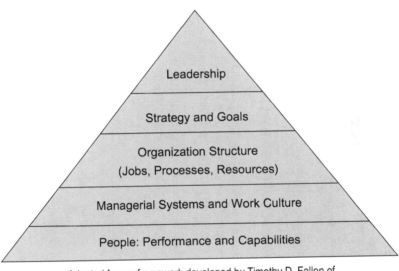

Adapted from a framework developed by Timothy D. Fallon of
TSI Consulting Partners. (2001)

FIGURE 11.3   Organizational Effectiveness Pyramid

At the top of the OE framework is leadership, the people in the key senior roles who set direction and vision for an organization. We place leaders in the top layer of this pyramid model, since they are responsible for articulating vision and direction into strategic goals. Strategic goals in turn define direction and clarify the path the organization seeks to follow. Goals dictate structure, which is the third layer in the pyramid model. Structure consists of several elements, including the functions and processes by which work is done and the technological resources available to support the work of the organization. Below this level in the model are managerial systems and culture. This layer represents the systems that guide work, providing feedback, motivation, incentives, and so forth. Culture is defined as the learned beliefs and traditions that are passed on from employees, generation to generation. We include culture in this layer with managerial systems, since culture acts, in essence, as an informal management system, influencing behavior and guiding actions.

At the bottom of our OE pyramid model are the people who populate the structure of the organization and attempt to do its work as guided by the managerial systems and culture. The reality of the training and performance improvement profession is that our "entry door" and access to influence is typically through this lowest layer in the OE model. That is, training and learning can shape and change the capability of the performers in the organization but have little influence to penetrate the higher layers in the OE framework. Nonetheless, it is these higher layers that, successively, have the greatest influence over successful impact. Consider this example: Imagine an ordinary company that manufactures and sells a product. Now imagine that this company asks us to provide training to its sales force in how to do a better job of closing sales to key accounts. Imagine further that we do so and that salespeople are indeed now more skilled in selecting key accounts to sell to, establishing rapport, understanding needs of prospects, and so forth. Let's now look at how flaws in the successively higher layers of the OE framework might frustrate the business impact of the training initiative. Imagine that

- Current management systems are such that district managers monitor and track the number of sales calls that salespeople make, using these data to influence their decisions about promotion and rewards. Because of managers' focus on this particular indicator, salespeople will have incentive to simply make more calls to more customers, regardless of the potential business value of these accounts. That is, they may forgo an opportunity to spend more time and effort with an especially tough account, even though that account could yield dramatic sales, simply because they need to complete more sales calls.
- Let's assume that the incentive and management issue was fixed. But the organizational structure is such that salespeople work in territories in which they have exclusive rights (that is, a salesperson from one territory is forbidden to work in the territory of another salesperson). But imagine that a potentially large account has recently merged with another company and now has buying centers that span more than one geographic territory. If our salespeople each separately approach this client, there is a good chance that they will not make a cohesive and coordinated sales pitch. In other words, the territory organizational structure could get in the way of closing a sale. Or imagine that a competitor's sales staff has recently acquired a sales analysis system that is linked, through expensive wireless remote technology, to salespeople's laptop computers. In other words, the competition can more quickly and accurately put together a

comprehensive proposal that is far more effective than what our staff can do. In either case, business impact is again severely diminished.

- Assume that all of the previous problems are taken care of. That is, our sales staff is given proper incentives and direction, and they have the best technology. Further, they have been reorganized into teams that can erase any geographical boundary that might interfere with meeting a customer's needs. But the leadership of the company is old and out of touch. They have carried on a family ownership tradition that has failed to grasp the realities of global commerce and a diverse market. Their product development and marketing strategy is seriously flawed and renders the company unable to compete in the emerging market. In other words, the best sales capability and performance cannot overcome the problems inherent in trying to sell the wrong products in the wrong markets.

This example, although drastically simplified, illustrates a triple reality of the training, learning, and performance improvement profession. First, our entry invitation is almost always at the lowest layer in the hierarchical OE model. Most often, we are invited to provide training to employees to enhance their capability to perform. At best, we may be invited in as "performance consultants," requested to work with the immediate performance environment, to build not only training but performance support tools and aids. In either case, we are constrained to operate only in the lowest layers of the organizational effectiveness framework.

The second reality is that the information we are able to glean and analyze in our engagement will come initially only from the lowest layers. We may, over time, learn more about the higher levels of the OE framework, but this information typically emerges slowly and disparately. Further, it is unlikely that any one person or single source in the organization sees or understands the larger picture. In other words, even if we *were* granted access, there really is no one who could fill in all of the information needed from all the layers to fill in a complete analysis of the OE framework as it bears on successful business performance.

The third reality is that there are relatively tough "membranes" between the layers in the model in most organizations. That is, it is hard to gain access and information from one successive layer to the next. It might be relatively easy, for example, to identify some management system factors that serve as obstacles to block performance improvement. It will be harder to gain the influence to make revisions in the system to remove or neutralize the obstacles. If the performance system obstacles are rooted in the organizational structure (which they are likely to be), it will be harder yet to influence a change in work processes or role definitions, since these are more firmly embedded.

The most difficult level to penetrate is the leadership itself. We found in one organization, for example, that a sales approval policy was undermining performance improvement in product quality. This company had a policy of not approving a sale until nearly the end of the fiscal quarter, so that only sales orders with the highest profit margins were approved. Thus, manufacturing orders were delayed until near the end of the quarter, causing a mad scramble in production to meet quarterly shipping deadlines. All of the compressed production was in turn causing quality defects, which was the initial issue for which we had been asked to provide training. It finally became clear that the sales approval policy was a means to make quarterly profit margins look as good as possible, which in turn drove stock prices on Wall Street. The executive mandating this policy was looking to retire in two years and needed high stock prices to assure a comfortable pension. No way were we going to get sufficient influence to change this reality. Only time, we recognized, would solve the root problem; in the meanwhile, the best we could do was offer training to streamline production and reduce worker stress during the end-of-quarter production rush.

The Strategic HIL Mission

We suggest that our rightful mission is to aim at the larger picture of overall organizational effectiveness. That is, eventually, we should do what we can to help build effective organizations. But this mission, of course, requires expertise well beyond that required to simply employ an HIL approach to learning and performance. An OE initiative, for example, may require assistance from experts in management systems, technological processes, strategic planning, personnel recruitment, and market analysis, to name a few. In no way do we suggest that an HIL practitioner should seek to master these areas of expertise. Nor do we propose that an HIL practitioner should seek to become a project or account manager to provide leadership to a comprehensive OE initiative.

What, then, is the proper role for the HIL practitioner vis-à-vis organizational effectiveness? Our response to this question is that the HIL practitioner should be a "humble and informed influencer." That is, the HIL practitioner should first be acutely aware of the limitations of a training/learning/performance improvement approach, recognizing that fixing performance problems will never provide the cure for a sick or broken organization. In all of our work, we should seek to educate our customers about the limitations of what we can accomplish and continuously seek to direct the attention of our customers upward through the framework.

When conducting an evaluation of a learning initiative, for example, we should make every effort to collect data from the higher levels in the framework and faithfully and accurately interpret and explain the ways in which higher-level factors have shaped our results, for better or for worse. We should also use every opportunity in meetings and interactions with senior staff to ask questions and build our understanding of management systems, business strategy, leadership capability, and so forth. When opportunities present themselves, we should prepare and sell proposals to move to higher levels of performance consultation, working our way into the second layer of management systems and culture. Here, we may need to partner with other experts (for example, compensation consultants or performance measurement technicians), but it is fully legitimate for the HIL practitioner to provide leadership to performance system improvement initiatives.

As problems and issues from higher levels in the framework become clearer, it is likely that efforts to influence and revise the organization will have to be handed off to others. As HIL practitioners, we have built strategic alliances with other consulting firms and experts with whom we can prepare joint proposals. We occasionally work in tandem, for example, with a business school from a university that specializes in executive education, a psychological assessment firm that specializes in employee selection, and a management consulting firm that specializes in strategy formulation and implementation. Sometimes we simply do our best to point out issues and problems to senior executives and provide referrals to other resources when we are able to do so with confidence.

Working effectively to steer OE improvements necessitates a careful balance and sensitive awareness of our own capabilities and limitations. On the one hand, we need to be aware of the limitations of what our core technology of learning and training can and cannot do. From this perspective, we are ever alert to issues and problems that we are not legitimately capable of dealing with. We resist the temptation to make ourselves somehow "full-service" experts, even though our clients may ask us to become involved in efforts that we are not rightfully equipped to handle. It is a truth of the consulting business (and all HIL work, internal or external, is consulting) that successful work with clients expands and deepens trust and reliance, and thus clients may want us to do additional work, even though it is not our strength. Here, we emphasize the need to "stick with our knitting." Our core expertise and capability is in learning and training. We can use the precepts, methods, and tools of HIL to be more effective in that role. But we must not undermine our effectiveness by diluting our energies and attentions away from our core capability. The better we are at what we do, the better we can serve our customers. Our advice to readers who, like us, love and are committed to what we do best—learning and training that impacts performance—is to stick with what we do best. We keep our eye on the larger goal of organizational effectiveness, but we invest our attention and expertise in our core arena of HIL.

Chapter Summary

Making the transition to an HIL approach almost always requires change, sometimes deep change, in long-standing training practices and beliefs, among both learning leaders and other key stakeholders in an organization. Above all, we suggest that learning leaders should proceed incrementally, not trying to solve all of their learning deficits at once or applying HIL thinking as an overall blanket solution. The transition to HIL must be conceived and managed as would any other organizational change process, paying special attention to factors that often resist or derail change efforts. Learning leaders are advised to move slowly, seek success in early efforts, move ahead on a project-by-project basis, and so forth. Readers are reminded as well that it is wise to conceive HIL initiatives as the beginning of a larger and more strategic effort to improve the overall effectiveness of the organizations in which they work.

Bibliography

Babbie, E. R. (1990). *Survey Research Methods*. Belmont, Calif.: Wadsworth.

Brethower, D. M., and K. A. Smalley. (1998). *Performance-Based Instruction: Linking Training to Business Results*. San Francisco: Pfeiffer/Jossey-Bass.

Brinkerhoff, R. O. (1987). *Achieving Results from Training*. San Francisco: Jossey-Bass.

Brinkerhoff, R. O. (ed.) (1989). "Evaluating Training Programs in Business and Industry." *New Directions for Program Evaluation* 44. San Francisco: Jossey-Bass.

Brinkerhoff, R. O., and S. J. Gill. (1994). *The Learning Alliance: Systems Thinking in Human Resource Development*. San Francisco: Jossey-Bass.

Brinkerhoff, R. O. and R. C. Messinger. (1999). *Strategic Employee Development: Manager's Guide*. San Francisco: Pfeiffer/Jossey-Bass.

Brinkerhoff, R. and M. Montesino. (1995). "Partnerships for Training Transfer: Lessons from a Corporate Study." *Human Resources Development Quarterly* 6, (winter): no. 2: 263–274.

Broad M., and J. Newstrom. (1992). *Transfer of Training: Action-Packed Strategies to Ensure High Payoff from Training Investments*. Reading, Mass.: Addison-Wesley.

Brookfield, S. D. (1991). *Understanding and Facilitating Adult Learning: A Comprehensive Analysis of Principles and Effective Practices*. San Francisco: Jossey-Bass.

Dick, W and L. Carey. (1990). *The Systematic Design of Instruction* (3rd ed.). Glenview, Ill.: Harper Collins.

Gagne, R. M. (1974). *Essentials of Learning for Instruction*. Hinsdale, Ill.: The Dryden Press.

Gayeski, D. M. (1998). Out-of-the-Box Instructional Design. *Training & Development* (April): 36–40.

Gilbert, T. (1996). *Human Competence: Engineering Worthy Performance*. Washington, DC: International Society for Performance Improvement/HRD Press.

Goleman, D. (1995). *Emotional Intelligence: Why It Can Matter More Than IQ*. New York: Bantam.

Gordon, J. and R. Zemke. (2000). The Attack on ISD. *Training* (April): 43–53.

HR Magazine. Lin Grensing Pophal. (2001). Motivate Managers to Review Performance. (March) vol. 46, no. 3: 35–38 (Society for Human Resources Management).

Kirkpatrick, D. L. (1976). *Evaluating Training Programs.* New York: McGraw-Hill.

Knowles, M. (1990). *The Adult Learner: A Neglected Species.* (4th ed.). Houston: Gulf Publishing.

Mager, R. F. (1997). *How to Turn Learners On Without Turning Them Off.* (3rd ed.). Atlanta, GA: The Center for Effective Performance.

Mager, R. F., and P. Pipe. (1997). *Analyzing Performance Problems.* (3rd ed.). Atlanta, GA: The Center for Effective Performance.

Marriam, S. B., and R. S. Caffarella. (1998). *Learning in Adulthood: A Comprehensive Guide.* San Francisco: Jossey-Bass.

Peters, T. (1999). *The Project 50.* New York: Alfred A. Knopf, Inc.

Phillips, J. J. (1997). *Handbook of Training Evaluation and Measurement Methods.* (3rd ed.). Houston: Gulf.

Robinson, D. G., and J. C. Robinson. (1989). *Training for Impact.* San Francisco: Jossey-Bass.

Robinson, D. G., and J. C. Robinson. (1996). *Performance Consulting: Moving Beyond Training.* San Francisco: Berrett-Koehler.

Rossett, A. (1987). *Training Needs Assessment.* Englewood Cliffs, N.J.: Educational Technology Publications.

Rummler, G. A., and A. P. Brache. (1995). *Improving Performance: How to Manage the White Space on the Organization Chart.* (2nd ed.). San Francisco: Jossey-Bass.

Swanson, R. A., and E. F. Holton III. (1999). *Results: How to Assess Performance, Learning and Perceptions in Organizations.* San Francisco: Berrett-Koehler.

Tannenbaum, S., and G. Yukl. (1992). Training and Development in Work Organizations. *Annual Review of Psychology* 43: 399–441.

Tracey, J. B, T. R. Hinkin, M. S. Tannenbaum, and J. E. Mathieu. (2001). The Influence of Individual Characteristics and the Work Environment on Varying Levels of Training Outcomes. *Human Resource Development Quarterly* 12 (1): 5–23.

Training. (2000). Industry Report 2000. (October) *Training* 37 (10): 45–63.

Urdan, T. A. and C. C. Weggen. (2000). *Corporate E-Learning: Exploring a New Frontier.* Research Report published by WR Hambrecht + Co. (March).

Zemke, R., and T. Kerlinger. (1982). *Figuring Things Out.* Reading, Mass.: Addison-Wesley.

Index

Made in the USA
Middletown, DE
24 December 2015